A Practical
Guide to
Feature-Driven
Development

ISBN 0-13-067615-2

9 780130 676153

90000

The Coad Series
Peter Coad, *Series Editor*

———■———

- Dave Astels, Granville Miller, Miroslav Novak
  A Practical Guide to eXtreme Programming

- Andy Carmichael, Dan Haywood
  Better Software Faster

- Donald Kranz, Ronald J. Norman
  A Practical Guide to Unified Process

- Jill Nicola, Mark Mayfield, Michael Abney
  Streamlined Object Modeling: Patterns, Rules, and Implementation

- Stephen R. Palmer, John M. Felsing
  A Practical Guide to Feature-Driven Development

- Jo Ellen Perry, Jeff Micke
  How to Get the Most Out of the Together ControlCenter

About the Series

The Coad Series' mission statement is: Improving the ways people work together. Each book in the series delivers practical keys for building lasting value into business by building people and their skills.

Peter Coad personally selects authors and books for this series—and works on a strategic level with each author during the development of his book.

About the Series Editor

Peter Coad is a business builder, model builder, and thought leader. As business builder, Peter leads TogetherSoft Corporation (www.togethersoft.com), growing the company nearly 12 times revenue in two years. As model builder, Peter has built hundreds of models for nearly every business imaginable, ever focusing on building competitive advantages into businesses. As thought leader, Peter writes books (six to date) and speaks at events worldwide. You can contact Peter at peter.coad@togethersoft.com.

A Practical Guide to Feature-Driven Development

*Stephen R. Palmer
and John M. Felsing*

Foreword by Peter Coad

Prentice Hall PTR
Upper Saddle River, NJ 07458
www.phptr.com

Library of Congress Cataloging-in-Publication Data is available.

Production Supervision: *Donna Cullen-Dolce*
Acquisitions Editor: *Paul Petralia*
Manufacturing Buyer: *Alexis Heydt-Long*
Cover Design: *Nina Scuderi*
Cover Design Director: *Jerry Votta*
Marketing Manager: *Debby van Dijk*
Cover art: *"Gravity" by M.C. Escher. Copyright 2001 Cordon Art—Baasm—Holland. All rights reserved.*

Copyright © 2002 by TogetherSoft Corporation
Prentice-Hall Inc.
Upper Saddle River, NJ 07458

Printed in the United States of America
ISBN 0-13-067615-2

Pearson Education LTD.
Pearson Education Australia PTY, Limited
Pearson Education Singapore, Pte. Ltd.
Pearson Education North Asia Ltd.
Pearson Education Canada, Ltd.
Pearson Educación de Mexico, S.A. de C.V.
Pearson Education—Japan
Pearson Education Malaysia, Pte. Ltd.

From Steve Palmer

To Suman, Mark, and Jared

For everything you give me. I don't deserve you.

From Mac Felsing

To Gina, Alex, Emilie, and Desiree

You give me determination, strength, focus, and above all, Love.

Contents

Acknowledgments

We need to thank all our friends, families, and colleagues past and present for their support, input, feedback and encouragement while writing this book.

We would especially like to thank Jeff De Luca and Peter Coad for first writing about Feature-Driven Development in their book *Java Modeling in Color with UML* [Coad99]. Also Jeff for his ability, courage, and commitment in creating a project environment where this sort of innovation could flourish, and Pete for so many insights, patterns, strategies, and techniques that made OO software analysis and design so accessible.

Thanks to the original cast of the PowerLender software development team in Singapore, especially Tan Siow Boon, Yeo Sai Cheong, Ajay Kumar Rana, Ju-Lia Tan, and James Tan, first for their willingness to adopt a new way of working, and second for their help in learning to apply FDD day after day for so many months. Too many to name individually but you know who you are.

Thanks to all the mentors at TogetherSoft who have contributed ideas, thoughts, and suggestions through countless discussions, e-mail exchanges and newsgroup threads. Special thanks to Lisa Juliani, our old "Mentor Operations Manager (MOM)," for helping get this book project started, and to Ken Ritchie, Greg Cathcart, Dan Massey, and Scott Schnier for their reviews, and continued encouragement and enthusiasm.

Also thanks to Paul Petralia, Donna Cullen-Dolce, and the rest of the team at Prentice Hall for the countless number of tasks, and their expert help and advice in turning our raw word-processor files into a real book. (As well as putting up with the quirks, foibles, and delays associated with working with two overworked, creative individuals.)

Finally, enormous thanks to our long-suffering wives for allowing us to neglect them for so many evenings and weekends to write these pages.

Foreword

To build anything of lasting value—software, systems, companies—building people must be at the heart-and-soul of all your do. "Process" is all about improving the ways people work together. A process is the family recipe, the secret sauce, the competitive edge, of human endeavor.

Everyone has his own collection of processes. So does every team. Making processes—good or bad—explicit is the first step to understanding what is going on, seeing what works and what doesn't, and looking with eyes of wisdom as to what is going on in one of life's many situations. Considering a process—the ways you are working together with others—is taking your thinking and going one level up. Feel pressure? Go one level up and take a look: Things begin to calm down right away; you begin to see more clearly. Feel panicked about what to do when, or what is most important? Go one level up. Having problems with a peer and just don't know where to turn? Go one level up. Having problems producing better software with others? Go one level up.

"Process" is about moving one level up, gaining new insights, inviting others to join you one level up to make strategic moves that will make the day-to-day realities so much more effective, palatable, and dare I say it: fun, rewarding, and satisfying.

Process, going one level up, is how one begins to understand what one is doing, what others are doing, what the people issues and dynamics are, what the bottlenecks and accelerators are, what the overall context is, what the expanded context is, and what to do about it all. One level up.

Problems happening? Go one level up and find out what to do. Goodness happening? Go one level up and discover ways you can engender goodness all the more.

May we all have the courage to reach one level up, that we might better connect with others, build meaningful relationships, build people, build lasting value—and truly succeed.

That brings us to the topic of this book, the topic of Feature-Driven Development (FDD). FDD is a collection of best practices, set into the context of an overall process, one level up from the day-to-day urgency—

at times even panic—experienced by business people and developers working together on mission-critical software-development projects.

A *Practical Guide to Feature-Driven Development* reveals the process, the secret recipe, that TogetherSoft and its clients use to produce world-class software. Jeff De Luca and I first described the recipe two years ago, in a short chapter in the book *Java Modeling in Color with* UML. Steve and Mac have gone far and beyond that initial description. FDD, as described herein, is significantly advanced by these two. I am most grateful for the work they have done and the many insights they chose to share.

FDD itself is one level up.

Read the book. Consider the recipe. Try it out. Adapt it as you would with any family recipe, making it your own, making it best fit the ingredients you have on hand. Read. Enjoy. And treasure the insights from Palmer and Felsing, one level up.

Sincerely,
Peter Coad
CEO and President, TogetherSoft Corporation
peter.coad@togethersoft.com

Preface

Feature-Driven Development (FDD) is a process designed and proven to deliver frequent, tangible, working results repeatedly. This is the first book to spell out the day-to-day details of using FDD on a real project, giving development team leaders all the information they need to apply FDD successfully to their situations.

What FDD Is!

FDD is a straightforward approach to producing systems that uses simple, easy-to-understand and easy-to-implement methods; problem-solving techniques; and reporting guidelines providing every stakeholder of a project with the information they need to make sound, timely decisions.

Programmers are provided with the information and supporting infrastructure they need to produce applications. Team leaders and managers get timely information about their teams and projects that allows them to reduce the project *risk*. Project managers and executive sponsors see the current project status and trouble areas so that they can actually make timely, informed decisions in a controlled, planned manner (no knee-jerk reactions). Reporting becomes easy, relatively painless, timely, and *accurate*!

Users (customers, sponsors, end users) can actually see areas of their business automated as the project progresses and give early, constructive feedback about the system while it is being developed. At the same time, the development team has the tools and information it needs to control "scope creep!"

FDD is *not* yet another process that takes up resources, time, and money but just doesn't produce the needed results. It is not another method whereby administrators, bureaucrats, and process-centric fanatics can focus everyone's time and energy on producing reams of printouts and signatures with nothing to show for it. FDD is not another set of process volumes that will sit on your shelf, collecting dust and impressing your supervisor, co-workers, and significant others with your knowledge of another less-than-useful set of directions for producing systems.

What FDD Is *Not*!

Why Should I Read this Book? (What's in it for Me?)

If any of the following questions apply to you, you will find the answers you are looking for on the following pages:

- Are you in charge of a group assigned to deliver a critical system with limited resources and short deadlines, and need help to organize the project?
- Are you tired of filling out so many process forms and reviewing so many documents that you don't have time to do your real work?
- Are you frustrated at the unfulfilled promises of process initiatives that claim to provide a way to deliver quality results repeatedly?
- Are you looking for a more efficient way to organize your team to streamline productivity, cut down on unnecessary interruptions, and improve the accuracy of reporting for your projects?
- Are you currently working on a project that is in trouble because the team has failed to produce a system?
- Do you want to add to the tools and techniques in your project management or team leader toolbox?

Prego (It's in There!)

Although FDD was first introduced in print in *Java Modeling in Color with UML* [Coad 99], we give a more thorough coverage of the topic. We point out the critical tips for success, as well as the pitfalls that may not be apparent from a cursory glance. Contents include:

- Who should use FDD
- The roles, artifacts, goals, and timelines
- Why FDD includes the practices and techniques that it does
- The driving forces behind the development of FDD
- Adapting the use of FDD to different styles of projects

FDD blends a number of industry-recognized best practices used successfully by Peter Coad, Jeff De Luca, and others in their consultancies. These practices are all driven from a client-valued feature perspective. It is the potent combination of these techniques and practices that makes FDD so compelling.

John M. Felsing (mfelsi01@sprintspectrum.com)

Stephen R. Palmer (sp@togethersoft.com)

December 2001

Introduction

A nswers: Why this book?

> *For enterprise-component modeling to be successful,*
> *it must live and breathe within a larger context, a*
> *software development process.*
> Coad, LeFebvre, De Luca [Coad 99]

Published in 1999, *Java Modeling in Color with* UML [Coad 99], often referred to as the "coloring book," devotes the first five of its six chapters to a discussion of a truly significant new object modeling technique called *modeling in color*. Those first five chapters are almost, but not quite, totally irrelevant to the discussion in the rest of this book. More relevant here—much more relevant—are the contents of that sixth chapter, hidden away at the back of the book. Chapter 6 of the coloring book was the first attempt to describe in print a particularly successful way of building complex software systems by significantly large development teams with members of varying talent, experience, background, and culture. The software development process that it described is called *Feature-Driven Development* (FDD), for want of a better name.

A Project in Trouble

What has become known as FDD was derived from work done on a large software development project in Singapore where Jeff De Luca was Project Manager, Peter Coad was Chief Architect, and Stephen Palmer (author) was Development Manager. The project was very ambitious, with a highly complex problem domain spanning three lines of business, from front office automation to backend legacy system integration.

The bank had already made one attempt at the project and failed. The project had inherited a skeptical user community, supportive but wary upper management, and what was left of a demoralized development team.

One of the key areas of risk that Jeff identified was the complexity of the problem domain. This demanded a level of ability and experience in domain object modeling beyond that of the current team. To mitigate this risk, Jeff persuaded Peter Coad to come to Singapore and work with the team to produce a resilient and flexible domain object model for the project.

To make a long story short, the result of Jeff, Peter, and others working together on this project was the discovery of the modeling in color technique and the creation of the FDD process—an agile, adaptive software development process that:

- Is highly iterative
- Emphasizes quality at each step
- Delivers frequent, tangible, working results
- Provides accurate and meaningful progress and status information with the minimum of overhead and disruption for the developers
- Is liked by clients, managers, and developers

Clients like FDD because they get to see real results early and progress reports written in terms that they understand.

Managers like FDD because it gives them a complete and accurate picture of project progress and status—the information they need to steer the project appropriately.

Developers like it because they get to work in small teams on small iterations and get to use the word *finished* frequently; they get to work on something new every few days. It involves them in analysis, design, and implementation. Analysis and design are not dictated by one or two elite analysts or architects. Developers also like FDD because it makes it easy to supply their managers with the status information they want with the minimum of effort and disruption.

Paul Szego, a Chief Programmer on the Singapore project, while signing author Steve Palmer's copy of the coloring book, wrote, "Who said software isn't fun? The best time I have had in a long time."

FDD answers positively the question, "What's in it for me?," for each role in the project. This contrasts with some processes used by managers to control developers because they feel the developers are not competent enough to be trusted; it also contrasts with processes used by developers to prevent themselves from being controlled because they do not feel their managers are competent enough to be trusted.

Since its introduction in the publication of the coloring book, FDD has proven effective within a growing number of development organizations. Its value is not restricted to salvaging projects in trouble; it is just as applicable to projects that are starting out, projects enhancing existing code, and projects tasked with creation of the second version of a system that was thrown together in a hurry last year.

FDD's underlying focus on producing frequent, tangible, working results at each level of the project (from developers to Chief Programmers, Chief Architects, Project Managers, Project Sponsors, and end users) makes it worthy of serious consideration by any software development organization that needs to deliver quality, business-critical software systems on time.

Those Responsible

Although a number of the Singapore project team members contributed to the development of FDD, there is no doubt that the main pair of villains involved were Jeff De Luca and Peter Coad.

Peter Coad is an industry-renowned object modeler, consultant, author, speaker, teacher, and wearer of Hawaiian shirts. Peter has designed hundreds of component and object systems, within nearly every industry imaginable.

Jeff De Luca, on the other hand, was schooled in the deep, dark arts of AS/400 operating system development at IBM's lonely laboratories in Rochester, Minnesota and is a highly successful, innovative, and experienced technical consultant and Project Manager. Pete has described him as "the best Project Manager I've ever worked with."

Why are they not writing this book? The simple answer is that they are both too busy building companies that build successful software applications. Jeff leads Nebulon Pty. Ltd. (www.nebulon.com) and is successfully using FDD to produce business systems for major clients in and around Melbourne, Australia. Pete is CEO of TogetherSoft (www. togethersoft.com), the company that produces the award-winning Together software development platform. All of the Unified Modeling Language (UML) diagrams in this book are constructed using TogetherSoft's Together ControlCenter software development platform.

Until now, people wanting information about FDD have been limited to the introduction in Chapter 6 of the coloring book [Coad 99], a little more discussion on the Nebulon Web site, and a few issues of the *Coad Letter* [Palmer], a monthly newsletter archived at www.togethercommunity. com and currently edited by Steve. The aims of this book are:

- To provide people with the in-depth information they have asked for about FDD
- To provide many practical hints and tips for applying FDD
- To discuss its development since the publication of the coloring book

If you are a developer or team leader, are involved in software development management in any way and need to make FDD work for you, or are simply interested in the whys and wherefores behind FDD, you are reading the right book.

Few, if any, of the ideas discussed are our own. Many of the ideas come from notes made by Jeff or Peter. Many of the ideas are inspired by the work of Fred Brooks [Brooks], Tom De Marco [De Marco], Luke Hohmann [Hohmann], and Gerald Weinberg [Weinberg 92, Weinberg 98]. In turn, much of their work builds on the work of Harlan Mills [Mills], Virginia Satir [Satir], Philip Crosby [Crosby], and others.

To attribute an idea to solely one person is naïveté; to attribute an idea solely to oneself is arrogance.

The principle of multiple minds taking a good idea and turning it into a great result pervades this book and FDD.

Reading This Book

The book is split into three sections:

1. Part 1 looks at some of the underlying principles and the important characteristics of any software development process and asks why it is so important. It then goes on to introduce the people, practices, and processes that comprise FDD. The section finishes with an introduction to tracking and reporting progress and work, and suggestions for report formats, design, and work packages.

2. Part 2 explores each process within FDD and provides extra hints, tips, and techniques to use when applying FDD.

3. Part 3 widens the discussion to answer the most frequently asked questions about FDD and to explore its impact on other important activities within a software development project that lie outside the process's targeted scope.

Making an Example

Writing a book about process is almost as mind-numbingly boring as reading one. In an attempt to keep you, the reader, awake until the end of the book, you'll find the authors suddenly bursting into role-play discussions at various points. We apologize, but it could be worse! Author Mac Felsing is a keen amateur opera singer; fortunately, printed media does not enable him to burst into song within these pages☺.

We use these role-play discussions to illustrate points within the context of a specific, small but realistic example project at Gary's Garage, a car dealership and servicing and repair shop.

Other books within this series are also using a similar example so that you can more readily compare the different approaches and processes described in the different books. We have chosen this example for two reasons:

1. It is large enough to present solid, real-world challenges.
2. We wanted to be able to present the contents of this book using a tangible, believable setting—one that you might relate to easily.

So, welcome to Gary's Garage. Gary owns the regional dealership franchise for a popular car manufacturer. At Gary's Garage, you can buy a new or quality used car, have your car serviced, and if unfortunately necessary, repaired. As the main dealer in the region, Gary also sells branded spare parts and accessories to other garages and to the general public. Gary and his team have volunteered to help specify and pilot a new sales and servicing management software system for the car manufacturer's dealerships.

Introducing...

The Development Team

- **Lisa, the Project Manager.** She is an experienced Project Manager for a small systems integrator and custom programming shop.
- **Steve, a Senior Developer.** He is experienced, intelligent, erudite, and British.
- **Mac, a Senior Developer.** He is just as experienced and intelligent as Steve but more handsome.
- **Various other extra staff as needed.** Don't you wish that staffing of projects was really this easy?

The Client Domain Experts

- **Mike the Mechanic.** As chief mechanic, Mike runs the servicing and repair workshop and a team of mechanics.
- **Stuart the Salesman.** He is in charge of the new and used car sales team and showrooms.
- **Sandy the Storeman (Parts Manager).** He is the parts manager, in charge of the spare parts inventory.
- **Rachel the Reception Manager.** She is in charge of scheduling services and repairs, and she handles customer relationships.
- **Anita the Accountant.** She runs a back office team, doing the books and payroll and managing the administrative side of the running a dealership franchise.

Steve: . . . Hey Mac, I'm told I'm going to be working with you on that car dealership project starting next week. What can you tell me about it?

Mac: Yeah! From initial discussions I've had with the Project Manager, Lisa, it's not as small a job as you'd first think, and wouldn't you know it; they want it up and running in 9 months. At least they've given us our pick of developers and team members. Lisa told me she wants a "proper process" used. I guess she does not want us experimenting with something like Extreme Programming on such a high-profile project. The team is likely to be too big for XP anyway . . . but the overhead of a really heavy process will make the schedule impossible. You're familiar with a good lightweight process, aren't you?

Steve: You mean Feature-Driven Development? Yes, I was the development manager on an important project where it was used very successfully. We can certainly use FDD. How about grabbing a meeting room, and I'll walk you through the ideas and concepts? . . .

Mac: Okay. I know Room 8 is free now. Let's grab a coffee on the way . . . .

Mac: . . . Just as I thought, Room 8 is free. It's a nice, quiet conference room with whiteboard, flipcharts, projector and projection screen, decent-sized working table, and comfortable chairs. We should have all we need.

Steve: More than enough! I don't think we'll need the projector; the whiteboard will do fine. I've picked up a couple of my favorite books on the topic, in case you ask me some hard questions, and we can grab anything else as we need it. Right! Where shall I start?

Mac: First I would like you to give me some general background so we can set a theoretical framework within which we can build and elaborate as we work on the project. That way, I will have a good understanding of what FDD is and how it works, and that will make it much easier to apply to our project.

Steve: Err . . . Okay!

part 1

Feature-Driven Development— Concepts

This section defines the roles, practices, processes, and progress reporting capabilities of Feature-Driven Development (FDD). It provides practical, useable answers to the following questions:

- Why do we have to manage software development?
- Who do we have to manage in software development?
- What do we have to manage in software development?
- How do we manage software development?
- How do we measure and track progress in software development?
- How do we document low-level design and implementation work?

Chapter 1 examines the current confusion, hype, and hysteria surrounding software development processes and asks why we need a formalized software development process.

Chapter 2 considers the influence of people and technology on a software development process and introduces the roles that people play in FDD.

Chapter 3 describes the collection of industry-recognized best practices that underlie FDD, why they are so valuable, and how they combine and support each other within FDD.

Chapter 4 defines the scope of FDD, identifying the processes within a development project that FDD covers and those it does not. The five processes within FDD are defined.

Chapter 5 shows how FDD captures data that makes accurate tracking and reporting of progress on the project relatively easy.

Chapter 6 demonstrates how to organize, plan, document, and audit the day-to-day design and implementation work being done on a project.

chapter 1

Process Pride:
The Pain and Relief

Answers: Why do we have to manage software development?

> *We think most process initiatives are silly. Well-*
> *intentioned managers and teams get so wrapped up*
> *in executing process that they forget that they are*
> *being paid for results, not process execution.*
>
> Coad, Lefebvre, De Luca [Coad 99]

The majority of nontrivial software projects fail to live up to expectations; they are late, over budget, and do not deliver all the needed functionality. Many software projects fail altogether.

**Process
Pride**

Developing complex software systems in teams of any significant size is hard, and when an important software project fails badly, pain and frustration are felt throughout an organization. Users, customers, executive sponsors, managers, developers, marketers, and sales and training staff are all affected in some way or another.

When confronted with this pain, organizations often look to formal processes, methodologies, and measurement systems for relief. Imposing a "proper process" is seen as a means for creating order out of the software development chaos:

> *If only we had the ultimate plan—a comprehensive set of steps that we could*
> *follow that would guarantee success. If only we had a better way of doing*
> *things, a better process. Then we would succeed...wouldn't we?*

This better process is seen as a silver bullet that will slay all the organization's software development woes. A working group or committee is set up and works for months to define, document, and deliver the new miracle-making process.

The Heavy Brigade

Many teams and organizations try to define a single, all-encompassing software development process for their organization. After all, if everyone in that organization created software in the same way, using the same process and producing the same types of documents, it would all become so much easier to manage. Wouldn't it?

The trouble is that software systems, technology, and organizations differ so much that any generalized approach to software development that truly spans the full spectrum of all the variations becomes far too general to be of practical use unless it then goes on to describe every possible role, activity, output, and step in detail. The resulting processes are usually documented in hundreds or even thousands of pages of activities and tasks, preconditions and postconditions, rules and guidelines, document templates and formats, and roles and responsibilities.

Some organizations have gone even further and have tried to define a single, all-encompassing software development process for an entire industry! Some companies even sell such processes!

Once these detailed, bulky processes are defined within an organization, a decree is usually issued, stating that all software development efforts, both big and small, must follow the new process. When problems in following these processes appear, the answer is to add more detail to improve the process, write down more information, and impose more order onto the chaos. However, the procedures used to review and approve suggested improvements to the new process are often difficult and drawn-out affairs. The result is a software development process that is inflexible and slow to adapt. Very quickly, more and more of the process is ignored, and its definition documents are left gathering dust on the shelf. Everyone goes back to what they were doing before the process was imposed, except that they may refer to the activities by different names to fool either themselves or their management into thinking that the new process is still being followed.

When successfully implemented, these processes are heavy on ceremony and administrative activity. Everyone looks busy doing something. Everyone has tasks to do, forms to fill out, meetings to attend, and status to report. Often, activity becomes a substitute for productivity. Communication between teams is achieved through the writing and reading of large, beautifully formatted documents. The result is an enormous volume of documentation, files, and records that rapidly become an overwhelming burden to read, fully understand, and keep up to date. The original desired end result—a software system—often becomes lost somewhere amidst all the activity and documentation.

Heavy, regimented processes make our project managers feel comfortable because they have something to hold on to, a guaranteed recipe for success: Their teams are "following the process." When they strike failure, they cannot be at fault because their teams were following the process; it is the process that failed, not the manager or the team. Obviously, a better process is needed so that another working group or committee is set up to define, document, and deliver the next new miracle-making process.

When we, as developers, are forced to follow one of these many unified processes, it feels as though our every step is dictated by the will of the all-powerful process. We no longer have to think, nor do we have the freedom to think—almost as though the process were wielding some sort of "Ruling Ring," such as that described in *The Lord of the Rings* [Tolkien]:

> *One Ring to rule them all, One Ring to find them,*
> *One Ring to bring them all and in the darkness bind them*
> *In the Land of Mordor where the Shadows lie.*
>
> JRR Tolkien [Tolkien]

Replace *Ring* with *Process* and *Mordor* with the name of your favorite thousand-page software development process. Go on! Try it! Does it fit?

Even when these processes work, they fail to deliver software fast enough to match the ever-quickening pace of change in today's business environments.

We need an alternative to the heavy process approach.

The Light Brigade

Recently, there has been a growing rebellion against heavy, high-ceremony processes. Out go the large documents. Out go the organizational walls separating customers, analysts, designers, and programmers. Out go the endless lists of detailed tasks, reports, and long meetings. However, as often happens in a rebellion, we swing from one extreme to another, and the baby, if not thrown out completely with the bath water, is left wobbling precariously on the edge of the bath.

If we are not careful, we lose the thinking before coding (analysis and design). We can also rapidly lose sight of the original scope and goals for the project. The result is a project out of control, building and rebuilding the wrong things, inability to deliver to a schedule, and a general lack of direction and coordination—in fact, all the very things that the heavy processes were intended to provide.

On October 25, 1854, at the battle of Balaclava, a misunderstood order sent 673 British light cavalrymen charging down a narrowing valley to make a frontal assault on a battery of Russian cannons. Also coming under fire from cannon and infantry on both sides of the valley, they were cut to ribbons; less than 200, almost all of them wounded, returned.

If not careful, in our eagerness to throw off the burden of heavy-weight processes, we charge headlong, straight into code and chaos, our very own *Charge of the Light Brigade* [Tennyson].

The Charge of the Light Brigade

Half a league, half a league,
Half a league onward,
All in the valley of Death
Rode the six hundred.
"Forward, the Light Brigade!
Charge for the guns!" he said:
Into the valley of Death
Rode the six hundred.

"Forward, the Light Brigade!"
Was there a man dismay'd?
Not tho' the soldier knew
Some one had blunder'd:
Theirs' not to make reply,
Theirs' not to reason why,
Theirs' but to do and die:
Into the valley of Death
Rode the six hundred.

Cannon to the right of them,
Cannon to the left of them,
Cannon in front of them
Volley'd and thunder'd;
Storm'd at with shot and shell,
Boldly they rode and well,
Into the Jaws of Death,
Into the mouth of Hell,
Rode the six hundred.

Flash'd all their sabres bare,
Flash'd as they turn'd in air,
Sabring the gunners there,
Charging an army, while
All the world wonder'd:
Plunged in the battery-smoke
Right thro' the line they broke;
Cossack and Russian
Reel'd from the sabre-stroke
Shatter'd and sunder'd.
Then they rode back, but not,
Not the six hundred.

Cannon to the right of them,
Cannon to the left of them,
Cannon behind them
Volley'd and thunder'd;
Storm'd at with shot and shell,
While horse and hero fell,
They that had fought so well
Came thro' the Jaws of Death,
Back from the mouth of Hell,
All that was left of them
Left of six hundred.

When can their glory fade?
O the wild charge they made!
All the world wonder'd.
Honour the charge they made!
Honour the Light Brigade,
Noble six hundred!

Alfred, Lord Tennyson *(1809–1892)* [Tennyson]

The courage, good intentions, effort, and skill of those who took part in the original charge is not in any doubt, but the cost was appallingly high: "*What do you mean, we are very late and very over budget? We delivered it, didn't we?*"

Although the Light Brigade did capture some Russian guns, they had charged the wrong ones: "*What do you mean, we haven't built what you wanted?*"

No one was able to follow the Light Brigade and secure the captured guns, so they had to be left for the enemy to recover:

"*What do you mean, what we've built is not useful?*"

"*What do you mean, you're going back to the old system?*"

Military historians still debate the chain of events that led to the heroic but insanely foolish charge of the Light Brigade.

"*Our development team can't deliver even the simplest projects! They are always late and never produce the systems we need!*"

"The executive sponsors keep changing their minds! We never have the resources or time to produce what they ask! They change the requirements at least two or three times before we can ever deliver anything! It's a wonder that we can deliver anything at all!"

The Search

The search for the ultimate process, the one and only true way to do software development, continues: high ceremony, low ceremony, heavyweight, lightweight, agile, iterative, incremental, full-lifecycle, user-centric, architecture-centric, feature-centric, and on and on. Process wars have replaced the method wars of the previous decade.

"'Play it again, Sam,'...only this time, call it something slightly different."

Ask yourself the following questions:

- Has executing a particular software development process become more important to you, your team, or your organization than achieving tangible, working results?
- Has executing a particular process in the name of quality become more important to you, your team, or your organization than producing quality results?
- Has following the "right process" become more important to you than delivering software on time, within budget, and with all the expected function?
- Does your current process encourage innovation and creativity or does it stifle them?
- Do you feel as though the process is in control of you, rather than you in control of the process?
- Do you spend more time arguing about process on object technology discussion forums than you do producing useful software?
- Do you feel that you no longer have to think to produce software, just follow a recipe, and everything will come out all right?
  - 2 weeks gathering requirements
  - 3 hours a week meeting to discuss status
  - 2 weeks designing
  - 4 weeks building and testing
  - 2 analysts, 15 programmers, 3 testers, 1 manager, and a partridge in a pear tree!
  - Mix well, put in small room together for the length of project, give it an impossible deadline, and let simmer for...

If we can answer yes to these questions, we are suffering the effects of process pride.

We must, *must* remember that a process is only a means to an end. Producing software is the ultimate goal of any software development effort. The process is only the set of tools used to achieve that goal! Process pride occurs when doing things the "right way" becomes more important than achieving the right results.

We need to beware of falling into that trap when talking about FDD. At the end of the day, we are being paid to produce software systems, not to follow some particular process, no matter how good we may think it is. We tend to forget that the process we follow—whether formal or informal, heavyweight or lightweight—is nothing more or less than a means to accomplish the goal of creating a software system.

So, with this warning *ring*ing in our ears, let's look at some fundamental concepts of a software development process.

Communication, Communication, and Communication

When we examine two developers writing a software application in their spare time, we see little that we would call a formal process. However, when we examine a project with hundreds of developers distributed across multiple locations working to develop a large software system, process often seems to be all we can see. Both examples do have process, but the first is much simpler and very informal. It is most likely maintained wholly within the minds and interactions of the two developers who, over time, have learned to communicate very effectively with each other. In larger projects, the processes tend to be both much more visible and much more formal, although you will still find many small "processes" in a large organization that are hidden, "understood," or part of the tribal knowledge and not recorded anywhere. In fact, the processes (not necessarily productive processes) that last the longest are those that become habit: "It's just the way we do things here." One goal for a process designer is to make the process straightforward to learn and remember so that following it becomes habit as quickly as possible.

So what are the fundamental differences between two developers writing software in a garage and thousand-person, multimillion-dollar software development efforts?

Those who work in the real estate industry tell us that the three most important aspects of real estate are location, location, and location. The software development process equivalent is communication, communication, and communication. Communication is taking place constantly within a software development process at every level. In fact, no process (work) can occur without it! In failed projects, communication or failure of it at some level is usually a major contributor to the project's downfall.

If we consider developers as nodes in a communication network, all potentially linked to each other by communications channels, there is only one channel between our two developers in their garage.

However, as we add more developers, the number of potential communication channels grows dramatically (Figure 1–1).

Between four developers, there are six potential communication links (Figure 1–2). Between 10, there are 45 potential links, and there are 4,950 potential communication links between 100 individuals on a team.

If not managed, there will be either too much time spent communicating, and nothing will get done, or too little communication, and results will not integrate and work together.

As a team grows larger, managing communication becomes increasingly difficult.

Language

Communication requires language. Within a development team, different subteams use different languages. Some of these languages are textual, others are graphical, and others are more mathematical in nature. There are languages for expressing requirements, defining interfaces, defining database tables, communicating analysis and design models, describing algorithms, and describing patterns; and there is a myriad of different programming languages for communicating instruc-

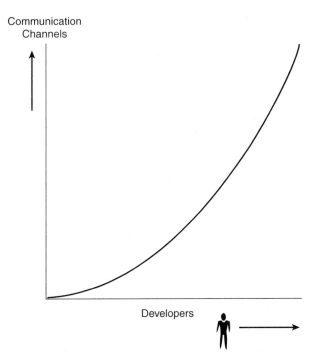

Communication Channels

Developers

Figure 1–1
The number of potential communication channels grows dramatically as developers are added.

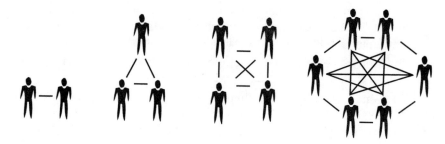

Figure 1–2
More developers means many more potential communication paths.

tions to a computer. Much of the work of a development team involves translating from one language to another (Figure 1–3).

Then, of course, to add to the mix, there are communication channels and languages required to communicate with customers, users, and sponsors of the project.

Each time we translate from one language to another, there is a potential for loss of information or for communicating the wrong information. Errors can occur when converting statements made during verbal interviews to structured requirements and diagrammatic models, adding documentation to the models, developing persistent storage models, and even creating the code. If information is not accurately transferred at each of these "interfaces," we have the potential for building the wrong system. Therefore, we want to keep the number of translations of infor-

Figure 1–3
Translating from one "language" to another.

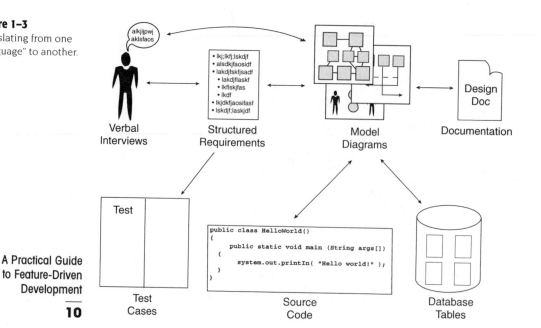

mation to a minimum and to automate as many of the translations as possible to reduce the chance that information is lost.

To further complicate matters, at each step along the way, the people involved in transferring the information may not know what they need to communicate. For example, users defining the system may not know what it is that they really need. They may end up describing task steps or symptoms of a larger problem without actually communicating the needed functionality. So, not only can we make errors in translating the information from one form or medium to another, we may even be translating the wrong information! Therefore, a good process uses numerous feedback loops to provide validation and verification as often and as early as possible.

Another big problem preventing communication is the fear of being wrong. If a user, manager, analyst, or developer is so afraid of being seen to have made a mistake that they withhold information, clear communication is obviously compromised, and the error is often compounded over time. It is proper that we should have accountability within a project but our software development processes should encourage and support an environment of trust and responsibility, rather than one of suspicion and fear of recrimination.

A software development process describes what to communicate, when to communicate, how to communicate, and with whom to communicate (most process descriptions will not tell you why; this is normally left for someone to write a book about!).

Mac: *...What sorts of communication will happen on this project? Obviously, the clients need to communicate their requirements to the development team.*

Steve: *Uh, huh! The team needs to find out what the client really wants the system to do but gathering requirements is hard because...*
- *Clients often have only a vague idea of what they want or what is possible.*
- *The development team often does not know the problem domain in depth.*
- *Development and business people often have very different personalities and styles of communication.*
- *The clients, analysts, and developers often lack a common language and terms, which aggravates miscommunication.*
- *And so on...*

Mac: *...And those working with the client on requirements will also have to take great care in communicating those requirements to the rest of the development team. Without clear communication of requirements, we cannot build the right system.*

Steve: *In return, the clients, managers, users, and sponsors are going to want to see the progress being made. If we do not give them the right level of detailed, accurate, and timely progress reports, they will not be able to intervene appropriately to resolve issues and steer the project. Worse still, they might intervene inappropriately, which could be disastrous.*

Mac: *What about communicating analysis, design, and implementation?*

Steve: *What about it?*

Mac: *Well, we generally split the development of software into four activities. In analysis, we try to understand the problem with little thought to the particular set of technologies that we are going to use to build the solution (technical architecture). In design, we map the results of our analysis to our intended technical architecture, making trade-offs and adding more detail as necessary. In implementation, we build our design, and in testing, we verify that the solution does, indeed, solve the problem.*

Steve: *Okay, I see what you mean! The Unified Modeling Language (UML), despite all its problems, has become the de facto standard graphical language for communicating object-oriented analysis and design results. Design patterns, programming language idioms, and coding standards help developers to communicate and verify that an implementation matches its design. And test cases, test results, defect reports, and fixes communicate quality and completeness to managers and the client.*

Mac: *We mustn't forget that the team responsible for deploying the new system needs to know the various software components that make up the system, what data needs to be loaded before the system can be used, and the exact format of that data. They are reliant on the development team to communicate all this to them.*

Steve: *And existing data may need to be "cleaned" and converted to the format of the new system. This involves communicating with the owners of the existing data. New machines and network links may be needed, so the deployment team also has to communicate with the operators and users at the site of the new equipment.*

Mac: *Finally, but not least important—although it often seems to be treated that way in my experience—the users of the new system will need to learn how to use it. The project team needs to communicate how to use the new system through online, context-sensitive help, user manuals, training courses, demonstrations, tips-of-the day messages, and so on.*

Steve: *Hmmm, it's already starting to sound complex. We will need to break the problem down and attack it a chunk at a time. That reminds me...*

Complexity

There is a limit to the amount of complexity mere humans can hold within their heads.

As the size of a software system grows, the complexity of that software system grows "at least as fast as the square of the size of the program" [Weinberg 92] and quickly outstrips the relatively fixed capacity of a human brain. Gerald Weinberg calls this law of software development *the size/complexity dynamic.*

The best strategy that we have for dealing with such large problems is decomposition. We break the problem down into smaller and smaller problems until we have reduced the size of the problems to something we can manage. We then go about solving each small problem, integrating the solutions to form the solution for the bigger problem.

Given enough time, our two friends in their garage could produce very large and complex software systems by solving one small problem after another. Adding more people to the team allows us to solve many of the small problems in parallel and deliver large systems more quickly. The more people we add, the more we can do in parallel.

Here's the catch: The more people we have working in parallel, the more likely it is that we will bump into communication and coordination problems. If there are significant dependencies between the problems being solved, we have to work hard at putting the right communication channels in place so that everyone has the information they need at the right time.

So we are back to managing communication again.

Mac: *Steve, What if we could arrange things so that the decomposed problems are completely independent of each other? Would that reduce the need for communication between groups of developers working on those problems and avoid having to manage the overhead of those communications?*

Steve: *That's a good point. It is an idea to consider when we discuss architecture [in Chapter 12, "Reducing Dependencies between Components"].*

Quality

According to Philip Crosby's definition [Crosby], quality can be simply defined as conformance to requirements—how often the software behaves as required. The question, as Gerald Weinberg [Weinberg 92] points out, is, whose requirements?

We can talk of quality in software development having both an external and internal face. A user talking about the quality of a system discusses the user interface, the response time, the reliability, and the ease of use of the system. A developer talking about quality discusses elegance of design; ease of maintenance and enhancement; and compliance to standards, patterns, and conventions.

These two faces are, of course, related. Low internal quality makes it much, much harder to maintain high external quality. This is especially true for incremental or iterative development where, after the first iteration or increment, we are constantly building on what we built before.

Recognizing when a design for an iteration is good enough is a very valuable skill. If we make the design too simple, we add to the rework that we must do in later iterations when we need to extend that functionality and when time pressure may be more intense. If we select a more general and complex design, we could be spending time building in flexibility that will never be used.

It often seems that developers have a natural complexity level; some developers always seem to make their designs too complex, and others always seem to oversimplify. Recognizing these tendencies in themselves helps developers make the appropriate trade-off decisions, as does a good knowledge of the problem domain. Whatever the trade-off decisions, it is important that they are made visible to others on the team— that communication word again.

The Quality Spectrum

Simply splitting quality into external and internal views is really too simple a model; users and developers are not the only people with opinions about a system's quality. Software managers will look at quality in terms of ease of maintenance and enhancement, compliance to standards and conventions, and ability to deliver it on time. Project sponsors will look at how well the system meets their business requirements. Does it allow them to meet a constantly changing business environment and be proactive in meeting the challenges that are ever present in the marketplace? When we add to this the views of testers, technical writers, technical support personnel, and so on, we see that we need to look at quality as a spectrum, with internal quality at one end and external quality at the other (Figure 1–4). Developers and software managers view the system more in terms of internal quality. System users and business sponsors tend to view the system more in terms of external quality.

Building in Quality

A naïve view associates quality with testing of code and testing with a separate test team that goes to work once coding is complete. This model has severe problems. It is reminiscent of "waterfall thinking." A waterfall approach to software development is:

1. Do all of the analysis first.
2. Then do all of the design.
3. Then do all of the coding.
4. Finally, test the system.

Figure 1–4
The quality spectrum.

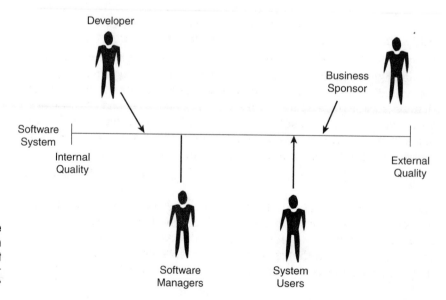

One of the most documented problems with a waterfall approach over the last couple of decades has been that mistakes made early in the process are often not found until very late in the process. The cost in finding an error later, rather than sooner, varies from study to study but is always much higher: "Observe that it is perhaps 100 times as costly to make a change to the requirements during system testing as it is to make the change during requirements definition."[Fairley]

One way to ease this problem is to split the project into iterations or increments so that the distance in time between analysis and test is reduced. If we test something earlier, we will find the problem earlier, and the cost of fixing it is reduced.

A complementary approach is to use practices that increase quality throughout the four activities. In other words, broaden the concept of quality so that it is more than just the testing of running code. Inspections are one such technique. Audits and metrics tools are another.

Mac: *So what you're saying is that, in earlier methods, they tried to improve quality by providing shorter iterations through the lifecycle and broadening the definition of quality to include more than just code without bugs.*

Steve: *Exactly! Both strategies attempt to provide earlier feedback on the correctness of what has been done so far.*

Mac: *So, by expanding the "definition" of quality to include things such as coding standards and measuring audits and metrics in the code, software managers are able to increase the quality of the delivered code because they are getting good feedback earlier in the lifecycle?*

Steve: *Yes, but remember that developers generally enjoy delivering quality work, too.*

People typically want to do "quality" work. Each individual developer has his or her own idea about the acceptable level of quality of a system and that is usually approximately the best quality that they have achieved in the past.

It is better to ask those developers who have a lower idea of quality to reach for a higher standard than to ask those with higher standards to reduce their ideas of acceptable quality. Our self-esteem is linked to the quality of what we produce. If we are consistently forced to produce what we consider to be low-quality work, we will lose self-esteem, resulting in lower morale and decreased productivity. On the other hand, if recognized as such, asking developers to produce a higher quality product than they would naturally do actually enhances their self-esteem—if they can do it.

Even if an organization standardizes on a level of acceptable internal quality, it may well be lower than that of the individual developer's ideas of acceptable quality. So, at the beginning of a project, the development team needs to agree on what is an acceptable level of internal quality and what is not. Obviously, this level cannot be lower than that of the organization (except in unusual circumstances) but may be set higher. This level of quality is made public in published design and coding standards and enforced primarily by some sort of design and code inspection (automated source code audits and source code formatters help to enforce code-naming and layout standards).

Mac: *If, as according to Crosby's working definition [Crosby], "quality is conformance to the requirements," we could specify things such as coding standards and the use of various algorithms and patterns, where appropriate, as requirements and could use techniques such as code inspections to detect and enforce these requirements. In other words, a software team can deal with important issues on a software project by creating a constraint in the form of a requirement for the project.*

Steve: *Yes, theoretically. In practice, I find that this use of the term* requirement *leads to confusion. I prefer to reserve it to mean the features and performance that the users desire in a software system. I prefer to talk of internal quality requirements as complying with standards, conventions, and practices.*

Also, requirements such as "The system will ship with no critical bugs" are useless because we cannot prove whether a system satisfies that requirement; we certainly cannot tell if a bug we do not know about is critical.

Mac: *Okay. What about a requirement that says the system will ship with no known critical bugs? We can measure that.*

Steve: *Yes we can, but it says very little about the quality of the system. In fact, the only thing we can say about the quality of system by this measure is that it is probably low in quality if we have a long list of known critical bugs. If this really was a measure of quality, we could "improve quality" by not testing at all; we would find no critical bugs and could ship whatever compiled cleanly because it would satisfy that so-called requirement. Even if we tested, how do we know whether our testers are any good? This is complete nonsense; it's just playing with figures and definitions.*

Mac: *Hmmm, not entirely convinced, but okay. However, I reserve the right to discuss this a bit more when talk about testing....*

In iterative, object-oriented software development where we want to reuse results, we need to ensure that internal quality is built in early so that we have quality to build on later. If we allow low-quality results at the start, we will find ourselves in a vicious cycle of low quality resulting in more low quality.

A word of caution: Be careful not to confuse quality with optimization. Great results can be made from combinations of suboptimal parts. Optimizing a small part may make no significant difference to the whole. An overly complicated, bug-ridden part or an incorrect implementation of a requirement, on the other hand, can be the cause of many problems in other parts.

In January 2000, a number of people, including Peter Coad and Jeff De Luca, were sitting in a room, discussing the purpose of a software development process. The result of that discussion was a statement similar to the following:

The purpose of a software development process is to enable and enforce the repeatable delivery of working software in a timely and cost-effective manner, supplying accurate and meaningful information to all key roles inside and outside a project with the minimum of disruption to developers.

When a process emphasizes only enforcement, it stifles creativity and innovation, and causes frustration for the developers who feel their ideas are considered of no worth. On the other side of the coin, when a process emphasizes only enabling, creativity and innovation are allowed to reign unbridled, causing frustration for managers and team leaders because everyone is doing their own thing, and results do not integrate. This is a constant balancing act. Any process should be monitored and reviewed for effectiveness and value, and should be modified when necessary to maintain its value to the organization.

Similarly, having hundreds of pages of steps to execute in an overly specified process demoralizes the team members to the point that they switch off their minds and blindly follow the steps. At the other extreme, process descriptions that are too vague, abstract, or general cause each one of us to make up our own way of doing things and to work harder than necessary to achieve the desired results.

The main mechanism for communication within the development team and between a development team and its client is often large documents. In a process that emphasizes the production of documents, care must be taken that the focus is not put on recording results when it should be on getting the results right—that the emphasis is put on achieving quality results instead of quality formatting of results.

If the overhead of producing progress and status reports is too high, it will not be done well, and the information they contain is more likely to be inaccurate or irrelevant. Without accurate and meaningful information, the feedback that managers get from the software process is useless or, even worse, late or inaccurate. Managers cannot take appropriate action if they do not know what is actually happening on a project. Worse still, they may take inappropriate action that increases rather than reduces the pain.

Summary

A *good process is well bounded*; it provides enough structure to guide innovation and creativity, constraining it to appropriate times and places.

A *good process clearly defines tasks. The tasks are focused on results* without specifying minutia, so that we progress efficiently but still have the freedom to adapt to unusual events or changes in circumstances.

A *good process produces accurate progress and status information* for team leaders, project managers, upper management, and the client, while minimizing the impact on the developer's time.

A *good process quickly becomes a matter of habit*, rather than a set of conscious acts. Developers do not want to have to consult a 3,000-page process manual every time they reach a new step in an activity.

A *good process helps a team to maintain quality and manage complexity*.

A *good process optimizes communication within and outside the team*.

chapter 2

Feature-Driven Development— Projects and People

A nswers: Who do we have to manage in software development?

> *No amount of process over-specification will make up for bad people. Far better: Staff your project with good people, do whatever it takes to keep them happy, and use simple, well-bounded processes to guide them along the way.*
>
> Coad, LeFebvre, De Luca [Coad 99]

In Chapter 1, we considered process from a relatively detached perspective. However, a software process must function within a context. That context is a software development project. Any project of any sort is little more than a collection of activities, resources, and communication channels, with at least one specific purpose or goal to achieve within a given time frame. However, this is a very general definition and could define a project for building a bridge, constructing an ocean liner, or landing a mission on Mars. Therefore, more specifically, what are the components of a software development project? They certainly include:

- *Some statement of purpose*, problem statement, or list of goals or very high-level requirements describing what the system needs to do. Without this, there is no reason for the project to exist.

- A *list of the roles* that people play on the project. When written down, this usually takes the form of an abstract organizational chart. Each different role requires a set of skills and a level of experience. Each role defines responsibilities and accountability.

- *People with the requisite skills and experience* to play the roles in the abstract organizational chart. Assigning people to the roles within the abstract organizational chart produces a concrete organization chart for the project.

- A *set of well-bounded processes* describing how these people playing their roles interact with each other to produce the desired software system.
- A *set of technologies*: programming languages, development tools, ready-built components, modules, and products.
- An *architecture*, a framework within which to construct the software system. The project may reuse an existing architecture. Alternatively, an appropriate framework may not exist, and one of the first activities of the project needs to produce and prove the architecture.

The statement of purpose does need to be sensible. It is nonsense to define a statement of purpose for a project that is not achievable within a reasonable time frame. For very ambitious programs, it is often better to identify several projects that can be run concurrently or as follow-on efforts. As we'll see, Feature-Driven Development (FDD) supports this need very nicely, indeed. The statement of purpose may also start off somewhat vaguely. Chapter 7, "Develop the Overall Model—Tips for the Chief Architect/Facilitator," suggests a useful exercise to help refine the statement of purpose.

The list of roles of a project team is like the players' positions in a sports team or the parts in a play or symphony. We need the software development equivalent of players, actors, and musicians to cast in those roles.

The processes describe the rules of the game, the acts of the play, or the movements in a symphony. They describe the framework through which all work is performed.

The technologies are the players' equipment, the props used in the play, or the musicians' instruments.

Likewise, the architectural framework is the marked pitch, the playing area, or the stage and scenery.

Mac: *What roles do we need on this project?*

Steve: *Well, obviously, the key roles are people representing the user or customer, developers, and testers. We already have Lisa as Project Manager to own it and steer it, but she will probably need some secretarial support.*

Mac: *Gary and his team are available to us as customer reps. The developers will need some support too, won't they? The IT department will provide the usual generic support but we'll need to provide more project-specific support.*

Steve: *Yes. Servers, network, databases, build system, configuration management. We need to try to cover the support of all these areas. And then there is managing the actual deployment, too.*

Mac: *Can we draw up an abstract organizational chart listing the roles we think we need?*

Steve: *Okay. I have an example from a previous project we can use as a starting point.* (Figure 2–1)

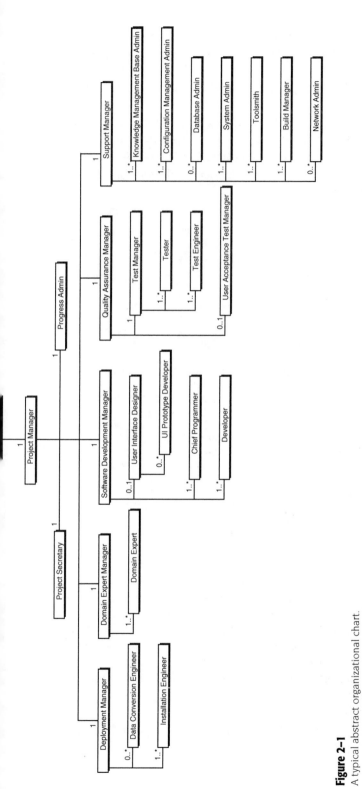

Figure 2-1

A typical abstract organizational chart.

21

Mac: *I'm not sure that we will need all of those roles on this project.*

Steve: *That's okay! It's just a starting point. We'll modify it to fit the project and resources we have.*

Mac: *I guess that we need to assign real people to these roles—start filling in names next to the roles.*

Steve: *Yes, and that's easier said than done. Sometimes, people are just not available or there is nobody qualified to play a certain role. It actually feels a bit like a soccer team manager selecting his team for the next game. We have a limited number of players in the squad from which to pick, and we may have to play someone "out of position" until we can sign a new player.*

Mac: *But it's more complicated than that. Remember, some people can play more than one role at once, and some roles can be played by multiple people....*

Note: Overdosing on UML

Unified Modeling Language (UML) is a graphical notation for describing software systems. With a little bending of the rules, it can also be useful in graphically describing software projects. Figure 2–1 is actually an abuse of the UML class diagram notation, with each role in the project represented as a class. Associations are used to suggest reporting lines, and multiplicities are used to suggest the number of people required in a role. We could represent instances of those roles by objects and draw a concrete organization chart for the project, using an object diagram. The UML actor notation might feel a more natural fit for roles within a project, but UML forbids the drawing of associations between actors, and the stickman graphic is clumsy to use in this context. UML activity diagrams are also obvious candidates for describing processes within a software development project and UML component diagrams could list the technologies used. However, beware of the temptation to overdose on notation where a simple text list is more than good enough. It is not a legal requirement to use every squiggle defined within UML. Throughout this book, we use UML extensively because it is the de facto industry standard, but we also use other formats and notations where we feel it communicates much better.

The Big Three

Coaches of sports teams are often spoken of as using a particular *system*, as are theatrical directors and symphony conductors. Let's consider a software development project as a system—a system for creating software. If a project is a system for building software, then the three biggest components of that system are people, process, and technology. Technology is obviously important, as is process, but it really is all about people. Jeff De Luca's first law of information technology states: "I.T. is 80% psychology and 20% technology."

In the anniversary edition of his book, *The Mythical Man-Month*, in a section entitled "People Are Everything (Well, Almost Everything)," Fred

Brooks [Brooks] says: "The quality of the people on a project, and their organization and management, are much more important factors in success than are the tools they use or the technical approaches they take."

The underlying thesis of Tom De Marco and Timothy Lister's famous book, *Peopleware: Productive Projects and Teams* [De Marco], is: "The major problems of our work are not so much technological as sociological in nature."

In Luke Hohmann's book, *Journey of the Software Professional: The Sociology of Computer Programming* [Hohmann], we read: "Although technology is important, Jim McCarthy got it right when he said: 'I see software development as primarily a sociological or cultural phenomenon.'"

Richard Fairley, in *Software Engineering Concepts* [Fairley] writes: "Software project managers must be effective in dealing with the factors that motivate and frustrate programmers."

Finally, Gerald Weinberg thought it important enough to write an entire book, *The Psychology of Computer Programming* [Weinberg 98].

Our own experience certainly does not disagree. Software development really is all about people. If it were not, it would be much, much easier.

Process and People

The temptation when designing a process or managing a project is to treat people as though they are no more than "resources." Many traditional project management tools, unfortunately, encourage this sort of thinking. It's as though the people in project teams are interchangeable, consistent, logical, software-producing machines, but thankfully people are not machines.

- People are emotional.
- People are fallible.
- People get tired.
- People get sick.
- People are all different.
- People are creative.
- People are innovative.
- People are resourceful.
- People can be inspired.
- People change as they grow older.
- People have lives outside of work.
- People leave for one reason or another.

Otherwise, it would be a dreadfully dreary industry to work in.

So, to be successful, unless it is to be used only by extraterrestrials, our process needs to take into consideration the peculiarities, strengths, and limitations of human beings.

Individual Productivity

To make things even more interesting, some human beings are much more productive than others. Results vary in the exact quantities but study after study has shown that good developers can be between 10 and 20 times more productive than poor developers (see almost every book in the reference section at the end of this book for details).

Do the math! Let's say that we hire four good developers instead of eight average developers. Even if the good developers are only four times more productive than the average developers and we have to pay the good developers twice as much as the average developers, we are still twice as productive for the same cost (Figure 2–2).

Figure 2–2
Cost and productivity of good vs. average developers.

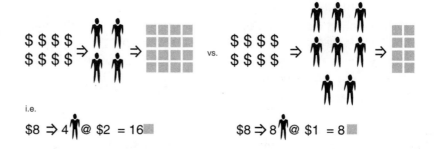

We have not even considered the reduction in communication and coordination headaches from managing half the number of people, the reduced cost of hardware, software, furniture, and office space, etc.

If you staff a team with great people, the process and technology should take care of themselves. It is not that great people do not need a formal process or do not use process. No, a good team will create a process if a useful one does not exist or will tailor an existing process to fit. They know they need a process and will, therefore, put one in place. They will also select appropriate technologies and use them well. This is part of what makes them great people.

You may say, "Okay. I'm sold! Where do I find these amazing developers?" Ah!...The problem! Great developers are not easy to find, and how do you tell the good from the average?

The big challenge is to attract good developers, recognize them, and keep them; after all, there is little point in going to all the effort of finding them if they are not going to want to stay.

Attracting, Recognizing, and Keeping Good People

An entire book could be written on each topic, so we will restrict ourselves to only a handful of basic ideas per topic.

Attracting Good People

Attracting good people means more than offering competitive salaries, standard benefits, and challenging work on the latest technologies. Nearly all organizations can promise these.

So, all other things being equal, what is it that attracts developers? Here are some of the additional benefits from one company's job advertisements* (with some of the authors' thoughts):

Weekly "Pizza Day"...*This company seems to have a sense of fun, and we like pizza.*

Free Starbucks Coffee and Soda ...*This company knows that developers traditionally live on fat, sugar, and caffeine.*

Monthly Book Allowance ...*This company knows that good developers read books on technology and software development to keep themselves up to date.*

Paid Certification Programs...*Professional development is important to this company.*

No Cubicles...*This company knows that a good working environment is important.*

Health Club Memberships...*This company values the health of its employees (and knows that its developers like fat, sugar, and caffeine too much!).*

Understanding how good developers think and what motivates them is key.

It sounds like this company understands developers and may be a cool place to work.

Another attractor is the core values of an organization or a team. Strong core values will attract people with similar core values. Togethersoft's core values are listed explicitly on its careers Web page, http://www.togethersoft.com/work_here.jsp, and Nebulon's are strongly implied on its Web site, http://www.nebulon.com/.

However, writing down core values on a Web page is no good if other visible qualities of the company do not reflect those core values. If a core value of a company is "always deliver quality" but that company's products are full of bugs, people are repelled instead of attracted by that core value.

---

*The company that advertises these benefits is Digital Focus (http://www.digital-focus.com), the home of Cliff Berg, author of Advanced Java: Development for Enterprise Applications *[Berg], several* Dr. Dobbs *articles [Dobbs], and the Java language guru on the project in Singapore, described in the Introduction to this book.*

Recognizing Good People

The next challenge is to recognize good people in the swarm of those attracted to our team or organization. It is important that strategies are devised for interviewing to help identify good people. Identify the characteristics you expect in the person you want for the job and develop an interview technique that will test for these characteristics. It sounds so obvious, but in practice, it is rarely done well, and an inappropriate Human Resources (HR)–devised default interview is often used instead.

Auditions are one highly recommended strategy. De Marco recommends that candidates present on a topic for 10–15 minutes in front of those they are likely to be working with if hired. If candidates are not going to fit in with the team well, it does not matter how knowledgeable they are, they are not going to be productive and may actually reduce the productivity of the team [De Marco].

TogetherSoft asks candidate mentors to present for 15 minutes on a non-technical topic of their choice, followed by a session of object modeling, where the candidate is asked to think out loud while modeling a simple problem domain. Representatives from all of the departments that work with the mentors are present and are asking themselves whether the candidate is someone they want to work with. A checklist of questions helps the reviewers to focus on specific aspects of the candidate's performance.

Because of the time and cost of arranging auditions, it is useful to have a couple of one-on-one screening interviews first, one by HR and one by someone from the hiring department. Again, some time spent designing a set of questions to highlight the desired qualities of the candidate is time well spent.

When auditions are not possible, instead of just sitting across a table firing questions at the candidates, work with them at a whiteboard, walking them through some standard scenarios and asking them to solve problems. Start with easy problems and increase the level of difficulty. Note the level of problem at which they start to have trouble and how they handle it. For developers, have problems that test implementation-level, design-level, and analysis-level thinking.

Proven experience in a particular role or a particular technology is obviously important, but both auditions and whiteboard sessions are looking for the ability to think, learn, and adapt as much as, if not more than, knowledge in a specific area.

> *The discussions aim at determining how smart a person is in an abstract sense—not simply how much people know about coding, testing, or a particular specialty, such as marketing. Bill Gates has been quoted as looking for four essential qualities in new hires: ambition, IQ, technical expertise, and business judgment, with IQ the most important. Famous general questions from Microsoft interviews include being asked to estimate the volume of water flowing down the Mississippi River and the number of gas stations in the United States. The answer does not matter as much as the approach a person takes to analyze the problem.*
>
> *Cusumano and Selby* [Cusumano]

Keeping Good People

Having gone to all the effort to attract and recognize good people, it makes sense to put some effort into keeping them. Losing anyone who is making a significant contribution to a project before its end is a blow to any team. It means that someone has to cover that person's responsibilities while a replacement is sought. It also changes the team dynamics, and the team has to learn to adjust to the change. Any replacement has to be brought up to speed, and that takes time, too. Therefore, it makes sense to keep people happy so that they stay for at least the duration of the project.

Work culture and environment are the main factors in retaining people. A culture of trust, a culture of excellence, and a culture that values people and encourages a sense of community—all these help people stay in a job.

Good, open communication encourages trust. As developers, we need to be able to trust our managers, and our managers need to feel that they can trust their developers. Processes that work on a need-to-know basis do not encourage trust. Quite the reverse; they encourage a sense of suspicion and insecurity. Most of us do not work for organizations that need to be run like military intelligence services. Those who do had accepted that culture as part of the job when they were hired.

Feeling you are part of something special, that your organization is the best at something, motivates people. In a culture pursuing excellence, you are always learning, trying to improve, trying to be the best. Good people thrive in environments such as this.

Feeling that your managers and peers value you is a super feeling. People who feel that management views them as interchangeable, easily replaced parts understandably feel less loyalty to their managers and organizations.

Regular, relaxed, informal communal events and activities, such as meals (Pizza Day), sports, games, and musical events, can all help to create a sense of community and belonging—taking on another team in the company at soccer or 10-pin bowling, for example. Going to see the latest Star Wars movie together or putting on a concert for charity are other examples. When you feel that you belong, you are less likely to consider leaving.

Work environment is also important. Providing an environment in which good people can excel is another good use of resources. It can take 15 minutes for people to re-immerse themselves in their work after an interruption. Phone calls, noise from across the room, slow or faulty hardware and software, having to get up to fetch a book because there are no bookshelves within reach, visitors wandering around saying "Hi" are examples of such interruptions.

The Roles People Play in FDD

The reality of life is that we are members of development teams of mixed ability and experience and from varying walks of life. We work in less-than-ideal environments and often have little power to change them. So we have to make the best of what we have.

FDD defines six key project roles and implicitly suggests a number of supporting and additional roles. The FDD roles, when combined with the FDD processes, organize a project so that individual strengths are fully utilized and support is available in areas of weakness.

Six Key Project Roles

1. The *Project Manager* (PM) is the administrative lead of the project responsible for reporting progress; managing budgets; fighting for headcount; and managing equipment, space, and resources, etc. As operator and maintainer of the project system, the Project Manager's job is to create and maintain an environment in which the system works best and where his or her team can work productively and excel. Part of that role involves shielding the development team from distractions by forces external to the project. Think of the Project Manager as operating the deflector shield on the front of Star Trek's USS *Enterprise* so that the project team behind can go about its work, safe from random elements floating in its direction. Random elements include overzealous CTOs or clients wanting to visit the team at a crucial moment in the project, HR personnel wanting a new form filled out by everyone and wanting it done today, building maintenance departments scheduling a fire-drill three days before a major milestone, the IT department wanting to do a stock take of the project's personal computers and printers, upper management deciding to restrict Internet access to a chosen few, an exotic new requirement request, and so on. An FDD Project Manager is not there to force team members to work but to enable them to work. The Project Manager has the ultimate say on scope, schedule, and staffing levels within the project. He or she steers the project through the administrative and financial obstacles confronting the project.

2. The *Chief Architect* (CA) is responsible for the overall design of the system. Although the Chief Architect has the last say, in FDD, he or she is responsible for running workshop design sessions where the team collaborates in the design of the system. This is a deeply technical role, requiring excellent technical and modeling skills, as well as good facilitation skills. The Chief Architect resolves disputes over design that the Chief Programmers cannot resolve themselves. For projects with both a complex problem domain and complicated technical architecture, the role may be split into domain architect

and technical architect roles. The Chief Architect has the last say on all design issues. He or she steers the project through the technical obstacles confronting the project.

3. The *Development Manager* is responsible for leading the day-to-day development activities. In a facilitating role requiring good technical skills, the Development Manager is responsible for resolving everyday conflicts for resources when the Chief Programmers cannot do it between themselves. In some projects, this role is combined with the Chief Architect or Project Manager role. The Development Manager has the ultimate say on developer resourcing conflicts within the project and steers the project through potential resource deadlock situations.

Note

Remember that these are role definitions, and one person can play multiple roles at once, and vice versa. It is very common to see these three roles shared by two people. Often, the same person will play Chief Architect and Development Manager. At other times, a master/apprentice relationship may be at work, with one person playing the majority of the Project Manager role, a high-level Chief Architect role, and mentoring/training another who gets to do project management tasks on occasion and plays Chief Architect and Development Manager on a day-to-day basis. On very large projects, a master/apprenticeship pairing may play each of the roles.

4. The *Chief Programmers* are experienced developers who have been through the entire software development lifecycle a few times. They participate in the high-level requirements analysis and design activities of the project and are responsible for leading small teams of three to six developers through low-level analysis, design, and development of the new software's features. Chief Programmers also work with other Chief Programmers to resolve day-to-day technical and resourcing issues. Self-driven to produce quality results on time, Chief Programmers combine great technical ability with enough people skills to lead small teams to produce results every few days. Other typical characteristics of Chief Programmers are that they are trusted and respected by both their managers and fellow developers, are determined to make the team succeed, and usually live the work.

5. The *Class Owners* are developers who work as members of small development teams under the guidance of a Chief Programmer to design, code, test, and document the features required by the new software system. Class Owners come in two stereotypical flavors and a myriad of shades in between; they are often talented developers who, with more experience, will

become able to play Chief Programmer roles in the future or are talented developers who are content to be master programmers and want nothing to do with leading or managing other people.

6. The *Domain Experts* are users, clients, sponsors, business analysts, or any mix of these. They use their deep knowledge of the business to explain to the developers in various levels of detail the tasks that the system must perform. They are the knowledge base that the developers rely on to enable them to deliver the correct system. Domain Experts need good verbal, written, and presentation skills. Their knowledge and participation are absolutely critical to the success of the system being built. Other important characteristics include seemingly infinite patience and endless enthusiasm about the promise of the new system.

Supporting Roles

For larger teams, the *Domain Manager* leads the Domain Experts and is responsible for resolving differences in opinions about requirements. In a small project, this role is often combined with that of the Project Manager role.

The *Release Manager* represents someone fussy enough to ensure that Chief Programmers report progress each week. They are thorough, ensuring that planned and actual dates are all entered properly and that charts are printed and distributed correctly. The release manager reports directly to the Project Manager. The name for the role comes from a regular, short progress meeting where Chief Programmers report on what has been "released" into the build since the last meeting. The role is analogous to the tracker role of Extreme Programming. The release manager may combine this role with a more general administrative assistant role to the Project Manager.

A *Language Lawyer* or *Language Guru* is a person who is responsible for knowing a programming language or a specific technology inside out. This role is especially useful on a project where a programming language or technology is being used for the first time; it is often played by a consultant brought in for the purpose. Once the team is up to speed with the language or technology, this role can be reduced until it disappears altogether.

The *Build Engineer* is responsible for setting up, maintaining, and running the regular build process. This includes managing the version control system, publishing any generated reports or documentation, and writing any build or deployment scripts. On larger projects, the version control manager or configuration manager may be a separate role or possibly part of another department.

The *Toolsmith* creates small development tools for the development team, test team, and data conversion team. Where necessary, this may include setting up and managing a database and Web site that acts as the team's knowledge repository. Many organizations have a centralized IT team that provides a generic service; the toolsmith writes tools that are specific to its project. It is a role that a fresh graduate or junior programmer can play.

The *System Administrator* configures, manages, and troubleshoots any servers and network of workstations specific to the project team. This includes the development environment and any specialized testing environments. The system administrator is also often involved in the initial deployment of the system into production.

On small systems, a single person may play all three of the build engineer, tool smith, and system engineer roles. In larger teams, multiple people may play each of these roles, and the system administrator role may be split into server administrator, network administrator, and database administrator.

Additional Roles

There are three more obvious roles required in any project:

1. *Testers* are responsible for independently verifying that the system's functions meet the users' requirements and that the system performs those functions correctly. Testers may be part of the project team or part of an independent quality assurance department.

2. *Deployers* convert existing data to the new formats required by the new system and work on the physical deployment of new releases of the system. Again, the deployment team may be part of the project team or part of some sort of operations and system administration department.

3. *Technical Writers* write and prepare online and printed user documentation. Technical writers in some organizations will have their own department that services all projects.

Project Patterns

Like all problem solving, including problem solving in software design, there are established patterns in building a software development project. A pattern describes a common, recurring problem in a particular environment, then describes the core of a solution in such a way that you can use the solution a million times without doing it exactly the same way twice [Alexander]. This is why, when we are struggling with a problem that we know others must have solved, we go looking for advice from an expert who has done it before and knows the patterns that work.

Good Project Managers, Architects, and Development Managers combine a mental catalog of patterns (Luke Hohmann in *Journey of the Software Professional: The Sociology of Computer Programming* [Hohmann], calls them *plans*) that have worked for them in the past with the ability to apply those patterns successfully again and again in slightly different situations. There are patterns for managing and interacting with different types of people. There are patterns for selecting and appropriately using technology on a project. A software development process is little more than an integrated collection of project patterns for setting the human communications structure and protocols within a project. These patterns often come in the form of "best industry practices" or recommended strategies and techniques.

Gerald Weinberg, in his series on quality software management [Weinberg 92], links patterns of behavior in software projects to mental models that managers and developers use (assumptions about the way people and things work). Some of these assumptions are not well thought through and may be false. Weinberg proposes that managers and developers examine their mental models and replace faulty ones with better models. Then, using these improved models, they can take more appropriate action during a project and move the team to a higher overall pattern of behavior.

For example, the mental model that says developers and months are interchangeable in a project plan is a seriously flawed mental model that leads Development Managers to apply the pattern of throwing in more manpower when a project starts to slip behind schedule, with generally disastrous consequences.

Another example is the mental model that says if we hire consultants from a big, established consultancy company, we will get useful advice. Many managers have recognized that a better mental model says if we hire consultants with proven experience where we lack it, we will get useful advice.

Summary

Projects consist of people, process, and technology, but by far the most important aspect is people. Looking to replace good people with a good process is a fool's quest.

However, given that we have done what we can to hire good people and keep them happy, if we can find a way repeatedly to create successful software-making systems, software development projects that produce the desired software on time and within budget, then we have the makings of a truly useful software development process.

FDD defines six key roles and implies a number of others:

- Project Manager
- Chief Architect
- Development Manager
- Chief Programmer
- Class Owner

Supporting roles include:

- Domain Manager
- Release Manager
- Language Guru
- Build Engineer
- Toolsmith
- System Administrator

Additional roles include:

- Testers
- Deployers
- Technical Writers

During the rest of the chapters in this section, we will meet and explore the key project roles in detail as we discuss the practices and processes within FDD. The supporting roles will also pop up occasionally. In Part 2, we present a number of hints, tips, and guidelines for the key roles. Discussion about the additional roles is left until the third and final part of the book.

chapter 3

Feature-Driven Development—Practices

A nswers: What do we have to manage?

> Good habits are a wonderful thing. They allow the
> team to carry out the basic steps, focusing on content
> and results, rather than process steps. This is best
> achieved when process steps are logical and their
> worth immediately obvious to each team member.
>
> Coad, LeFebvre, De Luca [Coad 99]

Integrating Best Practices

Like all good software development processes, Feature-Driven Development (FDD) is built around a core set of "best practices." The chosen practices are not new but this particular blend of the ingredients is new. Each practice complements and reinforces the others. The result is a whole greater than the sum of its parts; there is no single practice that underpins the entire process. A team could choose to implement just one or two of the practices but would not get the full benefit that occurs by using the whole FDD process.

Consider inspections, for example. They are decades old and have a mountain of evidence showing them to be a great tool. However, on their own, they are far from enough. No, it is the *right mix* of the ingredients in the *right amounts* at the *right times* that makes the FDD cake taste so good!

Mac: *Steve, are the processes within FDD rigid, or can we adapt them to fit the project, the team, and the organization?*

Steve: *FDD can certainly be adapted to a particular toolset and to teams of people with various levels of experience. It is this level of flexibility that makes FDD relatively easy to adopt within an organization.*

Mac: *So, you are telling me that for our project, we can pick and choose what we will implement and that's FDD?*

Steve: *Absolutely not! FDD is flexible and adaptable, but there are some best practices that need to be included in order for it to be an FDD process. I'll list the best practices that make up FDD. Take a look at it, and then we'll go over each one in detail.*

35

FDD Best Practices

The best practices that make up FDD are:

- Domain Object Modeling
- Developing by Feature
- Individual Class (Code) Ownership
- Feature Teams
- Inspections
- Regular Builds
- Configuration Management
- Reporting/Visibility of Results

Steve: *You could choose to implement a few of the practices and claim you are following a feature-centric process but I reserve the FDD name to mean that you are following all of the practices I've listed.*

Mac: *Okay, I can understand that distinction. Let's look at each practice in turn....*

Domain Object Modeling

Domain object modeling consists of building class diagrams depicting the significant types of objects within a problem domain and the relationships between them. Class diagrams are structural in nature and look a little like the more traditional entity-relationship diagrams of the relational database world. Two big differences are the inclusion of inheritance or generalization/specialization relationships and operations that specify how the objects behave. To support this behavioral view, it is usual to complement the class diagrams with a set of high-level sequence diagrams depicting explicitly how objects interact with each other to fulfill their responsibilities. The emphasis is on what questions objects of a particular class can answer and what calculations or services they can perform; there is less emphasis placed on determining exactly what attributes objects of a particular class might manage.

As analysts and developers learn of requirements from Domain Experts, they start forming mental images of the desired system. Unless they are very careful, they make assumptions about this imaginary design. These hidden assumptions can cause inconsistencies between different people's work, ambiguities in requirements documentation, and the omission of important details. Developing an overall domain object model (Figure 3–1) forces those assumptions out into the open—misunderstandings are resolved, holes in understanding are filled, and a much more complete, common understanding of the problem domain is formed.

In *Extreme Programming Explained*, Kent Beck offers the analogy that software construction is like driving a car [Beck 00]. Driving requires continual small course adjustments, using the steering wheel; you cannot simply point a car in the right direction and press the accelerator. Software construction, Beck says, is similar. Extending that analogy a bit further, a domain object model is like the road map that guides the journey; with it, you can reach your destination relatively quickly and easily without too many detours or a lot of backtracking; without it, you can very quickly end up lost or driving around in circles, continually reworking and refactoring the same pieces of code.

The domain object model provides an overall framework to which to add function, feature by feature. It helps to maintain the conceptual integrity of the system. Using it to guide them, feature teams produce better initial designs for each group of features. This reduces the amount of times a team has to refactor classes to add a new feature.

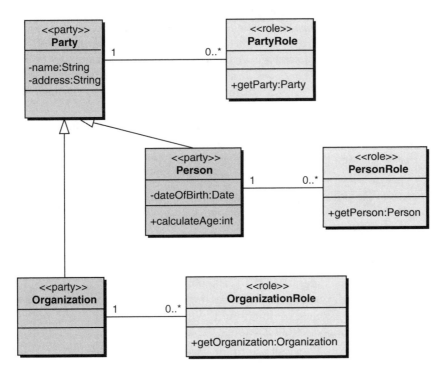

Figure 3–1
The early beginnings of a domain object model.

Domain Object Modeling is a form of object decomposition. The problem is broken down into the significant objects involved. The design and implementation of each object or class identified in the model is a smaller problem to solve. When the completed classes are combined, they form the solution to the larger problem.

The best technique the authors know for Domain Object Modeling is "modeling in color." Modeling in color uses four color-coded class arche-

Feature-Driven
Development—
Practices
—

types that interact in defined ways. The use of color adds a layer of "visually detectable" information to the model. Using this technique, a team or individual can very rapidly build a resilient, flexible, and extensible object model for a problem domain that communicates clearly and concisely.

FDD does not mandate the use of modeling in color and modeling in color does not require FDD. However, they do complement each other exceptionally well.

Mac: *I understand the analogy you used, but why is that so important to a software project? We have several very experienced programmers who will be working on our project. Some of them are used to listing the initial requirements, then going directly to coding. Sometimes they will prototype the system, but that's about as much of a model as they use.*

Steve: *For a very simple problem, that may be all right. However, the more complex the problem, the more imperative it is that the problem be adequately explored and explained. Source code is far too detailed a mechanism with which to do that. The information needs to be accessible to and understandable by all of those involved with specifying the requirements, as well as to those responsible for implementing them. A domain object model is a concise, relatively accessible, reuseable way of storing and communicating that information to everyone involved in the project.*

The old "building a house" analogy really fits here. I wouldn't mind building a kennel without plans and blueprints, but would I want a builder to build my home that way? Or would you want to live in a 30-story high-rise that was built without blueprints?

The domain object model provides a solid framework that can be built within when changes in the business environment require the system to change. It allows designers to add new features and capabilities to the system correctly; it greatly enhances the internal quality and robustness of the system.

Developing by Feature

Once we have identified the classes in our domain object model, we can design and implement each one in turn. Then, once we have completed a set of classes, we integrate them and hey, presto! We have part of our system. Easy!...Well, it's a nice dream!

Nontrivial projects that are run in this way have found that they end up delivering a system that does not do what the client requires. Also, classes in these systems are often overly complicated, containing methods and attributes that are never used while missing methods and attribute that are needed. We can produce the most elegant domain object model possible, but if it does not help us to provide the system's clients with the functionality for which they have asked, we have failed. It would be like building a fantastic office skyscraper but either leaving each floor unfurnished, uncarpeted, and without staff, or furnishing it with ornamental but impractical furniture and untrained staff.

In the "Process and People" section at the beginning of Chapter 2, we said that a key element in any project is some statement of purpose, problem statement, or list of goals or very high-level requirements describing what the system needs to do. Without this, there is no reason for the project to exist. This is the functionality that the system must provide for the project to be considered a success.

Every popular method or process contains some form of functional decomposition activity that breaks down this high-level statement into more manageable problems. Functional specification documents, use case models and use case descriptions, and user stories and features all represent functional requirements, and each representation has its own advantages and disadvantages.

Traditionally, we have taken the statement of purpose and broken it down into a number of smaller problems and defined a set of subsystems (or modules) to solve those smaller problems. Then, for each subsystem, we have broken its problem into a hierarchical list of functional requirements. When we have requirements granular enough that we know how to design and implement each of them, we can stop decomposing the problem. We then start designing and implementing each of our functional requirements. The project is driven and tracked by function; sets of functional requirements are given to developers to implement, and their progress is measured.

A major problem is that the functional requirements tend to mix user interface, data storage, and network communication functions with business functions. The result is that developers often spend large amounts of time working on the technical features at the expense of the business features. A project that delivers a system with the greatest persistence mechanism but no business features is a failure.

A good solution to this problem is to restrict our lists of functional requirements to those of value to a user or client and to ensure that requirements are phrased in language that the user or client can understand. We call these *client-valued functions*, or *features*. Once the features for a system have been identified, they are used to drive and track development in FDD. Delivering a piece of infrastructure may be important—even critical—to the project but it is of no significance to the client because it has no intrinsic business value. Showing progress in terms of features completed is something that the client can understand and assign value to. Clients can also prioritize features in terms of significance to the business.

Interestingly, Extreme Programming records functional requirements as user stories on index cards. In *Extreme Programming Explained*, a user story was described as "a name and a short paragraph describing the purpose of the story" [Beck 00]. A year later, in *Planning Extreme Programming Explained*, a user story is "nothing more than an agreement that the customer and developers will talk together about a feature," and a user story is "a chunk of functionality that is of value to the customer" [Beck 01].

Mac: What about use cases? Don't they do the same thing? Aren't both FDD and Extreme Programming reinventing the wheel here? Ivar Jacobson introduced the software development world to use cases back in 1992 [Jacobson 92]. He defines a use case as "a description of a set of sequence of actions, including variants, that a system performs that yields an observable result to a particular actor," where an actor is defined as "a coherent set of roles that users of use cases play when interacting with these use cases" [Jacobson, 99]. I know this is a bit of a mouthful but it sounds like a feature to me.

Steve: A bit of a mouthful!?!?

Mac: Okay, a big mouthful. All it really means is that you:

1. Identify the users of the system (both humans and other computer systems)
2. Identify what each user does (tasks)
3. Categorize users according to their tasks to form a set of user roles (actors)
4. Describe how the system will help each user role perform each of its tasks (use cases)

In other words, a use case approach is user-centric. It groups functional requirements by the type of user of those functions. Driving a project with use cases helps us to ensure that we are developing what users need. This sounds like a step forward, in my opinion.

Steve: I agree, the thinking and ideas behind use cases are good, and they sound great in theory. However, despite numerous successes, many projects have struggled to apply use cases successfully in practice.

My main problem with use cases is that their definition does not define at what level of granularity use cases should be written and what format and level of detail their contents should take. The result has been continuous, raging debates, both within teams and on public online discussion forums. For example, in the first edition of UML Distilled: Applying the Standard Object Modeling Language, Martin Fowler writes, "Ivar Jacobson says that for a 10-person-year project, he would expect about 20 use cases....In a recent project of about the same magnitude, I had more than 100 use cases" [Fowler].

This problem becomes worse when the wrong people are asked to write use cases at the wrong time. A team of analysts and Domain Experts used to writing traditional functional specifications is often asked to write all the use cases for a system before any modeling or prototyping is done. The result is often an inconsistent and incomplete set of use cases of mixed granularity, with differing levels of detail, mixing user interface and persistence details with business logic in an overdetailed description of the design of an imaginary system.

Mac: Sounds like you are talking from personal experience. One popular answer to this problem is to define long, comprehensive templates to follow when writing the contents of a use case. However, this makes the task of writing use cases expensive in terms of project schedule, and increased manpower is also required to keep the use cases up to date throughout a project.

Steve: And Project Managers following that approach need to be very careful not to become bogged down in endlessly writing and rewriting use cases; what one of our colleagues, Bob Youngblood, calls "death by use cases." As with anything new, it's best to *work with someone who knows what they are doing or at least to buy a book such as Advanced Use Case Modeling [Miller] and agree as a team to follow it.*

Mac: *So how do we avoid exactly the same problems with features? You've defined them as client-valued functions but there must be more to it than that, surely.*

Steve: *Yes...*

The term *feature* in FDD is very specific. A feature is a small, client-valued function expressed in the form:

<action> <result> <object>

with the appropriate prepositions between the action, result, and object.

Features Are Small

They are small enough to be implemented within two weeks. Two weeks is the upper limit. Most features are small enough to be implemented in a few hours or days. However, features are more than just accessor methods that simply return or set the value of an attribute. Any function that is too complex to be implemented within two weeks is further decomposed into smaller functions until each sub-problem is small enough to be called a feature. Specifying the level of granularity helps to avoid one of the problems frequently associated with use cases. Keeping features small also means clients see *measurable* progress on a *frequent* basis. This improves their confidence in the project and enables them to give valuable feedback early.

Features Are Client-Valued

In a business system, a feature maps to a step in some activity within a business process. In other systems, a feature equates to some step or option within a task being performed by a user.

Examples of features are:

- Calculate the *total* of a sale.
- Assess the *performance* of a salesman.
- Validate the *password* of a user.
- Retrieve the *balance* of a bank account.
- Authorize a *credit card transaction* of a card holder.
- Perform a *scheduled service* on a car.

As mentioned earlier, features are expressed in the form <action> <result> <object>. The explicit template provides some strong clues to the operations required in the system and the classes to which they should be applied. For example:

- "Calculate the *total* of a sale" suggests a calculateTotal() operation in a Sale class.
- "Assess the *performance* of a salesman" suggests an assessPerformance() operation in a Salesman class.
- "Determine the *validity of the password* of a user" suggests a determinePasswordValidity() operation on a User class that can then be simplified into a validatePassword() operation on the User class.

The use of a natural language, such as English, means that the technique is far from foolproof. However, after a little practice, it becomes a powerful source of clues to use in discovering or verifying operations and classes.

Mac: *So if I use the template to name my use cases and keep them to the two-week implementation limit, I would have the benefits of features and use cases? Use cases usually have preconditions, postconditions, and a description of what needs to happen. I could leave these empty to start with and fill them as development proceeds. That would avoid the analysis paralysis you warn of.*

Steve: *I suppose you could. I'm not sure what it buys you. One problem you might encounter by calling your features use cases is that you are going to confuse others who associate a different level of granularity, format, and application with the name use case.*

Another problem is that, although nearly every expert I have spoken to recently advocates writing use cases in parallel with building a domain object model, most people still try to write them before doing any modeling or prototyping. In fact, many people advocate using use cases or functional requirements to drive the building of a domain object model.

Mac: *Yes, I know, and I have seen the results many times! Function-heavy classes constantly accessing data-heavy classes, high coupling, low cohesion, and poor encapsulation. Yuck! I definitely prefer building the object model with Domain Experts first or at the same time as writing use cases. The functional decomposition and object-oriented decomposition are orthogonal approaches. Doing both helps to ensure that we deliver the function required within a structure that is robust and extensible.*

Class (Code) Ownership

Class (code) ownership in a development process denotes who (person or role) is ultimately responsible for the contents of a class (piece of code).

There are two general schools of thought on the subject of code ownership. One view is that of individual ownership, where distinct pieces or groupings of code are assigned to a single owner. Every currently popular object-oriented programming language uses the concept of a class to provide encapsulation; each class defines a single concept or type of entity. Therefore, it makes sense to make classes the smallest elements of code to which owners are assigned; code ownership becomes class ownership. This is the practice used within FDD; developers are assigned ownership of a set of classes from the domain object model.

Note

Throughout the rest of the book, we assume that the readers are using a popular object-oriented programming language such as Java, C++, Smalltalk, Eiffel, C#, etc. Therefore, we make the assumption that classes *are the programming language mechanism providing encapsulation (also polymorphism and inheritance). Where this is not the case, the reader is requested to translate* class *to whatever fundamental element provides information hiding, abstract typing, or data encapsulation in your programming language.*

The advantages of individual class ownership are many but include the following:

- An individual is assigned the responsibility for the conceptual integrity of that piece of code. As enhancements and new methods are added to the class, the owner will ensure that the purpose of the class is maintained and that the modifications fit properly.
- There is an expert available to explain how a particular piece of code works. This is especially important for complex or business-critical classes.
- The code owner can implement an enhancement faster than another developer of similar ability who is unfamiliar with that piece of code.
- The code owner personally has something that he or she can take pride in doing well.

The first classic problem with class ownership occurs when developer A wants to make some changes to his or her classes, but those changes are dependent on other changes being made in the classes owned by developer B. Developer A could be required to wait a significant amount of time if developer B is busy. Too many of these situations would obviously slow down the pace of the development team.

The second potential problem with individual class ownership that is often raised is that of risk of loss of knowledge about a class. If the owner of a set of classes should happen to leave the project suddenly for some reason, it could take considerable time for the team to understand how that developer's classes work. If the classes are significant, it could put the project schedule under pressure.

At the opposite end of the code ownership spectrum is the view promoted by Extreme Programming proponents, among others. In this world, all the developers in the team are responsible for all of the code. In other words, the team has collective ownership of the source code.

Collective ownership solves the problem of having to wait for someone else to modify code and can ease the risk of someone leaving because, at least in a small system, more than one person has worked on the code.

The main issue with collective ownership, however, is that in practice, it can quickly degenerate into nonownership or an ownership dictated by few dominant individuals on the team. Either nobody ends up being responsible for anything in the system or the dominant few try to do all the work because, in their opinion, they are the only competent members of the team. If nobody takes responsibility for ensuring the quality of a piece of code, it is highly unlikely that the resulting code will be of high quality. If a few dominant developers try to do everything, they may start off well but will soon find themselves overloaded and suffering from burnout. Obviously, teams that encounter these problems struggle to continue to deliver frequent, tangible, working results.

Mac: Hey, Steve. It appears that there is a swelling of opinion in the industry that says any team member should be allowed to change any piece of code. Many of our developers seem to like this idea, but FDD promotes individual class ownership. Is collective ownership an option?

Steve: Supporters of collective ownership claim that it works when combined with other complementary practices (see [Beck]):

- Pair programming—two developers working together at one personal computer or terminal to reduce the likelihood of introducing errors into the code and to shorten the time it takes a developer to learn and understand the system.
- Extensive unit testing to verify that new code functions as required and that refactored or updated code still functions as required.
- Coding standards compliance to improve the readability of code and to minimize errors due to misunderstanding of existing code.
- Continual integration of changes into the code base to reduce the likelihood that multiple programmer pairs need to access the same piece of code at the same time.

However, if we assume collective ownership, look at what could happen as developers work on features. For any given feature, the developer (or pair of developers) can add or modify operations and attributes of the classes that participate in the feature. A different pair, working on a different feature, can add or modify another operation in some of those same classes (Figure 3–2). In a large team, each method of a class could theoretically end up being written by a different developer.

Mac: My alarm bells are ringing at this point! With small classes and small teams, we might get away with this but on larger, more significant classes with a larger team,

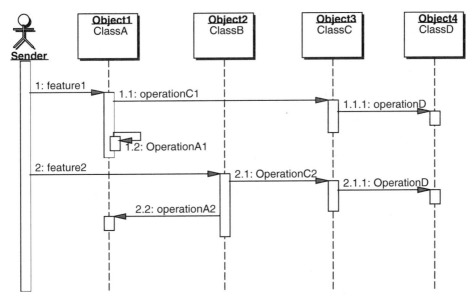

Figure 3–2
Features adding and enhancing operations in the same classes.

consistency and conceptual integrity, not to mention robustness, could become a major problem.

Steve: Exactly! The more minds working on a piece of work over time, the harder it is to maintain the conceptual integrity of that work [Brooks]. I believe the chances of the class evolving a consistent, elegant, efficient set of methods are greatly reduced if anyone and everyone can write a piece of it. I also think the need for rework and refactoring is going to be greatly increased.

Also, to modify a class correctly, the modifiers have to understand how its internals work. This can take time if those developers have not seen the class before or have not worked with it for a while. This is obviously going to take longer than if someone familiar with the code did the modification.

Mac: It sounds like individual class ownership is more likely to scale to our size of project and team. However, I can see that, in some cases within a project, collective ownership of parts of the model could be advantageous. Can we use combinations of individual and collective ownership and still call it FDD? Does FDD allow me to tailor the class ownership practice to the needs and structure of my team and organization?

Steve: You're not going to get arrested by the thought police, if that's what you mean. Also, let's not get hung up over a name of a process. We need to do what works for us and our organization. Having said that, I think as we cover the other practices in FDD, you'll find less and less of a reason to need collective ownership. The only areas where I personally might consider collective ownership is when building proof of concept prototypes for the technical architecture and user interface. When it comes to production code, I want to know that there is a single responsible person I can go to when there are issues with a particular class.

Mac: *I suppose there is no way of getting the benefits of both individual class ownership and collective ownership, is there? Or at least get close to that ideal?*

Steve: *Actually, I think the answer to that is yes! We need to combine class ownership with the use of feature teams and inspections.*

Feature Teams

Building a domain object model identifies the key classes in the problem domain. The class ownership practice assigns those classes to specific developers. We also know that we want to build, feature by feature.

So how do we best organize our class owners to build the features?

We assigned classes to owners to ensure that there was a single person responsible for the development of each class. We need to do the same for features. We need to assign each feature to an owner—somebody who is going to be responsible for ensuring that the feature is developed properly. The implementation of a feature is likely to involve more than one class and, therefore, more than one Class Owner. Thus, the feature owner is going to need to coordinate the efforts of multiple developers—a team lead job. Therefore, we pick some of our better developers, make them team leaders, and assign sets of features to each of them (we can think of a team leader as having an "inbox" of features that he or she is responsible to deliver).

Now that we have Class Owners and team leaders, let's form the development teams around these team leaders. Ah! We have a problem! How can we guarantee that all the Class Owners needed to code a particular feature will be in the same team? This is not an easy problem to solve.

We have four options:

1. We can go through each feature, listing the classes we think are involved, then try to separate the features into mutually exclusive sets. This feels like a good deal of design work just to form teams, and what if we get it slightly wrong? What if there are no convenient, mutually exclusive groupings of features? This does not sound like a repeatable step in the process.

2. We can allow teams to ask members of other teams to make changes to the code they own. However, now we are likely to be waiting for another developer in another team to make a change before we can complete our task. This is exactly the situation that led Extreme Programming to promote collective ownership.

3. We can drop class ownership and go with collective ownership and everything else that it requires to make it work. There is already a book in this series covering this option,

[Astels] and anyway, we know that collective ownership does not scale easily.

4. We can change the team memberships whenever this situation occurs so that a team leader always has the Class Owners he or she needs to build a feature. This is the only realistic option that will allow us both to develop by feature and to have Class Owners.

Actually, there is nothing that requires us to stick to a statically defined team structure. We can change to a more dynamic model. If we allow team leaders to form a new team for each feature they start to develop, they can pick the Class Owners they need for that feature. Once the feature is fully developed, the team is disbanded, and the team leader picks the Class Owners needed to form the team for the next feature. This can be repeated indefinitely until all the features required are developed.

This is a form of dynamic matrix management. Team leaders owning features pick developers based on their expertise (in this case, class ownership) to work in the *feature team* developing those features involving their classes (Figure 3–3).

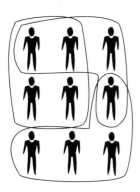

Feature teams are formed from class owners as needed.

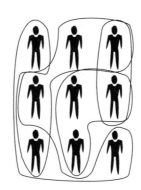

Figure 3–3
Feature teams.

Mac: *So are feature teams new? I remember that Harlan Mills suggested the idea of Chief Programmer teams back in 1971 [Brooks]. His idea is based on surgical teams, where a surgeon is supported by a number of talented and qualified people, each performing a specific role. In a Chief Programmer team, developers each have their own specific responsibility and support a lead developer.*

Steve: *Feature teams are similar but differ in two important aspects:*
- *The team leader acts as more of a coach for the team than some superprogrammer in charge of a bunch of junior or trainee programmers.*
- *The Class Owners' responsibilities are all similar to each other; it is the code that they are responsible for that differs.*

Every member of a feature team is responsible for playing their part in the success of the team. However, feature team leaders, as all good coaches know, are ultimately re-

sponsible for producing results. They own the features, and they are accountable for their successful delivery. Playing this team leader role well normally requires both ability and experience, so we call our feature team leaders Chief Programmers *in recognition of this and Mills'*[Brooks] *work.*

Mac: *Steve, this sounds incredibly flexible and may be the answer to a lot of the problems we have experienced in the past on our software projects, but what happens when a Chief Programmer guesses incorrectly about which classes are involved in the development of a feature? For example: What if a Chief Programmer thought three classes were needed to implement a given feature, and it turns out that two more are involved?*

Steve: *Easy! All the Chief Programmer needs to do is contact the appropriate Class Owner if they are not already in the team, verify their availability to work on the feature, and include them on the feature team. The Chief Programmer may have to discuss the availability of the extra developers with other Chief Programmers, if those developers are heavily loaded.*

Mac: *What happens if the Class Owners are working in too many teams and cannot take on another feature team for a few days? Does the feature team block?*

Steve: *Well, that feature team may block. However, remember that each Chief Programmer has this inbox of features assigned to him or her. If the Class Owners are not available to develop one feature, the Chief Programmer can pick a different feature to develop next, instead.*

Mac: *Even more flexible! I like this idea a lot! I guess, though, that there are some restrictions about which features a Chief Programmer can develop next.*

Steve: *Yes, there will be some dependencies between features to watch for, and some features will be higher priority than others and will need to be developed sooner rather than later, but that is about it.*

Mac: *Is there anything else interesting about feature teams?*

Steve: *A couple more points...*

Some things to note about feature teams:

- A feature team, due to the small size of features, remains small, typically three to six people.
- By definition, a feature team is comprised of all the Class Owners who need to modify or enhance one of their classes as part of the development of a particular feature. In other words, the feature team owns all the code it needs to change for that feature. There is no waiting for members of other teams to change code. So we have code ownership and a sense of collective ownership, too.
- Each member of a feature team contributes to the design and implementation of a feature under the guidance of a skilled, experienced developer. Applying multiple minds to evaluate multiple options and select the design that fits best reduces the risk of reliance on key developers or owners of specific classes.

- From time to time, Class Owners may find themselves members of multiple feature teams at the same time. This is not the norm but is not a problem, either. While waiting for others in one feature team, a Class Owner can be working on stuff for another feature team. Most developers can handle belonging to two or even three features teams concurrently for a short period of time. More than that leads to problems switching context from one team to another. Chief Programmers work together to resolve any problematic conflicts and to avoid overloading any particular developer.

- Chief Programmers are also Class Owners and take part in feature teams led by other Chief Programmers. This helps Chief Programmers to work with each other and keeps them close to the code (something most Chief Programmers like).

Inspections

FDD relies heavily on inspections to ensure high quality of designs and code. Many of us have sat through hours of boring, backbiting, finger-pointing sessions that were called *code reviews*, *design reviews*, or *peer reviews* and shudder at the thought of another process that demands inspections. We have all heard comments such as "Technical inspections, reviews, walkthroughs are a waste of time. They take too long, are of little real benefit, and result in too many arguments" or "I know my job! Why should I let others tell me how to design and write my code?"

However, when done well, inspections are very useful in improving the quality of design and code. Inspections have been recommended since the 1970s, and the evidence weighs heavily in their favor.

The Aetna Insurance Company found 82% of the errors in a program by using inspections and was able to decrease its development resources by 25%.

M.E. Fagan [Fagan]

In a group of 11 programs developed by the same group of people, the first 5 were developed without inspections. The remaining 6 were developed with inspections.

After all the programs were released to production, the first 5 had an average of 4.5 errors per 100 lines of code. The 6 that had been inspected had an average of only 0.82 errors per 100 lines of code.

Inspections cut the errors by over 80%....

In a software-maintenance organization, 55% of one-line maintenance changes were in error before code inspections were introduced. After inspections were introduced, only 2% of the changes were in error.

D.P. Freedman and G.M. Weinberg [Freedman]

IBM's 500,000-line Orbit project used 11 levels of inspections. It was delivered early and had only about 1% of the errors that would normally be expected.

T. Gilb [Gilb 88]

The average defect detection rate is only 24% for unit testing, 35% for function testing, and 45% for integration testing. In contrast, the average effectiveness of design and code inspections is 55 and 60% respectively.

C.L. Jones [Jones]

One client found that each downstream software error cost on average 5 hours. Others have found 9 hours (Thorn EMI, Reeve), 20 to 82 hours (IBM, Remus), and 30 hours (Shell) to fix downstream. This is compared to the cost of only one hour to find and fix using inspection.

T. Gilb and D. Graham [Gilb 93]

Need we say more?

Actually, there is a little more to say. The primary purpose of inspections is the detection of defects. When done well, there are also two very helpful secondary benefits of inspections:

1. Knowledge transfer. Inspections are a means to disseminate development culture and experience. By examining the code of experienced, knowledgeable developers and having them walk through their code, explaining the techniques they use, less experienced developers rapidly learn better coding practices.

2. Standards conformance. Once developers know that their code will not pass code inspection unless it conforms to the agreed design and coding standards, they are much more likely to conform.

Even though coding standards can be written (presumably by experienced developers) and distributed, they will not be followed (or maybe not even read) without the sort of encouragement provided by inspections.

Steve McConnell [McConnell 98]

We can make inspections even more useful by collecting various metrics and using them to improve our processes and techniques. For instance, as metrics on the type and number of defects found are captured and examined, common problem areas will be revealed. Once these problem areas are known, this can be fed back to the developers, and the development process can be tweaked to reduce the problem.

Of course, the catch is that little qualifying phrase that we have used a couple of times in the last few paragraphs—"when done well." Chapter 10, section titled "Verification: Design Inspection," and Chapter 11, section titled "Conduct a Code Inspection," provide hints and tips for achieving exactly this. We make a couple more general points here.

Inspections have to be done in a way that removes the fear of embarrassment or humiliation from the developer whose work is being inspected. Few developers like to be told that something they have sweated over for hours is wrong or could have been done better. Setting the inspection culture is key. Everyone needs to see inspections primarily as a great debugging tool and secondly as a great opportunity to learn from each other. Developers also need to understand that inspections are not a personal performance review[McConnell 93].

Inspections complement the small team and Chief Programmer–oriented structure of FDD beautifully. The mix of feature teams and inspections adds a new dimension. An entire feature team is on the hot seat, not just one individual. This removes much of the intensity and fear from the situation. The Chief Programmer controls the level of formality of each inspection, depending on the complexity and impact of the features being developed. Where design and code have no impact outside the feature team, an inspection will usually involve only the feature team members inspecting each other's work. Where there is significant impact, the Chief Programmer pulls in other Chief Programmers and developers both to verify the design and code and to communicate the impact of that design and code.

Regular Build Schedule

At regular intervals, we take all of the source code for the features that we have completed and the libraries and components on which it depends, and we build the complete system.

Some teams build weekly, others daily, and still others continuously. It really depends on the size of the project and the time it takes to build the system. If a system takes eight hours to build, a daily build is probably more than frequent enough.

A regular build helps to highlight integration errors early. This is especially true if the tests built by the feature teams to test individual features can be grouped together and run against the completed build to smoke out any inconsistencies that have managed to find their way into the build.

A regular build also ensures that there is always an up-to-date system that can be demonstrated to the client, even if that system does only a few simple tasks from a command line interface. Developing by feature, of course, also means that those simple tasks are of discernible value to the client.

A regular build process can also be enhanced to:

- Generate documentation using tools such as JavaSoft's Javadoc or Together's greatly enhanced documentation-generation capability.
- Run audit and metric scripts against the source code to highlight any potential problem areas and to check for standards compliance.
- Be used as a basis for building and running automated regression tests to verify that existing functionality remains unchanged after adding new features. This can be invaluable for both the client members and the development team.
- Construct new build and release notes, listing new features added, defects fixed, etc.

These results can then be automatically published on the project team or organization's intranet so that up-to-the-minute documentation is available to the whole team.

Configuration Management

Configuration management (CM) systems vary from the simple to the grotesquely complex.

Theoretically, an FDD project only requires a CM system to identify the source code for all the features that have been completed to date and to maintain a history of changes to classes as feature teams enhance them.

Realistically, a project's demands on a CM system will depend on the nature and complexity of the software being produced; for example, whether multiple versions of the software need to be maintained, whether different modules are required for different platforms or different customer installations, and so on. This is not explicitly related to the use of FDD; it is just business as usual on any sophisticated software development project where work is being done on different versions of a software system simultaneously.

It is a common fundamental mistake, however, to believe that only source code should be kept under version control. It is as important (maybe more important) to keep requirements documents, in whatever form they take, under version control so that a change history is maintained. This is especially true if the requirements form a legal commercial contract between two organizations.

Likewise, analysis and design artifacts should be kept under version control so that it is easy to see why any changes were made to them.

Test cases, test harnesses and scripts, and even test results should also be versioned-controlled so that history can be reviewed.

Any artifact that is used and maintained during the development of the system is a candidate for version control. Even contract documents with clients of the system that document the legal agreement for what is being built are candidates for versioning. The version of the process you are using and any changes and adjustments that may be made during the construction and maintenance of the system may need to be versioned and variances documented and signed by Project Managers or Chief Programmers. This is especially true for systems that fall under regulation of such governmental bodies as the U.S. Food and Drug Administration.

Reporting/Visibility of Results

Closely related to project control is the concept of "visibility," which refers to the ability to determine a project's true status....If the project team can't answer such questions, it doesn't have enough visibility to control its project.

The working software is a more accurate status report than any paper report could ever be.

Steve McConnell [McConnell 98]

It is far easier to steer a vehicle in the right direction if we can see precisely where we are and how fast we are moving. Knowing clearly where we are trying to go also helps enormously.

A similar situation exists for the managers and team leaders of a software project. Having an accurate picture of the current status of a project and knowing how quickly the development team is adding new functionality and the overall desired outcome provides team leads or managers with the information they need to steer a project correctly.

FDD is particularly strong in this area. FDD provides a simple, low-overhead method of collecting accurate and reliable status information and suggests a number of straightforward, intuitive report formats for reporting progress to all roles within and outside a project.

Chapter 5, "Progress," is dedicated to the subject of tracking and reporting progress on an FDD project, so we postpone any further discussion on the subject until then.

FDD blends a number of industry-recognized best practices into a cohesive whole. The best practices used in FDD are:

- *Domain Object Modeling*—a thorough exploration and explanation of the domain of the problem to be solved, resulting in a framework within which to add features.

Summary

- *Developing by Feature*—driving and tracking development through a functionally decomposed list of small, client-valued functions.

- *Individual Class Ownership*—having a single person who is responsible for the consistency, performance, and conceptual integrity of each class.

- *Feature Teams*—doing design activities in small, dynamically formed teams so that multiple minds are always applied to each design decision, and multiple design options are always evaluated before one is chosen.

- *Inspections*—applying the best-known defect-detection technique and leveraging the opportunities it provides to propagate good practice, conventions, and development culture.

- *Regular Builds*—ensuring that there is always a demonstrable system available and flushing out any integration issues that manage to get past the design and code inspections. Regular builds provide a known baseline to which to add more function and against which a quality assurance team can test.

- *Version Control*—identifying the latest versions of completed source code files and providing historical tracking of all information artifacts in the project.

- *Progress Reporting*—frequent, appropriate, and accurate progress reporting at all levels, inside and outside the project, based on completed work.

In the next chapter, we look at exactly how these practices blend together to form the five FDD processes.

chapter 4

Feature-Driven
Development—Processes

A nswers: How do we manage?

> With good habits in using simple, well-defined
> processes, the process itself moves from foreground to
> background. Team members focus on results rather
> than process micro-steps. Progress accelerates. The
> team reaches a new stride. The team performs!
> Coad, LeFebvre, De Luca [Coad 99]

Mac: *If we use FDD, will Lisa, our project manager, have all the tools she needs to manage and control the entire software development project and all of its activities? I guess I'm asking what FDD covers and what it leaves as an exercise for the reader.*

Steve: *FDD is specifically targeted at the actual design and construction of the software system. It focuses only on the specific activities and outputs needed to design and write software.*

Mac: *There are a lot of other activities going on in a typical software development project (Figure 4–1). Why aren't they included, too? Are they not considered important?*

Steve: *Most organizations have workable processes in place for many of those activities. The exception is the actual construction of the software. It seems that once past the creation of initial, high-level requirements, the processes simply do not work well until we reach system testing. The actual design and building of the software is the big problem. FDD is aimed precisely at that core, problem area.*

That doesn't mean that the other activities aren't important. They are extremely important, and we can certainly talk about them later. However, the majority of the pain in a development project is felt in the core activities between initial requirements and system test. If we cannot create code that does the right thing in the right way in a timely manner, then all the other activities are in vain, anyway.

Mac: *Some of the activities outside the scope of the FDD processes could produce input that is either used by FDD or that directly interacts with/impacts some of the FDD processes (e.g., initial requirements discussions, change request management, or the system, load and user acceptance testing). Is that interaction with FDD expected, and how is it managed?*

The Scope of Feature-Driven Development (FDD)

55

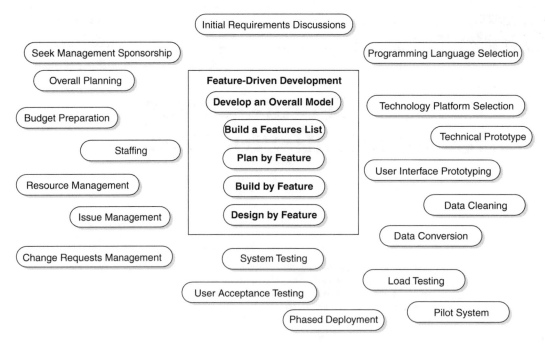

Figure 4–1
Some activities of a software development project.

Steve: As we go through the FDD process in more detail, you should be able to see how FDD works very neatly with the other important activities. You may even spot some opportunities to make some FDD-influenced improvements to your specialty areas of system and user acceptance testing, and to requirements change control.

Mac: Okay. Let's look at the core FDD process, then ...

FDD in Four Sentences

FDD starts with the creation of a domain object model in collaboration with Domain Experts. Using information from the modeling activity and from any other requirements activities that have taken place, the developers go on to create a features list. Then a rough plan is drawn up and responsibilities are assigned. Now we are ready to take small groups of features through a design and build iteration that lasts no longer than two weeks for each group and is often much shorter—sometimes only a matter of hours—repeating this process until there are no more features.

FDD consists of five processes (Figure 4–2). For the first process, domain and development team members work together under the guiding hand of an experienced object modeler (Chief Architect). Domain members present an initial high-level walkthrough of the scope of the system and its context. Then the domain members present more detailed walk-throughs of each area of the problem domain. After each walkthrough, the domain and development members work in small groups to produce object models for that area of the domain. Each small group presents its results to the team, and the team compares and discusses the various models, finally deciding on the most appropriate model for that domain area. The overall model shape is adjusted on the way, as necessary.

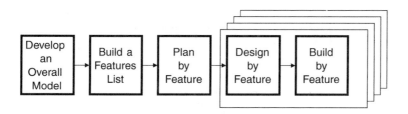

Figure 4–2
The five processes of FDD.

Building on the knowledge gathered during the initial modeling activity, the team next constructs as comprehensive a list of features as it can (Figure 4–3). A *feature* is defined as a small, client-valued function expressed in the form: <action> <result> <object> (e.g., *"calculate the total of a sale"*). Existing requirements documents, such as use cases or functional specs, are also used as input. The domain is reviewed, using a similar breakdown to that used by the Domain Experts when walking through the domain during the modeling activity. Within these domain areas, also called *major feature sets*, the features are grouped into feature sets. A feature set usually reflects a particular business activity. On initial compilation, the users and sponsors of the system review the feature list for validity and completeness.

The third process is to sequence the feature sets or major feature sets (depending on the size of the system) into a high-level plan and assign them to Chief Programmers. Feature sets are sequenced, depending on priority and dependencies. Also, the classes identified in the modeling activity are assigned to individual developers; the owner of a class is responsible for its development. In large projects, major milestone timeframes may be set that time-box the completion of a number of feature sets. For example, a time box of three months might be set to complete the first few feature sets and formally demonstrate the results to upper management. The team can also use the time box milestone to reset the plan formally and gain management approval for the change. For shorter projects, it's usually unnecessary to include this level of formality in the plan.

Processes 4 and 5 are the development engine room. A Chief Programmer selects a small group of features to develop over the next few days (no longer than two weeks). He or she identifies the classes likely to be involved, and the corresponding class owners form the feature team for this iteration. This feature team works out detailed sequence diagrams for the features and writes class and method prologues. The team then conducts a design inspection. After a successful inspection, the class owners add the actual code for their classes, unit test, integrate, and hold a code inspection. Once the Chief Programmer is satisfied, the completed features are promoted to the main build, and processes 4 and 5 repeat with the next group of features.

Figure 4–3

The five processes of FDD with their outputs.

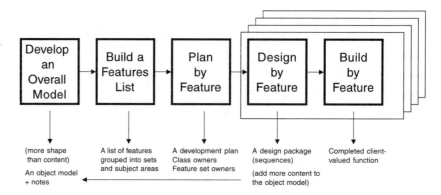

Mac: *So FDD consists of only five processes! That seems simple enough, almost too simple. I have a couple of questions. The diagram shows iteration in the last two steps but doesn't indicate iteration in the first three processes or in the overall process itself. So, is it really an iterative process? If so, where can it iterate, and how is that controlled?*

Steve: *Within the context of a single FDD project, we are iterating through the design-by-feature and build-by-feature processes (4 and 5), designing and building to completion one feature or a small group of features per iteration. We do a reasonable amount of work up front in processes 1 and 3. This ensures that when we have multiple feature teams iterating rapidly through processes 4 and 5, the output from those iterations does converge toward the desired overall result.*

The ideal is to model the entire problem domain that lies within the scope of the project in process 1. However, things often fall short of ideal. If, during the modeling, it becomes obvious that more time is needed to clarify requirements in a particular area (possibly because clients or users need management time and decisions), then we might choose to postpone the modeling of that area. Once the requirements are in better shape, the modeling team can be reformed to complete the object model in that area; the features for that area listed; and the plan, feature set assignments, and class ownership lists updated. So in that sense, yes, you can iterate through processes 1–3 again.

For truly large development efforts, you often find that members of management have already decided to break the effort into several projects, some of which they might run concurrently and some of which might be run sequentially, depending on the business priority, availability of developers, and dependencies between the projects. Where the true scope of a project is discovered only during the modeling in process 1, the Project Manager needs to sit down with management to decide whether to break the project into several smaller projects, each with reduced scope. One criterion to use is that each project should be delivering something of real benefit to its clients.

Once a project is over, a new project can certainly select more areas of the problem domain that were outside of the scope of the original project, model those, and add new features. So in that sense, all five FDD processes can be iterated.

Mac: What about identifying new requirements or features once you have started? How does that affect the project?

Steve: New requirements and features should be controlled by a change management process, which includes reviewing the impact to cost, schedule, and quality, that adding new requirements to any software project can have. Then a decision can be made regarding whether to add them to the current project or leave them for a subsequent project. Let's leave discussing change management in detail until a little later (Chapter 14, "Requirements Change Management").

Mac: Okay, but I also want to know whether and how this applies to projects that are enhancing an existing system or customizing a core software product for a specific customer.

Steve: Good question! Much will depend on the starting point. Adding more features to a system already built using FDD is simply more of the same. Repeat the process but start with the existing object model and features list, and extend them. Obviously, the work may also lead to some refinement of the existing object model and software. Careful documentation of any changes is needed, and I'll show you how that can be achieved without enormous overhead (Chapter 6, "Chief Programmer Work Packages"). Where software does not have an existing object model, it is almost certainly going to be beneficial to create one. Tools such as TogetherSoft's Together ControlCenter can help reverse-engineer an existing code base. Depending on the result of the reverse engineering, it may be desirable to produce a more ideal object model by performing process 1 for the core system, anyway. Comparing the two models gives the Chief Architect and Project Manager a better idea of the cost of refactoring some of the existing system versus trying to bend the new features to fit within the existing model.

Now, before you ask me any more good questions, I really want to walk you through the five FDD processes in detail. However, before I can do that, I need to tell you a little about the format that was used when writing them down...

Have you ever tried to make all your developers follow a hundred-page process manual? Peter Coad tells the tale of writing a 110-page process manual and finding that the developers only ever read the four-page summary at the back [Coad 99].

Each of the five processes in FDD is described on one or two sheets of letter-sized (A4 for those outside the United States) paper. This is all the developers need and most likely all you will be able to get them to

FDD in Detail

Feature-Driven
Development—
Processes
___

read, anyway. It actually takes extra effort to write with simplicity, clarity, and brevity (if this book is too long, it is because we ran out of time within which to make it shorter).

Having someone who has done it before and who can answer process questions as they arise is an approach that is far more likely to see success than telling the developers to look it up in a hundred-page document. Once the Development Manager and Chief Programmers "get it," they can provide all the day-to-day help needed to guide those working with them.

The FDD Process Template

M. A. Rajashima introduced the Entry-Tasks-Verification-eXit (ETVX) template to Jeff De Luca, the Singapore Project Manager described in the Introduction for this book. Using this template, each FDD process is described in four sections (Table 4–1):

Table 4–1
The ETVX Template

Section	Description
Entry	A brief overview of the process and a set of criteria that must be met before we can start the process
Tasks	A list of tasks to perform as part of that process
Verification	The means by which it is verified that the process has been completed satisfactorily: Is the result good enough?
Exit	A list of the outputs from the process

The tasks within each process are split into a header bar and a short text description (Figure 4–4). The header bar contains the name of the task, the role responsible for that task, and an indicator to say whether the task is optional or mandatory ("required").

Edward Tufte's magnificent book, *Envisioning Information* [Tufte], inspired the use of color or shading for layering and separation. This makes it easier to see the outline and then the detail. Also, you can run your eye down the table headings easily to see whether your role is involved. The overall result is a simple and clear structure that concisely communicates what the different people need to do in each activity.

Sometimes, organizations in industries such as pharmaceuticals, health care, or government contractors cannot accept a process written on five sheets of paper—more formality is required for legal or political

Form the Modeling Team	Project Manager	Required

The modeling team consists of permanent members from the domain and development areas, specifically, the domain experts and the chief programmers. Rotate other project staff through the modeling sessions so that everyone gets a chance to participate and to see the process in action.

Conduct a Domain Walkthrough	Modeling Team	Required

A domain expert gives an overview of the domain area to be modeled. This should include information that is related to this domain area but not necessarily a part of its implementation.

Figure 4–4
Task descriptions in FDD.

reasons. We hope the hints and tips in the following chapters will help anyone tasked with writing the hundreds of process manual pages required to satisfy the legal regulations and organizational policies involved.

One possible place to start would be to apply the ETVX template to each of the tasks in the processes to make those more formal; the task description becomes the overview of this new subprocess. Next, define formal templates for each of the outputs and provide forms for those responsible for each task to sign off when complete.

You could also provide the processes as Web pages on an intranet and link each task heading to another page with as much justification, rationale, hints, and tips as desired. However, do not expect many of your developers to ever read it.

The rest of us who work in less regulated industries where legal and contractual accountability are less burdensome can be thankful that we deal with only five double-sided pages of formal process description.

ETVX, Use Cases, and Operations

The ETVX template will look vaguely familiar to those folks who use a formal template for writing use case content. Both these techniques describe what something does (algorithm), given a set of assumptions about conditions at the start (preconditions). Both describe results at the end of that activity (post conditions). Of course, many use case templates are far more complicated, but the general pattern for describing "behavior" is there.

Those practicing "program by contract" and more formal specification methods also use preconditions and post conditions. Here, the behavior is defined without specifying how it is implemented; an algorithm description or the actual source code is needed to describe the implementation.

The idea of preconditions and post conditions seems pervasive in the description of behavior of all kinds of systems.

The verification section of the ETVX template provides something extra. It describes how to verify the quality of the result to ensure that it is "good enough." Use cases describe the actions of a deterministic computer system. ETVX is describing the actions of a software development project—a human system. The human system has points in which value judgments are made about the quality of a design, a piece of code, a list of requirements, and a project plan.

A computer can certainly be used to help make those value judgments. For example, a set of automated audit checks and metric scripts can be run against a piece of code to highlight potential problems. The result of the checks can be used to help assess the quality of the code. However, a computer is not usually trusted to make the value judgments itself.

The FDD Processes

The five process descriptions that follow have been enhanced since the publication of the coloring book [Coad 99] to make certain aspects clearer and more precise. The essential principles and practices remain exactly the same.

In subsequent chapters, we will highlight and explain the differences between the coloring book process descriptions and the improved versions published here.

FDD Process 1: Develop an Overall Model

An initial project-wide activity with domain and development members working together under the guidance of an experienced object modeler in the role of Chief Architect.

Domain Experts perform a high-level walkthrough of the scope of the system and its context. They then perform detailed domain walkthroughs for each area of the domain that is to be modeled. After each domain walkthrough, small groups are formed with a mix of domain and development staff. Each small group composes its own model in support of the domain walkthrough and presents its results for peer review and discussion. One of the proposed models or a merge of the models is selected by consensus and becomes the model for that domain area. The domain area model is merged into the overall model, adjusting model shape as required.

The object model is then updated iteratively with content by process 4, Design by Feature.

Entry Criteria

- Domain Experts, Chief Programmers, and the Chief Architect have been selected for the project.

Tasks

Form the Modeling Team	Project Manager	Required

The modeling team consists of permanent members from the domain and development areas, specifically, the Domain Experts and the Chief Programmers. Rotate other project staff through the modeling sessions so that everyone gets a chance to participate and to see the process in action.

Conduct a Domain Walkthrough	Modeling Team	Required

A Domain Expert gives an overview of the domain area to be modeled. This should include information that is related to this domain area but not necessarily a part of its implementation.

Study Documents	Modeling Team	Optional

The team studies available reference or requirements documents, such as object models, functional requirements (traditional or use-case format), and user guides.

Develop Small Group Models	Modeling Team in Small Groups	Required

Forming groups of no more than three, each small group composes a model in support of the domain area. The Chief Architect may propose a "straw man" model to facilitate the progress of the teams. Occasionally, the groups may also sketch one or more informal sequence diagrams to test the model shape.

Develop a Team Model	Modeling Team	Required

A member from each small group presents that group's proposed model for the domain area. The Chief Architect may also propose further model alternatives. The modeling team selects one of the proposed models or composes a model by merging ideas from the proposed models.

Refine the Overall Object Model	Chief Architect, Modeling Team	Required

Every so often, the team updates the overall object model with the new model shapes produced by iterations of the previous two tasks.

Write Model Notes	Chief Architect, Chief Programmers	Required

Notes on detailed or complex model shapes and on significant model alternatives are made for future reference by the project.

Verification

Internal and External Assessment	Modeling Team, Business	Required

Domain Experts actively participating in the process provide internal or self-assessment. External assessment is made on an as-needed basis by referring back to the business (users) for ratification or clarification of issues that affect the model.

Exit Criteria

To exit the process, the modeling team must produce an object model to the satisfaction of the Chief Architect. The object model consists of:

- Class diagrams focusing on model shape, the classes in the domain, how are they connected to one another and under what constraints, plus any operations and attributes identified.
- Sequence diagram(s), if any.
- Notes capturing why a particular model shape was chosen and/or what alternatives were considered.

FDD Process 2: Build a Features List

An initial project-wide activity to identify all the features needed to support the requirements.

A team usually comprising just the Chief Programmers from process 1 is formed to decompose the domain functionally. Based on the partitioning of the domain by the Domain Experts in process 1, the team breaks the domain into a number of *areas* (*major feature sets*). Each area is further broken into a number of *activities* (*feature sets*). Each step within an activity is identified as a feature. The result is a hierarchically categorized features list.

Entry Criteria

- The modeling team has successfully completed FDD process 1, Develop an Overall Model.

Tasks

Form the Features List Team	Project Manager, Development Manager	Required

The features list team comprises the Chief Programmers from the modeling team in process 1.

Build the Features List	Features List Team	Required

Using the knowledge obtained from process 1, the features list team identifies features. The team may also use any existing reference or requirements documents, such as object models, functional requirements (traditional or use-case format), and user guides, noting the source document against any features identified in this way.

This task is a simple functional decomposition, starting with the partitioning of the domain used by the Domain Experts for their domain area walkthroughs in process 1. The domain is decomposed into *areas* (*major feature sets*) that comprise *activities* (*feature sets*) that comprise *features*, each of which represents a step in an activity.

Features are granular functions expressed in client-valued terms, using the naming template:

$$<action> <result><object>$$

For example, "calculate the total of a sale" and "calculate the total quantity sold by a retail outlet for an item description."

Features are granular. A feature should take no more than two weeks to complete but not be so granular as to be at the level of simple getter and setter operations. Two weeks is an upper limit; most features take less than this amount of time. When a step looks larger, the team breaks the step into smaller steps that then become features.

Verification

Modeling team members actively participating in the process provide internal or self-assessment. External assessment is made on an as-needed basis by referring back to the Domain Experts from the modeling team or the business (users) for ratification or clarification of issues that affect the features list.

Exit Criteria

To exit the process, the features list team must produce the features list to the satisfaction of the Project Manager and Development Manager. The features list consists of:

- A list of major feature sets (areas)

- For each major feature set, a list of feature sets (activities) within that major feature set

- A list of features for each feature set (activity), each representing a step in the activity of that feature set

FDD Process 3: Plan by Feature

An initial project-wide activity to produce the development plan.

The Project Manager, Development Manager, and Chief Programmers plan the order that the features are to be implemented, based on feature dependencies, load across the development team, and the complexity of the features to be implemented. The main tasks in this process are not a strict sequence. Like many planning activities, they are considered together, with refinements made from one or more tasks, then considering the others again. A typical scenario is to consider the development sequence, then consider the assignment of feature sets to Chief Programmers and, in doing so, consider which of the key classes (only) are assigned to which developers (remembering that a Chief Programmer is also a developer). When this balance is achieved and the development sequence and assignment of feature sets to Chief Programmers is essentially completed, the class ownership is completed (beyond the key classes that were already considered for ownership).

Entry Criteria
- The features list team has successfully completed FDD process 2, Build a Features List.

Tasks

Form the Planning Team	Project Manager	Required

The planning team consists of the Project Manager, Development Manager, and Chief Programmers.

Determine the Development Sequence	Planning Team	Required

The planning team assigns a date (month and year only) for completion of each feature set. The identification of the feature set and the completion date (and, thus, the development sequence) is based on:
- Dependencies between features in terms of classes involved
- Balancing of load across class owners
- Complexity of the features to be implemented
- Bringing forward of high-risk or complex feature sets
- Consideration of any external (visible) milestones, such as betas, previews, feedback checkpoints, and the "whole products" that satisfy such milestones

Assign Feature Sets to Chief Programmers	Planning Team	Required

The planning team assigns Chief Programmers as owners of feature sets. The assignment is based on:
- Development sequence
- Dependencies between features in terms of classes involved

- Balancing of load across class owners (remembering that Chief Programmers are also class owners)
- Complexity of the features to be implemented

Assign Classes to Developers	Planning Team	Required

The planning team assigns developers as class owners. Developers own multiple classes. The assignment of classes to developers is based on:

- Balancing of load across developers
- Complexity of the classes
- Expected usage (e.g., high use) of the classes
- Development sequence

Verification

Self-Assessment	Planning Team	Required

The planning is a team activity, so self-assessment is achieved by the active participation of the Project Manager and Development Manager with the Chief Programmers, who use the knowledge they gained from process 1 to help make better informed decisions.

Exit Criteria

To exit the process, the planning team must produce the development plan to the satisfaction of the Project Manager and Development Manager. The development plan consists of:

- Feature sets with completion dates (month and year)
- Major feature sets with completion dates (month and year) derived from the last completion date of their respective feature sets
- Chief Programmers assigned to feature sets
- The list of classes and the developers that own them (the class owner list)

FDD Process 4: Design by Feature

A per-feature activity to produce the feature(s) *design package*.

A number of features are scheduled for development by assigning them to a Chief Programmer. The Chief Programmer selects features for development from his or her "inbox" of assigned features. Operationally, it is often the case that the Chief Programmer schedules small groups of features at a time for development. He or she may choose multiple features that happen to use the same classes (therefore, developers). Such a group of features forms a *Chief Programmer Work Package*.

The Chief Programmer then forms a *feature team* by identifying the owners of the classes (developers) likely to be involved in the development of the selected feature(s). This team produces the detailed sequence diagram(s) for the selected feature(s). The Chief Programmer then refines the object model, based on the content of the sequence diagram(s). The developers write class and method prologues. A design inspection is held.

Entry Criteria

- The planning team has successfully completed FDD process 3, Plan by Feature.

Tasks

Form a Feature Team	Chief Programmer	Required

The Chief Programmer identifies the classes likely to be involved in the design of this group of features. From the class ownership list, the Chief Programmer identifies the developers needed to form the feature team. As part of this step, the Chief Programmer starts a new design package for the feature(s) as part of the work package.

Conduct a Domain Walkthrough	Domain Expert	Optional

At the request of the Chief Programmer, a Domain Expert walks the feature team through details of algorithms, rules, formulas, and data elements needed for the feature to be designed. This is an optional task, based on the complexity of the feature and/or its interactions.

Study the Referenced Documents	Feature Team	Optional

The feature team studies the documents referenced in the features list for the feature(s) to be designed and any other pertinent documents, including any confirmation memos, screen designs, and external system interface specifications. This is an optional task, based on the complexity of the feature and/or its interactions and the existence of such documents.

Develop the Sequence Diagram(s)	Feature Team	Required

The feature team develops the detailed sequence diagram(s) required for each feature being designed. The team writes up and records any alternative designs, design decisions, assumptions, requirements clarifications, and notes in the design alternatives or notes section of the design package.

Refine the Object Model	Chief Programmer	Required

The Chief Programmer creates a *feature team area* for the feature(s). This area is either a directory on a file server, a directory on his or her personal computer (backed up by the Chief Programmer, as required), or utilizes work area support in the project's version control system. The feature team uses the feature team area to share work in progress and make it visible among the feature team but not to the rest of the project.

The Chief Programmer refines the model to add additional classes, operations, and attributes and/or to make changes to existing classes, operations, or attributes, based on the sequence diagram(s) defined for the feature(s). The associated implementation language source files are updated (either manually or automatically by some tool) in the *feature team area*. The Chief Programmer creates model diagrams in a publishable format.

Write Class and Method Prologue	Feature Team	Required

Using the updated implementation language source files from the "Refine the Object Model" task in the feature team area, each class owner writes the class and method prologues for each item defined by the feature and sequence diagram(s). This includes parameter types, return types, exceptions, and messages.

Design Inspection	Feature Team	Required

The feature team conducts a design inspection, either before or after the unit test task. Other project members may participate; the Chief Programmer makes the decision to inspect within the feature team or with other project team members. On acceptance, a to-do list is created per affected class, and each team member adds his or her tasks to their to-do list.

Verification

Design Inspection	Feature Team	Required

A successful design inspection is the verification of the output of this process. The design inspection task is described above.

Exit Criteria

To exit the process, the feature team must produce a successfully inspected design package. The design package comprises:

- A covering memo, or paper, that integrates and describes the design package so that it stands on its own for reviewers
- The referenced requirements (if any) in the form of documents and all related confirmation memos and supporting documentation
- The sequence diagram(s)
- Design alternatives (if any)
- The object model with new/updated classes, methods, and attributes
- The <your tool>-generated output for the class and method prologues created or modified by this design
- The to-do task-list entries for action items on affected classes for each team member

FDD Process 5: Build by Feature

A per-feature activity to produce a completed client-valued function (feature).

Working from the design package produced during the Design by Feature process, the class owners implement the items necessary for their classes to support the design for the feature(s) in the work package. The code developed is then unit-tested and code-inspected, the order of which is determined by the Chief Programmer. After a successful code inspection, the code is promoted to the build.

Entry Criteria

- The feature team has successfully completed FDD process 4, Design by Feature, for the selected feature(s). That is, the design package from process 4 has been successfully inspected.

Tasks

Implement Classes and Methods	Feature Team	Required

The class owners implement the items necessary to satisfy the requirements on their classes for the feature(s) in the work package. This includes the development of any unit-testing code needed.

Conduct a Code Inspection	Feature Team	Required

The feature team conducts a code inspection, either before or after the unit test task. The Chief Programmer decides whether to inspect within the feature team or with other project team members. The decision to inspect before or after unit test is also that of the Chief Programmer.

Unit Test	Feature Team	Required

Each class owner tests their code to ensure that all requirements on their classes for the feature(s) in the work package are satisfied. The Chief Programmer determines what, if any, feature team-level unit testing is required—in other words, what testing across the classes developed for the feature(s) is required.

Promote to the Build	Chief Programmer, Feature Team	Required

Classes can be promoted to the build only after a successful code inspection and unit test. The Chief Programmer is the integration point for the entire feature(s) and responsible for tracking the promotion of the classes involved (either by promoting them personally or through feedback from the developers in the feature team).

Verification

A successful code inspection plus the successful completion of unit test is the verification of the output of this process. The code inspection and unit test tasks are described above.

Exit Criteria

To exit the process, the feature team must complete the development of one or more whole features (client-valued functions). To do this, it must have promoted to the build the set of new and enhanced classes that support those features, and those classes must have been successfully code-inspected and unit-tested.

FDD tackles the key core problem area in software development—that of constructing the right software correctly and on time.

FDD does enough work up front to provide a resilient conceptual framework within which to work—the domain object model (structure) and features list (requirements). The highly iterative, self-organizing, controlled chaos of the Design by Feature and Build by Feature iterations provides an agile operational framework that can quickly adapt to change.

This balanced approach advocated by FDD avoids the *analysis paralysis* often found in teams following traditional processes with long analysis phases (simply unworkable for short-duration projects with business requirements changing monthly, if not weekly). However, FDD also avoids the large amounts of unnecessary reworking of code that are almost guaranteed when a team dives straight into coding without any reasonable shared understanding of the problem to be solved.

Like other agile processes, FDD is designed to enable teams to deliver real results more quickly, without compromising quality. It is highly iterative, people-focused, and results-oriented. FDD breaks down the traditional walls separating domain and business experts/analysts from designers and implementers; analysts are dragged out of their abstractions and participate first-hand with the developers and users in the construction of the system.

FDD is essentially described in five short processes, each consisting of one to two pages, following a simple ETVX template.

Other development activities, such as defining/gathering initial requirements, change management, and formal testing, provide input to or use the output of the core FDD processes.

chapter 5

Feature-Driven Development—Progress

A nswers: How do we measure and track progress?

> We plan for and track each DBF/BBF milestone. Re-member that the total time from beginning to end is two weeks or less. So these milestones are very tiny—maybe 'inch pebbles.' The combination of small client-valued features and these six DBF/BBF mile-stones is the secret behind FDD's remarkable ability to track progress with precision.
>
> Coad, LeFebvre, De Luca [Coad 99]

Time: A Scarce Resource

Much has been written about time being a limited resource. In software projects, this is often painfully true.

1. Software projects are often time-boxed or have required completion dates that are inflexible. In projects that have limited resources, are working with *bleeding-edge* technologies, have poorly defined requirements, or contain combinations of all three; a mandated time limit can be a major obstacle for delivering a project. It may, in fact, make the project undeliverable!

2. Process methodologies and project management practices often have administrative requirements that team members must complete as part of the work of producing a deliverable product. Activities such as status reporting, filling out various forms and checkpoints, and attending numerous status meetings are a few examples of this. These activities, unless contractually required, *do not contribute* to the actual completion of the project. In fact, they are responsible for consuming a valuable resource, namely, *time!* They are also usually dismissed as either inconsequential or just the normal "cost of doing business."

Consider a project team of 20 persons working on a three-month project. If each team member works 40 hours per week at 80% efficiency (6.4 available hours per day, assuming a 5-day week) and 4.3 weeks per month on average, this yields 137.6 available hours per person for the project and 2,752 available hours in total for the project.

Let's say that it takes 30 minutes per week per person to report time and status, an additional hour per week per person for status meetings, two hours per week filling out required process forms, and an additional 30 minutes per week for e-mails, phone calls, and "visits from the boss" on project status and time reporting. That's an additional 0.8 hours, or 48 minutes of the available project work time per day per person (4 hours per week)—12.5% of the remaining available project time spent on "nonproductive" activities. That takes 344 hours, or over 10.5 man-weeks (344/32 = 10.75) away from the total project time (the hours used are a characteristic example, based on experience, not actual figures).

The challenge, then, is to find a way to minimize activities such as time and status collection, status meetings, useless forms, and nonproductive communication activities by making the capture of that information as automatic and simple as possible.

Estimating Progress

Martin Fowler and Kent Beck, in *Planning Extreme Programming* [Beck 01], say that asking a developer for a percentage of completeness for a task generates a nearly meaningless answer.

As a developer, have you ever been in a situation where you were asked to *guess*timate how far along on a task you were or how close you were to finishing? It was a guess because you were unsure of the actual size, scope, or complexity of the task at which you were laboring. Also, the time required to produce an accurate answer would significantly delay the completion of the task.

As a team lead or Project Manager, you will probably have encountered many developers who have dived into coding without thinking enough first. These developers are often 90% complete in a matter of days, 95% complete in a month, 99% complete in six months; then they depart for a better job in 12 months, leaving the work "99.9% complete."

Feature-Driven Development (FDD) does not ask feature teams for a percentage of completeness. FDD *tells* feature teams what percentage complete they are!

FDD uses the percentage of completeness of each feature to produce summary progress reports accurately to all levels of management within and outside the project team. The coloring book [Coad 99] suggests one particular way of spatially organizing progress reports for upper management, sponsors, and clients that uses a simple color-coding scheme to communicate more effectively. We discuss these in more detail and add suggestions for additional reports to the various interested parties within the project.

It should also be said that the FDD processes do not dictate what reports are produced or their format. It merely enables the reports to be produced accurately and with a minimum of effort.

Mac: *What you're saying is that FDD provides accurate reporting as a result of using the process and recording progress?*

Steve: *Yes! That's one of the biggest issues encountered with many of the other software development processes that I've used. The reporting of status is either so inaccurate as to be useless or misleading, or it takes so much effort to do on the part of the developer that it never gets done—and actually takes valuable time away from the project.*

We start by defining six milestones for each feature. We iterate through the feature list, performing the Design by Feature (DBF)/Build by Feature (BBF) processes for each feature. The first three milestones are completed during the Design by Feature process. The last three milestones are completed during the Build by Feature process. The six milestones are completed sequentially for each feature being developed (Table 5–1).

Track by Feature

Table 5–1
The Six Milestones of Feature Development

Design by Feature			Build by Feature		
Domain Walkthrough	Design	Design Inspection	Code	Code Inspection	Promote to Build

1. The *Domain Walkthrough* milestone is attained on completing the *domain walkthrough* and the optional task of *studying the referenced documents*.

2. The *Design* milestone is attained on completion of the three tasks:
   - Develop the Sequence Diagram(s),
   - Refine the Object Model,
   - Write Class and Method Prologues

3. The *Design Inspection* milestone is attained on successfully passing the design inspection task.

4. The *Code* milestone is attained on completion of the implement classes and methods task and, if unit testing is being done before code inspection, on completion of the unit test task.

5. The *Code Inspection* milestone is attained on completion of the code inspection task. This includes the completion of any modifications required by the inspection and the completion of any unit testing performed after the code inspection.

6. The *Promote to Build* milestone is attained when all the code for a feature has been checked into the version control system used to generate "the build."

The key point here is that a milestone is reported complete *only* when all work for that task has been finished and verified to be so. No estimation is required or allowed!

Each of these milestones is, therefore, very explicitly defined to satisfy Fred Brooks' observation that "rarely will a man lie about milestone progress, if the milestone is so sharp that he can't deceive himself" [Brooks]. This is a deep and really key point about FDD and why it is so effective and operational; the milestones are the key to the accurate tracking.

Of course, we need to ask the Chief Programmers to indicate when each of the milestones is reached. A tick in a box allows us to determine where we are currently; having the Chief Programmers record the actual date a milestone is reached enables us to examine the progress at specific points in time and to plot trends in progress over time.

Mac: *So, by using well-defined milestones for the Design by Feature and Build by Feature processes of FDD, you're saying that we can accurately report actual progress and eliminate the guesswork.*

Steve: *Exactly!*

Mac: *How do we capture this information? You mentioned that the Chief Programmers check off the milestone in a box. Do we need a special software package to do this?*

Steve: *No. In fact, having to enter information into an online form could slow things down. I guess a laptop or hand-held device might work but I've found that the best way to do this is for the Chief Programmers to be given printouts of the work packages (see Chapter 6, "Chief Programmer Work Packages") that they are working on and to have them scribble the dates in the boxes as they go along. At regular intervals, most usually once a week, the Chief Programmers meet to present their scribblings to the release manager, who oversees the actual data entry and processing.*

Reporting to the Development Team

By tracking the dates that each of the milestones is attained for each feature, we can produce a large report, listing every feature, which Chief Programmer owns each feature, and the dates of each milestone achievement so far. This can be posted on a suitable wall in the development team area, in some place visible and accessible to the project team. Near the coffee machine or water cooler is often a good place.

We can also use a simple coloring scheme to show the status of each feature. For example, we can leave a feature white if it has not been started; color it yellow if it is in progress, and green when it is complete. This simple coloring scheme allows people to stand back from the wall and get a good visual feel for the overall status of the project, then walk up to the wall to zoom in on particular areas in more detail. Unfortunately, it does not work quite so well in grayscale. Thankfully a cheap, color inkjet printer does more than an adequate job. Table 5–2 is an example of tracking milestones.

Table 5-2

Tracking Feature Development

#	Feature Name	Chief Prog.	Domain Walkthru	Design	Design Inspection	Code	Code Inspection	Promote to Build
1	Schedule a *service* for a car	srp	12/10	12/10	15/10	17/10	19/10	22/10
2	Edit a *customer's details* in the customer list	srp	12/10	12/10	15/10	17/10	19/10	22/10
3	Edit the *service schedule* for a car model	srp	22/10	22/10	24/10	29/10	30/10	31/10
4	Edit a *service descrip* of a service schedule	srp	22/10	22/10	24/10	29/10	30/10	31/10
5	Edit the *task list* of a service description	srp	22/10	22/10	24/10	29/10	30/10	31/10
6	Edit the *parts list* of a service description	srp	22/10	22/10	24/10	29/10	30/10	31/10
7	Reserve the list *of parts* for a service	srp	22/10	22/10	24/10	29/10	30/10	31/10
8	Send a *service reminder* to a customer	srp	22/10	22/10	24/10	29/10	30/10	31/10
9	Edit a *service* in the workshop calendar	srp	22/10	22/10	24/10	29/10	30/10	31/10

Mac: *If we have daily builds, do we need to print this wall chart every day? That would be a full-time job.*

Steve: *No, we usually print it only after a release meeting, and that is usually held only once or, at most, twice a week. This is usually more than frequently enough for any project of any significant size. For a small project, we could have a mini-release meeting at the end of each day and update the wall chart accordingly.*

Mac: *If we had an online system that Chief Programmers could use to enter dates as they went along, then we could have an up-to-the-minute view of the feature chart on-line.*

Steve: *Yes, there is a great deal of fun that could be had building useful visualizations of the data and a virtual representation of the big wall chart. However, we do not want to get carried away and spend more time than necessary producing wonderful charts and reports when we could be adding function to the requested system, instead. Common sense needs to prevail.*

Mac: *Agreed! We are being paid to produce results, not status reports. It might make a nice project sometime, though.*

Reporting to the Chief Programmers and Project Manager

With our sharp milestones defined, we next assign a percentage weighting to each of them (Table 5–3).

Now we can say that a feature that has reached the coding stage is 1 + 40 + 3 = 44% complete. Notice that we *count only the milestones that have been reached* and do not take any work in progress into account. In this example, we may be 90% through the coding tasks but it has not been completed, so it is not counted.

Table 5–3
Percentage Weighting Assigned to Milestones

Design by Feature			Build by Feature		
Domain Walkthrough	Design	Design Inspection	Code	Code Inspection	Promote to Build
1%	40%	3%	45%	10%	1%

This might seem strange at first glance, but the error is small because each feature is granular and represents no more than two weeks of time. In this respect, the reporting lags a little behind the work (usually during design or code milestones), but does err on the conservative side. Using only completed tasks to report status means that we are measuring accomplished goals, rather than estimated progress.

"Mister Scot, have you always multiplied your repair estimates by a factor of four?"

"Certainly, Sir. How else can I keep my reputation as a miracle worker?"
Captain James T Kirk and Chief Engineer Montgomery Scot,
Star Trek III, The Search for Spock, Paramount Picture Corporation 1984

The weighting percentages assigned to each milestone in Table 5–3 are a starting point. It is important that the percentages reflect reality as closely as possible. If, for instance, we know that domain walkthroughs in our organization take 5% of the effort, not 1%, that design takes only 20%, and that design inspections really use 10%, not 3%, of the effort, then our weightings should reflect this. This is true even if the weightings in our organization differ from industry averages. The whole point of doing this is to produce accurate reports and not kid ourselves or management about progress.

Mac: *We've never done projects this way before. I don't have a feel for how close those percentages are to the actual performance of our team and organization. How do we deal with that?*

Steve: *The percentages I presented were really a starting point and can be used for the first couple of projects or subprojects. Then, as the actual performance information is captured, you can adjust the percentages for any follow-on projects. If you do adjust them, you should record that information as to when and why, and make that information available to the entire organization.*

The weightings should not be changed while features are in the process of being developed without the knowledge of the sponsor, client, and upper management because a shift in the weightings could lead to lower overall completeness percentage (as we will see later), and that would take some explaining at the next progress review with that audience. In a large project, there might be planned review points, with big milestones marking the end of a specific time box or the completion of a specified number of features. These make good points to review progress and agree on an adjustment of weightings with sponsors, clients, and upper management.

We can now calculate the percentage of completeness for every feature in the feature list. We can easily roll up the percentage figures for each feature in a feature set to calculate the percentage of completeness for each feature set. We can do the same for each major feature set and for the whole project. We can also easily count the number of features not started, the number in progress, and the number completed for the project or a particular time box within the project and produce a report such as the one shown in Figure 5–1.

Feature-Driven
Development—
Progress

Workshop Management Feature Area

Feature Set	Number of Features	Number Not Started	Number in Progress	Number Completed	Percentage Complete
Scheduling a Service	19	9	8	2	27.7%
Performing a Service	15	8	7	0	30.1%
Billing a Service	6	5	0	1	16.6%
Booking in a Repair	13	2	2	9	75%
Total	**53**	**24**	**17**	**12**	**38.7%**

Car Sales Management Feature Area

Feature Set	Number of Features	Number Not Started	Number in Progress	Number Completed	Percentage Complete
Ordering a New Car	16	9	4	3	30%
Selling a Forecourt Car	7	0	0	7	100%
Selling an Approved Car	7	0	0	7	100%
Trading in an Old Car	15	5	0	10	66.7%
Arranging Financing	13	1	3	9	78%
Total	**58**	**15**	**7**	**36**	**63.9%**
...	...	...	...	...	
Complete Project Total	**164**	**64**	**32**	**58**	**45%**

Figure 5–1
Progress totals summary report.

If we generate the data for this report on a regular basis, for example, every Wednesday afternoon, we can plot trends over time to show rates of progress. For example, we can plot and graph the number of features completed each week (Figure 5–2).

This is very useful for the Chief Programmers and Project Managers to determine whether the underlying rate of feature completion is increasing, decreasing, or stable.

This sort of graph can also be used to demonstrate the positive impact of discovering and purchasing a useful third-party component; the line suddenly shoots up steeply. It can also be useful in communicating to upper management, sponsors, and clients the negative impact of doing things such as a major formal system demonstration; the line goes almost flat for three weeks as the team prepares for the demo, does the demo, and recovers from it.

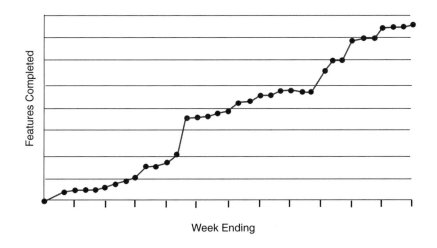

Figure 5–2
Features completed vs. weeks elapsed.

Mac: Hey, Steve. Why does the chart from your previous project show a large jump in the number of features completed? What happened there? Did you suddenly all become hyper productive?

Steve: Well, sort of. We found, bought, and integrated a third-party component that provided a large number of spreadsheet-like features that we needed. A large number of features ticked off the list, and it was a great illustration to show management and developers the benefits of reusable components.

Mac: Very cool! And the flat bits? What happened there? How come the productivity dropped?

Steve: The worse flatline, where we completed little over a period of three weeks, was when management suddenly decided it would be good to do a major formal system demonstration to show everyone the progress so far. It meant that the project leadership and some of the Chief Programmers were working on the logistics of this formal demonstration instead of resolving issues and ensuring that features were properly completed.

Again, being able to show management the flatline helped to persuade them to give us more notice the next time. Work didn't stop, it just didn't get finished; once the demo was over, the completion rate picked up again quickly.

Mac: *What about the smaller dips? I guess those could show people on vacation or sick.*

Steve: *Could be. I honestly do not remember. There were public holidays and other scheduled major progress review points but I couldn't match them up with dips in the graph with any certainty.*

Mac: *Might be worth annotating the graph with significant events next time to help show exactly why output dropped.*

Steve: *Yes, good idea. I'll remember to do that on this project.*

All sorts of graphs can be plotted and mathematics applied to produce statistics and metrics, none of which would be possible without the data provided by tracking the six milestones at the level of each feature.

Reporting to Sponsors and Upper Management

When it comes to preparing progress reports for management, clients, and sponsors, we do not need to report on every individual feature; reporting on major feature sets and their feature sets is more than good enough at this level.

We want to communicate the status of the project clearly and concisely. A gentle graphical representation of each feature set plus the use of color again can aid communication enormously. We again use yellow to mean work in progress, green to mean completed, and white to mean not started.

We also add red, indicating that something needs attention (in other words, something is slipping behind schedule). We can do this because we have the planned dates that were estimated in process 3 for each feature set. Therefore, if a feature set is not completed by the estimated planned date, it shows up in red.

Figure 5–3 shows each feature set represented by a rectangle divided into three bands: top, middle, and lower.

The top band is the biggest compartment and contains the name of the feature set, followed by the number of features in the feature set, followed by the percentage completed for that feature set. This compartment is set to the background color appropriate for the status of the feature set.

The middle band shows a progress bar graphically representing the percentage of completeness. The progress bar is green, the completed color.

The lower band contains the planned completion date estimated in process 3 and remains white until completed, whereupon it turns green to match the other two bands.

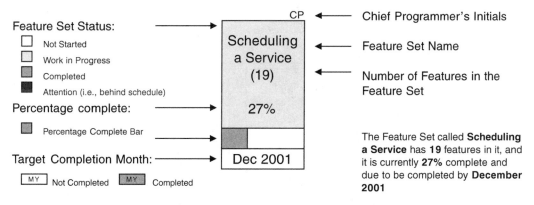

Figure 5-3
Progress of the Scheduling a Service feature set.

Just to add a little bit of incentive to the Chief Programmers, although they are not normally the type of people who need it, their initials are printed at the top right-hand corner of each of the feature sets they own.

Feature sets are arranged horizontally inside larger rectangles representing the major feature sets of the system (Figure 5–4). Each page of paper contains a number of major feature sets so that the final report consists of a few pages of colored rectangles.

Keep the layout the same for each report sent to upper management, sponsors, and clients so that it is easy to look back at previous reports and see (hopefully) green appearing in increasing amounts, red appearing, then disappearing, and a similar amount of yellow throughout the middle part of the project.

Clients, upper management, and sponsors soon learn to ask why a feature set is red and why another feature set has been yellow for a long time and still has not turned green. They should also be concerned if they see the Chief Programmer initials changing frequently in the report. This could indicate a number of things, nearly all of them negative, including:

- High turnover in the team personnel
- Frequent reassignments, hiding a Chief Programmer who is not delivering
- A Project Manager desperately trying to control a runaway project

Mac: You could have some fun animating the changes in color over time in this report.
Steve: It isn't high on my priority list. ☺

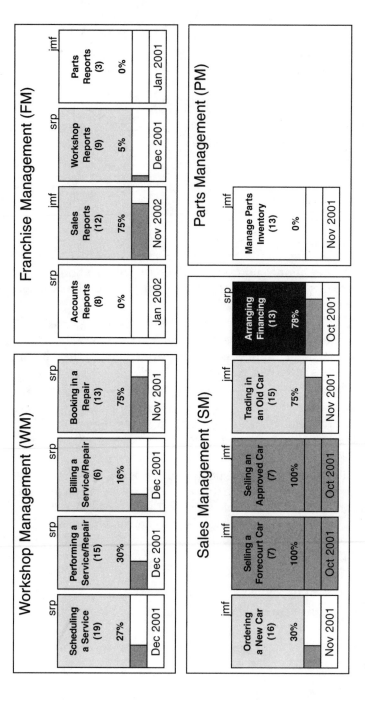

Figure 5–4
Feature sets progress report.

Mac: *I really like this. It seems to be much easier than trying to explain a detailed Gantt chart to a group of senior business managers. Gantt charts manage to cram an enormous amount of information into one diagram but they can get very complicated.*

Steve: *And they can be abused. I've seen one project present a Gantt chart that was pages of tasks, all with the same start and end dates—the start and end of the project. It was just page after page of bars going from one end of the page to another. As far as I could tell, the project lead was essentially saying, "We are not sure but we think we are going to be very busy doing a lot of work for the whole duration of the project."*

Mac: *That is extreme! I've seen Gantt charts used very well, and they can be simple enough when done at a high level. There are a couple of things shown on a Gantt chart that are not shown in your parking lot chart. The first is start dates and the second is dependencies.*

Steve: *Correct. We capture only completion dates and not start dates or actual hours worked on a particular task. You could extend the scheme to capture these. You might want this if you usually have people working on multiple projects at a time and have to account for the time spent on each. I'd prefer to keep it as simple as possible if we can.*

Mac: *Yes. Knowing what's completed and what is not is probably enough. Another thing to bear in mind, though, is that people do not like change. Suddenly turning up at a major project status meeting with a new style of report may not go down too well. We need to be gentle! I'll find out the type of report that upper management, sponsors, and clients usually expect. We can then decide whether that report communicates progress well enough and can be easily produced with minimum disruption to the developers. If it can, there seems to be little reason to change it. If it does need changing, we'll take both to the first status meeting and try to get management to agree to adopt the new format.*

Steve: *Fair enough. It will not affect us on this project but if you ever try to use the color-coding abroad sometime, it is worth checking that the colors are still appropriate. Different colors have different symbolism in different countries. You have to be careful and not overly rigid about the color scheme. It is far better to find the appropriate color scheme for the culture and use that.*

So far, we have looked at tracking progress. In the last section, we also compared progress against a plan and used that information to highlight problem areas to upper management, sponsors, and clients. Can we do the same at the Chief Programmer level? The answer is yes.

We can ask the Chief Programmers to provide plan dates for each of the six DBF/BBF milestones for the features they are about to start working on. Then we can compare the actual dates with the planned dates and color the features red that are behind schedule. In this way, we are treating each DBF/BBF iteration as some sort of micro project, with the Chief Programmer as both the architect and Project Manager.

We can now add another column to our project report (Figure 5–5)...

... and add planned dates to the wall chart, coloring behind-schedule features accordingly (Table 5–4).

Chief Programmer Plans

Feature-Driven Development—Progress

Workshop Management Feature Area

Feature Set	Number of Features	Number Not Started	Number in Progress	Number Behind	Number Completed	Percentage Complete
Scheduling a Service	19	9	7	1	2	27.7%
Performing a Service	15	8	7	0	0	30.1%
Billing a Service	6	5	0	0	1	16.6%
Booking in a Repair	13	2	2	0	9	75%
Total	**53**	**24**	**17**	**2**	**12**	**38.7%**

Car Sales Management Feature Area

Feature Set	Number of Features	Number Not Started	Number in Progress	Number Behind	Number Completed	Percentage Complete
Ordering a New Car	16	9	2	0	3	30%
Selling a Forecourt Car	7	0	0	0	7	100%
Selling an Approved Car	7	0	0	0	7	100%
Trading in an Old Car	15	5	0	0	10	66.7%
Arranging Financing	13	1	1	2	9	78%
Total	**58**	**15**	**7**	**2**	**36**	**63.9%**
...	...	...	...		...	
Complete Project Total	**164**	**64**	**24**	**8**	**58**	**45%**

Figure 5-5
Tracking progress of features (column added for features behind schedule).

Table 5–4

Tracking Behind-Schedule Features

#	Feature Name	Chief Prog.	Domain Walkthrough		Design		Design Inspection		Code		Code Inspection		Promote to Build	
			Plan	Actual	Plan	Actual	Plan	Actual	Plan	Actual	Plan	Actual	Plan	Actual
1	Schedule a *service* for a car	srp	12/10	12/10	12/10	12/10	15/10	15/10	17/10	17/10	19/10	19/10	22/10	22/10
2	Edit a *customer's details* in the customer list	srp	12/10	12/10	12/10	12/10	15/10	15/10	17/10	17/10	19/10	19/10	22/10	22/10
3	Edit the *service schedule* for a car model	srp	22/10	22/10	22/10	23/10	24/10	24/10	29/10		30/10		31/10	
4	Edit a *service description* of a service schedule	srp	22/10	22/10	22/10	23/10	24/10	24/10	29/10		30/10		31/10	
5	Edit the *task list* of a service description	srp	22/10	22/10	22/10	23/10	24/10	24/10	29/10		30/10		31/10	
6	Edit the *parts list* of a service description	srp	22/10	22/10	22/10	23/10	24/10	24/10	29/10		30/10		31/10	
7	Reserve the list of parts for a service	srp	22/10	22/10	22/10	23/10	24/10	24/10	29/10		30/10		31/10	
8	Send a *service reminder* to a customer	srp	22/10	22/10	22/10	23/10	24/10	24/10	29/10		30/10		31/10	
9	Edit a *service scheduled* in the workshop calendar	srp	22/10	22/10	22/10	23/10	24/10	24/10	29/10		30/10		31/10	
...		srp												
20	Make a *mechanic assignment* for a service	srp												
21	Record a *service performed* for a car	srp	25/10	25/10	26/10	26/10	31/10		2/11		5/11		7/11	
22	Record *any ad hoc notes* for a service	srp	25/10	25/10	26/10	26/10	31/10		2/11		5/11		7/11	
23	Record a list of parts used for a service	srp	25/10	25/10	26/10	26/10	31/10		2/11		5/11		7/11	
24	Record a *total of labor time* for a service	srp	25/10	25/10	26/10	26/10	31/10		2/11		5/11		7/11	
...		...	...	...	...	...	...	...	...	...	...	...	...	...
35	Calculate a total cost of parts used for a service	srp												
36	Calculate a total cost of labor for a service	srp												
37	Calculate a tax total for a service	srp												
38	Generate an invoice for a service	srp												
39	Process a *payment received* for a service	srp												
40	Generate a *receipt* for a payment	srp	1/10	1/10	2/10	2/10	4/10	4/10	8/10	8/10	9/10	10/10	9/10	10/10
41	Edit *problem details* for a repair	srp	10/10	10/10	10/10	11/10	15/10	15/10	19/10	19/10	22/10	22/10	24/10	24/10
42	Edit a *repair scheduled* in the workshop calendar	srp	10/10	10/10	10/10	11/10	15/10	15/10	19/10	19/10	22/10	22/10	24/10	24/10
43	Add the *details of a car* to the list of cars	srp	10/10	10/10	10/10	11/10	15/10	15/10	19/10	19/10	22/10	22/10	24/10	24/10
43	Add the *details of a car* to a repair	srp	10/10	10/10	10/10	11/10	15/10	15/10	19/10	19/10	22/10	22/10	24/10	24/10

(continued)

Table 5-4

Tracking Behind-Schedule Features

#	Feature Name	Chief Prog.	Domain Walkthrough		Design		Design Inspection		Code		Code Inspection		Promote to Build	
			Plan	Actual	Plan	Actual	Plan	Actual	Plan	Actual	Plan	Actual	Plan	Actual
...	...	...	...	...	...	...	...	...	...	...	...	...	...	...
54	Update the *model catalogue* from the makers info	jmf												
55	Create a *new order* for a car model	jmf	1/10	1/10	2/10	3/10	4/10	5/10	9/10	10/10	11/10	11/10	12/10	12/10
56	Edit the *optional items* for a new car order	jmf	1/10	1/10	2/10	3/10	4/10	5/10	9/10	9/10	11/10	11/10	12/10	12/10
57	Cancel a *car order* for a customer	jmf	1/10	1/10	2/10	3/10	4/10	5/10	9/10	9/10	11/10	11/10	12/10	12/10
58	Submit a *new car order* to the manufacturer	jmf	15/10	18/10	19/10	19/10	22/10	22/10	26/10		29/10		31/10	
59	Print an *order confirmation* for the customer	jmf	15/10	18/10	19/10	19/10	22/10	22/10	26/10		29/10		31/10	
...	...	...	...	...	...	...	...	...	...	...	...	...	...	...
99	Submit an *application for finance* for a customer	srp	1/10	1/10	2/10	2/10	4/10	4/10	8/10	8/10	9/10	10/10	9/10	10/10
100	Approve an *application for finance* for a customer	srp	1/10		2/10		4/10		8/10		9/10		9/10	
	Blocked: Waiting for management decision on exact routing of application approval notification													
101	Accept *financing* for a customer	srp	1/10		2/10		4/10		8/10		9/10		9/10	
	Behind Schedule: Barry on sick leave for 4 days													
	Behind Schedule: Barry still catching up after being ill last week													
...	...	...	...	...	...	...	...	...	...	...	...	...	...	...

Gary's Garage: Feature List - Progress (Date 26/10)

We can also ask the Chief Programmers to supply the release manager with a one-line reason to explain why the feature is behind schedule at each release meeting. We print the reason underneath the feature on the wall chart. For every release meeting that the feature remains behind schedule, another one-line reason is added. The result is that the red area on the wall chart grows over time until the problem is sorted out. The growing patch of red shouts louder and louder at the Chief Programmer and the Project Manager until someone does something about it. Once the feature is back on schedule, the reasons are no longer printed.

Feature Kills

Visibility of results is a great motivator to encourage continued or increased levels of performance. One way this can be approached is through *feature kills*, which can be a fun and effective way of promoting team interaction, healthy competition, and better performance.

After each release meeting, the release manager prints out a sheet of paper containing a green icon for every completed feature that a developer has worked on. A second row of red icons represents every feature the developer is currently working on that is behind schedule. Each developer must display all "kills" and "misses" prominently at his or her workstation.

As well as being a bit of fun, this sends a couple of messages to the developers:

1. It is important to meet planned dates.
2. The performance of the feature team dictates the number of kills and misses you get, so it is the performance of the feature team that is important; not the performance of any one individual on the team.

The feature kills method is not something we need to keep running for the life of a project. Once the message has gotten through and hitting deadlines has become the norm rather than the exception, we can stop playing the feature kills game. The novelty does wear off after a while, anyway, and there is no point spending time to produce the "kill sheets" every week if the team is no longer benefiting from it.

Summary

FDD uses six sharply defined milestones to track progress of each feature through processes 4 and 5, Design by Feature and Build by Feature.

By assigning percentages of completeness to each of the milestones, we can tell how complete a feature is. Rolling these percentages up allows us to show how complete each feature set is, how complete each feature area is, and how complete the entire project is.

We can use this information to provide easily understood progress reports for various levels of management within and external to the project.

Collecting the data at regular points over time allows us to plot various graphs and to measure the rate of feature completion over time.

FDD does not mandate the style of reporting, but it certainly enables highly accurate progress tracking and reporting, using a few simple tools and a minimum of administrative overhead.

chapter 6

Feature-Driven Development—Packages

Answers: How do we document low-level design and implementation work?

> *We've seen far too many technologists going beyond what is needed, and in extreme cases striving for (unattainable) perfection on one part of a project, without considering the other parts they compromise by doing so.*
>
> Coad, LeFebvre, De Luca [Coad 99]

Mac: *In other projects, we had detailed design specifications; detailed planning documents; and folders for code, documentation, and meeting notes. All that information is important. How and where is it captured in FDD?*

Steve: *We use the Chief Programmer work package as the focal point for capturing this information. The Project Manager, Chief Architect, and Chief Programmers should determine what information is needed for the specific project and how and where it should be captured. The work package becomes the place to go for all this information.*

Mac: *How does it work?*

Chief Programmer Work Packages

Chief Programmer work packages are a combined planning, design, recording, and auditing tool. They replace traditional large, monolithic, design specification documents by a specification consisting of short, loosely integrated (hyperlinked) documents produced when needed through collaboration within a feature team.

How much and what sort of documentation should we create and keep for each iteration through the Design by Feature (DBF) and Build by Feature (BBF) activities?

The information captured during any project includes:

1. Design and development artifacts (what was done, how it was done, and why it was done that way)

2. Planning, scheduling, and progress tracking (when were things done, when they were supposed to have been done, and how well were they done)

3. Responsibilities (who did what)

We do not want to force developers to spend significant time creating unnecessarily large volumes of design documentation and project plans; many of us working on short-duration projects (those running on so-called Internet time) can no longer afford the luxury of the time required, and few developers relish the task. The resulting documents are also hard to maintain, seldom fully read *and* understood, and they are frequently lost or become seriously out of date over time.

Lost and out-of-date requirements, analysis, and design documentation also negatively impacts other teams, such as user manual writers and proposal writers replying to detailed requests for quotation (RFQs). In the third part of this book, we look at some of the ways that FDD can improve the communication between the core development team and other teams within the software development project or organization.

The documentation that we create and keep for Design by Feature/Build by Feature iterations is defined by the tasks. Each of the tasks produces an output of some kind that we could record. For example, the DBF task *Form the Feature Team* results in a list of developers, and the BBF task *Implement Classes and Methods* obviously results in a set of updated source code files.

Once we have decided what documentation to keep, the next problem is how to link it all together in a way that makes sense. Imagine that we were doing this manually: A Chief Programmer prints out a copy of the Design by Feature and Build by Feature processes for his or her next iteration, assigns a unique name or number to the iteration, and writes it on the top of the printout. Next, the Chief Programmer lists the name or ID of the features included in that iteration on the printout. Then, to track progress, the Chief Programmer writes the completion date next to each task as it is completed.

If we leave enough space under each task, we could also ask the Chief Programmer to write down the names of the developers in the feature team and the names of any files produced as the result of each task. The printout becomes the integration point for all the documentation created during an iteration. At this point, you are probably thinking, "What if, instead of printing out a copy of the DBF and BBF processes, we used an online form instead?" Yes!

Imagine that a Chief Programmer has identified the feature or group of features to be developed in the next iteration. He or she requests a new work package for that iteration, giving the iteration a unique name or ID number. Next, the Chief Programmer specifies the features to be implemented in the iteration. If we already have a table of features for the project, the work package can automatically display the specified feature's details. If each feature in our project table is hyperlinked to the relevant supporting documents (use cases, functional specification sections, or domain walkthrough notes), the work package can also automatically list the relevant documents to study in the third task of Design by Feature (*Study the Referenced Documents*).

The Design by Feature task *Form the Feature Team* requires the Chief Programmer to remember or look up the owners of the classes involved in the iteration. If we already have a table or file on our project intranet relating developers to the classes they own, the work package can accept the names of the classes involved and look up and automatically list the developers required in the feature team.

We could even extend the work package to include hyperlinks automatically to the current version of the Javadoc output (or documentation generated by TogetherSoft's Together) for the classes involved.

Under each task heading, we then capture the results in some electronic form and provide hyperlinks to those results as the tasks are performed. For example, these outputs would include notes from the domain walkthrough task and inspection results (details of the inspections, such as the list of defects found, may be too much of an overhead without a dedicated administrator to do the data entry, or they could be scanned). Figures 6–1 and 6–2 are examples of work packages.

FDD does not dictate the exact format of a work package, just the concept, leaving us to do what is both achievable and appropriate for our particular mix of technologies and organizational constraints. Figure 6–1 literally takes the process descriptions and replaces a task's detailed description with lists of outputs from those tasks. Figure 6–2 groups the outputs more functionally.

Work Package: AR2345

Form the Feature Team						Chief Programmer: Fred					Required
Feature ID	**Walkthrough**		**Design**		**Design Review**		**Development**		**Code Inspection**		**Promote To Build**
	Planned	Actual	Planned	Actual	Planned	Actual	Planned	Actual	Planned	Actual	Planned	Actual
1007	19/3/1998	7/5/1998	7/5/1998	7/5/1998	14/5/1998	15/5/1998	18/5/1998	21/5/1998	20/5/1998	26/5/1998	22/5/1998	26/5/1998
1008	19/3/1998	7/5/1998	7/5/1998	7/5/1998	14/5/1998	15/5/1998	18/5/1998	21/5/1998	20/5/1998	26/5/1998	22/5/1998	26/5/1998
1009	19/3/1998	7/5/1998	7/5/1998	7/5/1998	14/5/1998	15/5/1998	18/5/1998	21/5/1998	20/5/1998	26/5/1998	22/5/1998	26/5/1998
1010	19/3/1998	7/5/1998	7/5/1998	7/5/1998	14/5/1998	15/5/1998	18/5/1998	21/5/1998	20/5/1998	26/5/1998	22/5/1998	

Package	Class	Class Owner	Class Version	Unit Test Results
com...application.	ApplicationForm	Fred	2.3	Passed
com...approval.	Approval Request	Larry	1.5	Passed
com...user.	User	Dilbert	3.2	Passed
com...user.	UserAuthorization	Sally	4.0	Passed
com...user.	OfficerAssignment	Sally	8.0	Passed
com...user.	OfficerCode	Sally	2.1	

Domain Walkthrough	Domain Expert: Arnold	Optional

Walkthrough Meeting Notes
Follow-Up Questions and Answers

Study the Referenced Documents	Feature Team	Required

Use Case: Specifying/Updating User ID for Officer Code	1.01
Use Case: Viewing the List of Officer Codes and their User IDs	1.0
Policy Manual	1998

Develop the Sequence Diagram(s)	Feature Team	Required

Sequence Diagram Name	Feature
can Approve	1007
check Borrower	1008
check Limits	009
get Default Authority	1007
submit Application	1010

Refine the Object Model	Chief Programmer	Required

Class Diagram Name	Feature
Authorizing Limits	1007
Officer Codes and Users	1008

Write Class and Method Prologue	Feature Team	Required

Click on class names in Class and Class Owners section for documentation

Design Inspection	Feature Team	Required

Reviewers:

Location:

Date: Time Started: Time Finished:

Defects comments and suggestions

Result:

Accepted:	Rejected:
As is	With Major Changes
With Minor Modifications	Total Rework

Figure 6–1

One possible work package layout.

Implement Classes and Methods	Feature Team	Required

Click on class names in <u>Class and Class Owners</u> section for documentation

Unit Test	Feature Team	Required

Click on unit test column in <u>Class and Class Owners</u> section for unit tests and results

Code Inspection	Feature Team	Required

Reviewers:

Location:

  Date: Time Started: Time Finished:

Defects comments and suggestions

Result:

Accepted:	**Rejected:**
As is	With Major Changes
With Minor Modifications	Total Rework

Promote to the Build	Chief Programmer, Feature Team	Required

Click on version column in <u>Class and Class Owners</u> section for class change history

Figure 6–1

One possible work package layout (continued).

Work Package:1007-1010

Features

ID	Walkthrough		Design		Design Review		Development		Code Inspection		Promote to Build	
	Planned	Actual	Planned	Actual	Planned	Actual	Planned	Actual	Planned	Actual	Planned	Actual
1007	19/3/1998	7/5/1998	7/5/1998	7/5/1998	14/5/1998	15/5/1998	18/5/1998	21/5/1998	20/5/1998	26/5/1998	22/5/1998	26/5/1998
1008	19/3/1998	7/5/1998	7/5/1998	7/5/1998	14/5/1998	15/5/1998	18/5/1998	21/5/1998	20/5/1998	26/5/1998	22/5/1998	26/5/1998
1009	19/3/1998	7/5/1998	7/5/1998	7/5/1998	14/5/1998	15/5/1998	18/5/1998	21/5/1998	20/5/1998	26/5/1998	22/5/1998	26/5/1998
1010	19/3/1998	7/5/1998	7/5/1998	7/5/1998	14/5/1998	15/5/1998	18/5/1998	21/5/1998	20/5/1998	26/5/1998	22/5/1998	

Classes and Owners

ID	Class Name	Owner	Promoted Version
1049	ApplicationForm	Fred	23
1058	ApprovalRequest	Larry	15
1171	User	Dilbert	32
1172	UserAuthorization	Sally	4
1174	OfficerAssignment	Sally	8
1345	OfficerCode	Sally	2

Requirements

ID	Description
1104	Use Case: Specifying/Updating User ID for Officer Code
1105	Use Case: Viewing the List of Officer Codes and their User IDs
1987	Domain Walkthrough Notes

Diagrams

ID	Type	Description	Feature
1795	Class	Authorizing Limits	1007
1794	Class	Officer Codes and Users	1009
1796	Sequence	Can Approve	1007
1797	Sequence	Check Borrower	1008
1798	Sequence	Check Limits	009
1799	Sequence	Get Default Authority	1007
1800	Sequence	Submit Application	1010

Notes

ID	Description
1801	Design Alternatives

Inspections

Design	Code

Figure 6–2
A work package listing task outputs functionally.

Another variation is to be able to pull out only the design and implementation artifacts into a design package that can be reviewed independently of the planning and tracking information. Again, this is nothing special, just combining loosely integrated documents to provide the views of the data desired.

A table of contents for a typical design specification might resemble the following outline:

1. Introduction
   a. Overview
   b. Intended Audience
   c. How to Read this Document
   d. Terms and Definitions
2. Requirements
   a. Functional Requirement 1
      i. Constraint 1
      ii. Constraint 2
      iii. ...
   b. Functional Requirement 2
      i. Constraint 1
      ii. Constraint 2
      iii. ...
   c. Functional Requirement 3
      i. Constraint 1
      ii. Constraint 2
      iii. ...
3. User Interface (if applicable)
4. How to Use this Component
5. Application Programming Interface
6. Internal Design of Component
7. Error, Warning, and Information Messages
8. Alternative Designs Considered

Compare this with the contents of a design package, and you'll notice that much of the content is similar. Traditionally, one or two developers would be responsible for writing such a document, and it would need an extensive review before coding could start. In the meantime, the requirements might have changed and the authors forced to make major modifications to the document before submitting it for review again.

Instead, the feature team members have created much of the content of the work package together as they worked through the Design by Feature/Build by Feature processes. This helps to reduce the number of design errors and spreads the responsibility for the design across the team. Also, the fine granularity of the iterations spreads the documentation load over time. Reviews are done earlier and in smaller chunks, helping to find requirements issues earlier.

The Chief Programmers and developers like work packages because, when working in two or three feature teams concurrently, they can look at the work package and immediately see how far the teams are through the iterations. All the relevant information for that iteration is immediately accessible from one place—a great convenience tool.

The project management team also really appreciates the details and information contained in the work packages.

Mac: *I noticed that the first programmer work package example you used was the combined Entry-Tasks-Verification-Exit (ETVX) template forms for process steps 4 and 5, Design by Feature and Build by Feature, with links to the actual documents. The other examples were more like reports. Are there any specific rules or guidelines to follow in creating the work packages?*

Steve: *The aim is to provide the level of process and artifact documentation necessary for the success of the project. The Project Sponsor, Project Manager, Chief Architect, and Chief Programmers should determine this at the start of the project. Any changes to this during the project should be recorded with a reason for the change and who authorized it, and should be part of the project summary information. The purpose is to provide the amount of documentation and paperwork necessary to the successful completion and delivery of the project.*

Mac: *It also sounds like this is a collaborative effort, where the documentation is produced when and where it is needed, instead of having a small group or individual try to create it all up front. It's more like the documentation is created iteratively, as well the actual system.*

Steve: *That's a very important difference. It helps to eliminate process bottlenecks, where the entire team is waiting on the work of a few individuals in order to start work!*

When You Have to Produce a Mountain of Paper

Sometimes, for legal reasons, you have to create large amounts of documentation. Products, such as Together ControlCenter, that can take comments from source code files and generate documentation conforming to specified templates, go a long way toward easing the pain of producing such volumes of formal documentation. Keeping the documentation in the source code also decreases the chances that it will get lost and increases the chances that it is up to date.

Rather than having one or two developers concentrate on writing large, monolithic volumes of design documentation, FDD encourages feature teams to collaborate and produce a set of loosely integrated design and implementation documents (as many as possible generated by some tool) and to link them together into named design packages or work packages that combine both design results and planning and tracking information.

Also, a more loosely integrated structure to the documentation makes it easier to integrate information, notes, and content to support user manuals and help text writers (more on this topic in Chapter 14, in the section titled "User Documentation").

part 2

Feature-Driven Development—The Five Processes in Practice

Having described the Feature-Driven Development (FDD) process in Part 1, we now move on to provide a series of hints and tips for each task in the five FDD processes.

It must be emphasized that the hints and tips are just that. They in no way form a rigid set of steps or form part of the definition of FDD. To try to make them do so would result in a very rigid process and severely reduce the agile and adaptive nature of FDD.

This part is organized into five chapters, one for each process in FDD. Each chapter starts with a Unified Modeling Language (UML) activity diagram of its process and contains a section for each task in that process. Within each section, the hints and tips are arranged by role so that the reader can quickly find the tips for his or her role in that task.

Chapter 7 describes the tricks of the trade that we have learned in performing the *Develop an Overall Object Model* process, including some well-worn tips on facilitating these modeling sessions.

Chapter 8 deals with the often-misunderstood *Build a Features List* process.

Chapter 9 presents the factors that need to be considered when following the *Plan by Feature* process.

Chapter 10 discusses the *Design by Feature* process and includes hints and tips on holding peer reviews or inspections, with emphasis on design inspections.

Chapter 11 probes the details of the deceptively easy-looking *Build by Feature* process. Included are some tips and tricks specifically for   **103**

source code inspections and the use of a shared storage area by feature team members.

More examples and discussions from the Car Dealership case study are provided throughout to illustrate the points being made.

Where appropriate, we also describe adjustments made to the processes after the coloring book [Coad 99] was published and explain the rationale behind those changes.

chapter 7

Develop an Overall Object Model

Although *Develop an Overall Object Model* (Figure 7–1) is the first step in FDD, some of the project team may have been working on the project for some time by now. Depending on the circumstances, the project team may have already put together a small prototype and a business justification to gain upper management sponsorship. There may even have been a formal requirements-gathering activity. Or the project team may be adding functionality to an existing problem domain and have a lot of existing documentation and design information. This is okay. One of the great strengths of FDD is its flexibility. You don't have to start from scratch! FDD will leverage the work already done, using it as a starting point to refine and add more detail to what is already there.

However, with the start of the modeling process, the project moves up a gear, more of the project team become involved, and management or sponsors have given the project the green light or at least have given permission to do the first three processes within FDD so that an informed development plan can be presented and reviewed.

In other cases, the start of the modeling signals one of the first meetings of the project team. In this case, the startup speed will be slower as the team explores the scope of the problem domain and brainstorms about the capabilities of the desired system.

The use of FDD reduces or eliminates the old paradigm of "do my work and toss it over the wall to the next unsuspecting victim," preferring instead a more collaborative approach. At the end of the modeling process, we should have:

1. An overall object model of the problem domain for the project. This model concentrates on the identification of major classes, their important responsibilities, and the relationships between them. More detailed classes, attributes, and operations are added in processes 4 and 5.

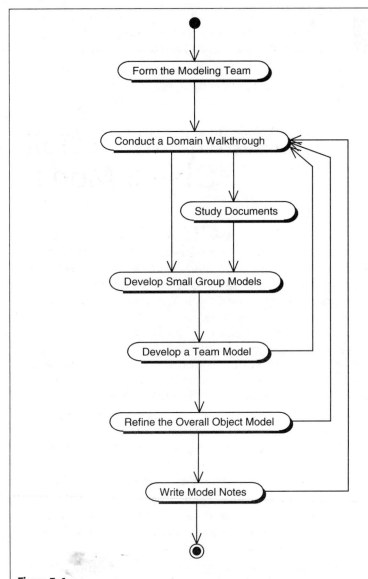

Figure 7-1

Develop an Overall Object Model:

An initial project-wide activity with domain and development members working together under the guidance of an experienced object modeler in the role of Chief Architect.

Domain Experts perform a high-level walkthrough of the scope of the system and its context. They then perform detailed domain walkthroughs for each area of the domain that is to be modeled. After each domain walkthrough, small groups are formed, with a mix of domain and development staff. Each small group composes its own model in support of the domain walkthrough and presents its results for peer review and discussion. One of the proposed models or a merge of the models is selected by consensus and becomes the model for that domain area. The domain area model is merged into the overall model, adjusting model shape as required.

The object model is then updated iteratively with content by process 4, *Design by Feature*.

2. High-level sequence diagrams illustrating the model's ability to support some of the more complex functional requirements. Again, detail is postponed until processes 4 and 5.

3. A collection of notes augmenting and annotating the overall object model, including major analysis and design decisions made and the alternative designs rejected.

To achieve these results, we recommend an accelerated approach to performing and communicating analysis. We use a series of facilitated workshop sessions similar to the Joint Application Design (JAD) style of working sessions. This workshop-style approach has a number of advantages, including:

Facilitating Object Modeling Sessions

1. Involving people from both sides of the analysis/development wall

2. Applying multiple minds to the same problem concurrently

3. Quickly standardizing on the use of much of the vague problem domain terminology used

4. Early identification and resolution of many assumptions, preconceived ideas, and omissions in the minds of key team members

5. A full and common understanding of the purposes and goals of the project

6. A shared conceptual framework around which detailed requirements can be discussed

It is also a great way to build momentum and a sense of teamwork, purpose, and expectancy for the project.

However, as you might expect, the modeling sessions can be very intense and often emotive affairs. Therefore, before looking at each task within this process, we present some tips on facilitating these sessions.

Tips for the Chief Architect/Facilitator

1. The best environment we have found for this activity is a large, conference-style room with a good mix of natural light and wall space on which to stick flipchart pad sheets. A whiteboard or two, or even a whiteboard wall is a plus. Beware of small, cramped rooms with limited capacity and wall space. Also, make sure that the temperature and airflow can be controlled or are acceptable. If you don't have a room immediately available, consider an off-site facility. It is well worth the price.

2. We strongly recommend that the first time a team works in this style, the facilitator use the first 15 to 20 minutes after

initial introductions to explain the four-stage development cycle (Figure 7–2) of a team and work with the team to produce a set of norms.

Figure 7–2
The four-stage development cycle.

Every team goes through four stages of development:

1. **Forming**: Everyone is polite, no one wants to rock the boat or appear silly. Real opinions are withheld, and discussions are superficial. Productivity as a result is not high.

2. **Storming**: Differences in opinion emerge, discussions become more intense, people start speaking their minds, disagreements are voiced—sometimes heatedly. Again, productivity is not high.

3. **Norming**: The group learns how to communicate and work with each other; the group starts to produce significant results. Productivity improves.

4. **Performing:** The team is working to individual strengths to produce outstanding results. Productivity is very high.

The important lesson for the team to learn is that the stages are a sequence. We cannot get to norming without going through forming and storming first. The group should see storming as something positive: "Good, we have reached the storming stage. We are making progress. Let's work through this and get to norming."

A second important lesson is that a team will drop back to an earlier stage at times. The intensity required in the performing stage is not sustainable over a long period of time. The team will drop back to norming every now and then to recharge its batteries. Changes in team membership and possibly circumstances will also cause the team to drop back all the way to the forming stage. The size of the changes will dictate how quickly the team can get back through forming and storming to norming and performing again.

Norms

Example Norms

- *Have fun*
- *One speaks, all listen; listen to understand*
- *Everyone participates, no one dominates*
- *It's okay to disagree*
- *It's okay to ask questions*
- *Protect all ideas*
- *Respect time limits*
- *Anyone can call "time out"*
- *Electronic devices turned off or to "vibrate"*
- *All conversation to be in English*

Agreeing on a set of ground rules for communicating during team sessions is a useful way to help a team through the forming and storming stages (we call these ground rules *norms*, as in norms of behavior, not in honor of the character from the old *Cheers* TV sitcom).

Work with the team to identify and establish the norms they want to work within during these sessions. Write them on a flipchart and stick them on a wall; then, any team members can call a breach of norms if they see one happening. Norms used for one project team can be used, adapted, or added to for other projects as well. (Reuse is a wonderful thing!)

Some useful norms are:

- *One speaks, all listen; listen to understand.* Avoid missing information and having arguments where parties are in "violent agreement" with each other by agreeing to have only one person speaking at any one time and by agreeing to listen carefully to that person to understand fully what they are saying.

- *Everyone participates; no one dominates.* Ask the quieter people to commit to speaking up and the louder people to commit to shutting up every now and again.

- It's OK *to disagree.* Agree to allow people to disagree, especially with their boss, if he or she is present.

- It's OK *to ask questions*. If something is unclear to someone, they should have no qualms about asking a question, even if it seems a dumb question. It is especially important to check assumptions.
- *Protect all ideas*. All ideas expressed, no matter how "out there" they might be, are important. A weird idea with a twist from someone else could become a breakthrough idea.
- *Respect time limits*. Agree to start and end sessions and breaks promptly to avoid wasting time.

And so on. . . .

Acknowledgment

Although certainly not new, the team development cycle, norms, Plus/ Deltas, and the Rat Hole List are collectively known within TogetherSoft as "Lessons Learnt from Fred," in honor of Fred Racey, a professional facilitator based in North Carolina.

Fred introduced the "lessons" to Pete while working with him on a particular project in 1997. Pete took them on board, wrote about them in an issue (#40) of the Coad Letter [Palmer], entitled "Lessons Learnt from Fred," and used the techniques to great effect on the Singapore project and subsequent projects. They have become standard operating procedures at TogetherSoft and are used on all TogetherSoft workshops. Try them; they really do work well.

Also, for those interested in this sort of stuff, compare the team development cycle with the Satir Change Model, discussed in Chapter 15, "People and Change," and note the similarities between the stages in each.

3. Recommended materials include:
- *Flipchart pads and stands*. Ideally, we would like one flipchart stand for every three people in the modeling team, though this is not critical. The modeling team will easily demolish two or three standard-size flipchart pads in a week.
- *Post-It® notes*. Here, we want the standard 3-inch square size. The modeling in color technique uses the usual four pastel shades of pink, yellow, green, and blue. More colors are distraction. Do not use them.
- *Permanent marker pens*. These should not be too thick because it makes it hard to write clearly on the Post-It® notes. Also, beware of marker pens that bleed through paper (like some whiteboard markers); their contribution to the décor may not be universally well received.

- *Pencils and erasers* for tentatively drawing associations and names until the small group is confident enough to ink them in.

- *Correcting tape* for removing associations and names that the small group was overconfident of.

- *Masking tape* for hanging flipchart sheets on the wall. The Post-It® note style flipchart pads that stick to the wall on their own reduce the need for the tape. However, it is still needed if you want to hang the sheets in landscape orientation.

- *Whistle* for the facilitator to use to get the attention of the team when working in small groups.

- *Ball* to use as a token during intense team discussion; only the person currently holding the ball may speak. When done speaking, the ball is passed to the next person who wants to speak. This is a great tool for enforcing the "one speaks, all listen" norm until it becomes a team habit.

- CD *player* to provide background music during small group work. Especially useful to keep people engaged immediately after lunch by playing something up-tempo.

4. Work together to produce a statement of purpose for the system. An extremely useful but simple warm-up activity is to break into groups of three for about 10 minutes and prepare a concise statement of purpose for the system to be produced/enhanced. The statement should capture the core business reasons why the system is being built/enhanced. Use no more than 25 words; keep it concise and high level. Avoid technology terms such as *scaleable* (it sounds like a characteristic of a fish or a rock face); the purpose should communicate to the Domain Experts.

Get each small group to read out its result. As a team, compare and contrast the results, highlight good words and phrases in each, then volunteer two or three people to merge the small group statements into one statement while the others are on the next coffee/tea/juice/soda break.

In doing this, the team gets some initial practice at splitting into and working in small groups, presenting results and comparing them. The facilitator sees the group in action for the first time and can note the initial group dynamics and personalities in the team.

The result also provides a focus for the team and the project. It makes explicit the overall goals and the critical success factors. The team may tweak the statement occasionally as requirements become clearer but the team can now answer, in a couple of sentences, the question, What does this system do?

This is a useful exercise, even if the team has inherited a statement of purpose prepared earlier, because it helps the team to explore that statement of purpose to understand fully what is important and why.

Steve: *Okay, Mac, what have we got for a statement of purpose for the car dealership?*

Mac: *Merging the small group suggestions, we have ended up with "To track orders and sales of new and quality used cars, schedule and record servicing and repairs of cars, and process invoices and payments." We kept it very high level and around 25 words or less.*

Steve: *Not bad! Not bad at all!*

Mac: *It still seems like a lot to implement in the time given. I don't feel comfortable with something this big and complex. It also seems like we're leaving out a lot of detail.*

Steve: *It's certainly good enough to start with. And good enough to keep the team focused on what we're trying to achieve. We haven't chiseled it on stone tablets yet; we can fine-tune it as we learn more about the domain and the customer's needs during the initial modeling . . .*

The *Form the Modeling Team* Task

Form the Modeling Team	Project Manager	Required

The modeling team consists of permanent members from the domain and development areas, specifically, the Domain Experts and the Chief Programmers. Rotate other project staff through the modeling sessions so that everyone gets a chance to participate and to see the process in action.

Expected Results

The output from this task is obviously the list of names of the people chosen to form the modeling team with the role each will play within the modeling team, Chief Architect, Domain Expert, or modeler.

Participation

The process description assigns this task to the Project Manager. However, the split of responsibilities between Project Manager and Chief Architect often differs between organizations. In some organizations, where the Project Manager role is almost entirely administrative, the Chief Architect might perform this task better than the Project Manager.

Most likely, the Project Manager and Chief Architect will perform this task together, with the Project Manager taking ultimate responsibility for the team membership. Of course, this all assumes the Chief Architect for the project has been identified. If not, the Project Manager's first job is obviously to find a Chief Architect for the project.

Tips for the Project Manager/Chief Architect

1. An ideal team size is between 6 and 12 people in addition to the Chief Architect/Facilitator. This allows the team to split into multiple smaller teams of two or preferably three. Any more than 12 becomes hard to facilitate, and we are into diminishing returns for each additional person participating. Any less than six and the team members tire quickly because they are required to participate more intensely.

2. For larger teams, keep a core team and rotate the other development team staff through in ones or twos so that they get a feel for the process, the domain, and the object modeling techniques. If the room is big enough, others can also sit in and observe (no participation allowed).

3. The members of the team should include the Chief Programmers, Domain Experts, and some of the better analytical developers. A mix of two-thirds developers and one-third Domain Experts seems to work well because, when working in threes, each pair of developers has a Domain Expert to provide domain guidance.

4. A skilled Facilitator is required during the object modeling. It is an intense and crucial time. A skilled Chief Architect is also required to ensure that the resulting object model is the best possible. A person who can play both of these roles at the same time is a great but odd commodity.

Mac: *So the roles for this session are:*
- *Chief Architect: Responsible for facilitating the session and for ensuring that a high-quality object model is delivered as a result.*
- *Modelers: Chief Programmers plus some of the more analytically minded developers to work in small groups with the Domain Experts to construct and present object models.*
- *Domain Experts: Responsible for presenting the business requirements in a series of walkthroughs and for working in small groups with the modelers.*

I normally prefer that a Facilitator not be a stakeholder in the project. The Facilitator role is to facilitate and focus the group objectively on delivering the goals and outcomes of the session. Therefore, actual and perceived neutrality is essential. If it is perceived that there is a bias or predisposition on the part of the Facilitator, the outcomes tend to become biased or, in the worst case, the sessions may break down and fail to reach the objectives at all. The idea of this type of session is to reach a real consensus, and it often requires a balance of objectivity and neutrality on the part of the Facilitator.

Steve: *It depends on the group and the caliber of the Chief Architect. Many teams work successfully without a separate, independent Facilitator, given an agreed set of norms or ground rules and a Chief Architect whose ability and experience is respected. A good Chief Architect, by definition, will defend both good ideas and good principles.*

Develop an Overall
Object Model

113

An independent Facilitator or mentor would be useful where there are known estab-lished "camps" within a team or several strong personalities that are likely to clash. Also, as with any new activity, it is useful to have someone who has done it before to guide you through the first one.

Mac: *Well, as you have done this before successfully, I think that makes you the ideal candidate to lead the modeling sessions for the Gary's Garage project.*

Steve: *Hmmm, I did rather drop myself in it there, didn't I? Okay, I'll take on that role but I may let you lead some of the later sessions so that you learn how to do it, too. So with myself as Chief Architect, the other members of the modeling team will be:*

- *Domain Experts: Gary, Mike the mechanic, and Rachel the reception man-ager. Stuart the salesman, Sandy the store man (parts manager), and Anita the accountant are available to help when we are considering the areas they work in.*
- *Modelers: You, Mac, plus three more Chief Programmers, I would think, and a couple of the other developers so that we have two developers per Do-main Expert. Let's work with Lisa the Project Manager to nail down exactly who this should be.*

Mac: *Okay, sounds like a plan.*

The *Conduct a Domain Walkthrough Task*

Conduct a Domain Walkthrough	Modeling Team	Required

A Domain Expert gives an overview of the domain area to be modeled. This should in-clude information that is related to this domain area but not necessarily a part of its implementation.

Expected Results

The members of the modeling team are encouraged to take notes during this activity. Therefore, the minimum output from this task con-sists of the collection of those notes. As discussed below, the walk-throughs could also be written up using any suitable or mandated for-mat. They could also be videoed for use as a training aid for those joining the project later.

Participation

The modeling team has been selected and is now gathered in the "modeling room," ready to start iterating through this and the next few tasks for each area of the problem domain under consideration. The Chief Architect (or a professional Facilitator) is facilitating. The first do-main walkthrough will usually be a broad, high-level introduction to the problem domain and scope of the project. The Project Manager is not normally present but may be in the room to help kick off this first ses-sion. Subsequent domain walkthroughs are more detailed presentations of a particular area of the problem domain.

Tips for the Facilitator/Chief Architect

1. Let the Domain Experts break up the domain into chunks that they can present. The breaks will often fall naturally around major business or functional areas that the system has to support.

2. The first overview walkthrough and the next few domain walkthroughs may be significantly longer but, as the team becomes more familiar with the domain, the walkthroughs should average between 15 and 20 minutes. Much more and you will exceed the modeling team's natural span of attention and have too much to model in the small groups; it is better to take more small bites than to bite off more than can be chewed easily.

3. Have a piece of flipchart paper entitled *Rat Holes* stuck on the wall somewhere. Whenever a presentation or discussion drifts off course or gets stuck on a particular issue, someone calls out "Rat Hole," and the issue can be written down on this chart so that it is not forgotten. The presentation or discussion should then continue back on course. It's not that the issue isn't important or not worthy of discussion. It is just not within the scope of the particular presentation or discussion, or quickly resolvable in the modeling session context. After the session, we can schedule time to address the Rat Hole issues or take them up with the appropriate person.

4. Watch out for technically aware Domain Experts making assumptions about the design or implementation of the new system. Allowing an assumption into the modeling may waste a lot of time and could lead to a brittle domain model if not recognized and challenged. Technically aware Domain Experts may also suggest abstractions during their walkthroughs to deal with thorny domain areas. Again, these must be thoroughly tested to avoid wrong turns.

5. If you have the resources to do so, it is a good idea to capture the walkthroughs on video. They become a great internal training aid for new people joining the project. They can also be referred to if the organization's upper echelons require a detailed, formal writeup of requirements. However, the modeling team should still be encouraged to take notes; they form an incomplete but much more concise record, and information is much easier to access from notes than is some point made on videotape.

6. If the Domain Experts are having a hard time in breaking the domain down, it can be useful to enlist the aid of the whole team in making an informal features list to help the Domain Experts organize their thinking. In small groups ask the teams

to list important features under four categories. The four categories are:

- Setting Up—features that must be in place before the doors of the business open, before most users can use the system to do their jobs.

- Conducting Business—features that are needed while the doors of the business are open; features used by most users to do their jobs.

- Analyzing Results—features desired for when the doors of the business close at the end of the shift, day, month, quarter, or year; features used by managers or supervisors to assess performance and quality.

- System Interaction—features that require coordination with other systems.

Note

Building an informal features list is a required step in the coloring book [Coad 99] but we found in practice that it misled people into thinking that it was a significant activity within process 1. It is not and is unnecessary if high-level requirements work has already been performed before the start of process 1. The current process description omits this step from the description, and we include it here as a tip, instead.

Tips for the Domain Experts

1. First, we are aiming to communicate to the modeling team how the business works and why it does things the way it does. What are the legal requirements? What is organization policy? What is fundamentally unchanged in the way this sort of business has operated in the last 50 years? Secondly, we want to communicate the users' and clients' points of pain—the difficult, tedious, repetitive, time-consuming chores and day-to-day problems that they face. The purpose of the walkthrough is not to suggest design or implementation; there is plenty of time for that in the next task, and we want to avoid prejudicing the modeling.

2. Draw diagrams on whiteboards or flipcharts. Give specific useful examples that illustrate the rules and structures in the business. Do not bore people to death with endless, beautiful PowerPoint slides.

3. Answer questions honestly. If you do not know the answer, say so, and let it be added to the Rat Hole list as a question to be followed up at the next break or with the Project Man-

ager. You do not have to defend the way the business works but you should be open to suggestions on improving the way it works. Ninety-nine suggestions may be useless but one may be a significant improvement or result in a large simplification in the new system.

Tips for the Modeling Team

1. Feel free to ask questions of the Domain Expert giving the walkthrough. However, do not shoot the messenger. In other words, do not treat the Domain Experts as though they are personally responsible for some stupidity in the business process. Even if they are responsible, it is unlikely to be helpful to rip them to shreds over it. Gently suggest an improvement instead.

2. Take notes. For business systems, particularly note events or activities that take place and their order, if any. Note people, organizations, places, and things that participate in those events or activities. Note categories of organizations, places, and things that are mentioned. Also note major business rules and roles. At the end of a session (a few hours, a day, a week, a month, as decided by the Chief Architect), a subset of the modeling team needs to write up its notes to augment the object model.

Mac: One modeling session role we do not have is that of a scribe. Wouldn't that be a useful role?

Steve: Yes, it would be useful if you can get one . . . and one who can do shorthand. There is nothing worse than having to keep stopping a creative meeting so that the scribe can catch up. Also, with today's input devices, there is no way a scribe could record all the walkthroughs, model shapes, suggestions, etc., on a personal computer as they are being discussed, so the scribe's notes have to be typed up afterward, anyway.

Mac: So the modeling team members all take notes and combine their notes at the end so that if one has missed something important, another will have captured it.

Steve: That's the way I have found works best in the absence of a shorthand secretary with enough technical knowledge to record the proceedings accurately.

Mac: A rare person. I agree it's not a good idea to mandate that role. . . .

The *Study Documents Task*

The team studies available reference or requirements documents, such as object models, functional requirements (traditional or use-case format), and user guides.

Expected Results

This activity augments the domain walkthrough activity, especially where the area under consideration has highly detailed algorithms or data item requirements. As a result of this activity, the modeling team members are expected to have familiarized themselves with the relevant documents and made notes of any key points within them that could affect the shape of the object model. The task is obviously dependent on there being suitable documents available. Occasionally, it may fall to a Domain Expert to produce a suitable document where none exists for the relevant algorithms and data items.

Participation

The whole modeling team participates in this activity, and depending on the size and complexity of the documents involved, the team may remain together in the modeling room or break to perform the task at members' own desks/offices/cubicles. Obviously, this is only an option if the modeling room is located near to the modeling team members' desks/offices/cubicles or if this is going to be the last task for the day.

Tips for the Chief Architect/Domain Experts

1. If there are functional specifications, formal requirements documents, use cases, policy manuals, user interface prototypes or storyboards, documents explaining standard algorithms, equations and formulae for the domain available, provide one or more copies for the modeling team.

2. A Domain Expert may like to refer to or walk through a particular document as part of a domain walkthrough. However, the walkthrough should consist of more than the reading out loud of a document.

3. Existing data models are useful for adding attributes to the object model later and an interesting exercise in comparison, once the initial modeling is complete. However, bringing an existing data model into the modeling activity can seriously prejudice the modelers. A good data model will look similar to a good object model but there are significant differences (inheritance, operations, many-to-many associations), and we also do not want to repeat any mistakes made in the design

of the existing data model or make our own mistakes based on assumptions about the data model.

4. In traditional software development, we often spend a great deal of time rewriting material that exists in other documents. Instead of doing this, make the existing documents available and read them. If you can make them available online so you can hyperlink to them from design and implementations results, this is even better.

5. If you are going to take a break and separate to read through the documents, make sure you agree on a time to reconvene. You can always then agree to separate again if the team needs more time. Remember also that the team needs to find only the key points and characteristics that will affect the object model shape, so it is unusual to spend more than 30 to 45 minutes on this task.

The team starts to model the servicing of cars at Gary's Garage:

Mike: . . . *and so each model of car has different regular servicing intervals; then, of course, there are the unexpected repairs that need scheduling and recording. To recap then, my biggest headache that I want solved is accurately recording which mechanic gets assigned to which service, and which of them actually does the service so we can make sure the mechanics get equal amounts of work.*

Steve: *Thanks for that walkthrough, Mike. Are there any documents for the servicing area of the domain that would be helpful to study? I'm especially thinking of some of the rules that the car manufacturer insists upon that you mentioned.*

Mike: *The franchise Policy Manual outlines the rules and guidelines that the garage must comply with when servicing cars made by the manufacturer. I have some copies here of the relevant sections.*

Mac: *We also have a small set of high-level use cases that were written for the current system.*

Steve: *Okay, I suggest we break for lunch early and spend half an hour or so looking through those before we get back together at 2:00 pm.*

Develop Small Group Models   Modeling Team in Small Groups   Required

The *Develop Small Group Models* Task

Forming groups of no more than three, each small group composes a model in support of the domain area. The Chief Architect may propose a "strawman" model to facilitate the progress of the teams. Occasionally, the groups may also sketch one or more informal sequence diagrams to test the model shape.

Expected Results

The output of this task is a flipchart-sized piece of paper from each small group within the modeling team, showing a class/sequence dia-

Develop an Overall Object Model

119

gram of the area being modeled. The diagram is usually drawn using Post-It® notes and marker pens so that it is clearly visible to the whole modeling team when presented.

Participation

Domain Experts and modelers within the modeling team form small groups of two or three and pick one part of the modeling room in which to work together to build these models. The Chief Architect normally floats, picking up on ideas and discussions from each of the groups. The groups could use breakout rooms, if available, but when the teams remain in the same room, they often overhear useful snippets of information or ideas from the other groups. It is also harder to bring the teams back together again if they are in breakout rooms. The Chief Architect, in the absence of a professional Facilitator, determines the time spent in the small groups and calls the teams back to present their results.

Tips for the Chief Architect /Facilitator

1. In practice, we have found that teams of four or more are less efficient than those of two or three. The fourth member becomes a *manager* and starts *managing* the group. It is also hard for the fourth member to see what is going on and to participate when the team is on one side of a table, the large sheet of paper in front of one person, with the other two members on either side. Hanging the paper on the wall and working standing up provides more space but gets physically tiring after a while.

2. Deliberately mixing up the sub teams every now and again lets people work with others, helps the team gel as a whole, and avoids the formation of little cliques of like-minded people.

3. If you have a couple of difficult people who insist on dominating the teams they are in, put them together and, if necessary, make up the third yourself.

4. Fifteen to twenty minutes is a reasonable amount of time to let the small groups work before reviewing progress as a whole team. It is not a sin, however, to go a little longer if all the teams request extra time. Thirty minutes is probably a good time to call a stop, though; beyond 30 minutes, and the teams may diverge too far, making it hard to come to a consensus in the next task.

Tips for the Modeling Team

1. The best tools for modeling in small groups are Post-It® notes, marker pens, and large sheets of paper (flipchart size).

Use Post-It® notes to represent classes and arrange them on the paper, using a pencil to draw in tentative associations and a marker pen once you have decided an association is good.

2. An in-depth description of the modeling in color technique is beyond the scope of this book, and this book is not printed in color, so it's much harder to see the benefit. We refer readers to the coloring book [Coad 99] for more information. For those who want a quick refresher:

When modeling, we look for four categories of problem domain (PD) class, the four class archetypes:

1. *Moment/Interval* (MI) (Pink)—a moment or interval in time (event or activity) that must be tracked for business or legal reasons.
2. *Role* (Yellow)—a role played by someone, something, or some place, a way of participating.
3. *Party, Place, Thing* (PPT) (Green)—a role player, a uniquely identifiable entity.
4. *Description* (Desc) (Blue)—a catalog-like entry, a set of values or characteristics that apply again and again.

The archetypes suggest typical attributes and methods for their classes. The archetypes also suggest typical interactions between classes of different archetypes (Figure 7–3).

The domain neutral component (DNC) is a pattern of archetypes that occurs again and again within PD object models, especially those of business systems (Figure 7–4).

Mac and Steve work with a Domain Expert, Mike the mechanic, in a small group modeling session:

Mac: *Mike, so far we have a Car class and a Model class to track cars and car makes and models, and we have connected the Car to a class representing a Service.*

Steve: *Right! The Car class belongs to the Thing archetype. The Service is a business event or activity we need to remember, so it's a Moment-Interval, and instances of the Model class are like entries in a catalog, so Model belongs to the Description archetype. What else do we need?*

Mike: *How do we know which mechanic serviced which car and how much to pay the mechanic? Also, what about the owner of the car? We have to bill them.*

Mac: *Money things are important! Sounds like two classes belonging to the Role archetype. Let's add Mechanic and CarOwner as classes.*

Steve: *I like the Mechanic class but I'm not so sure we need another class for the car owner. What sort of attributes and operations will that class have?*

Mac: *Okay, let's put a question mark on CarOwner for now. . . . [Figure 7–5]*

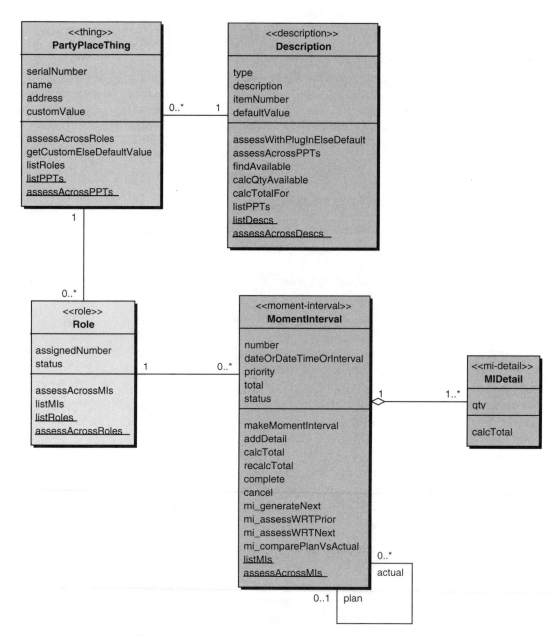

Figure 7–3
The four class archetypes.

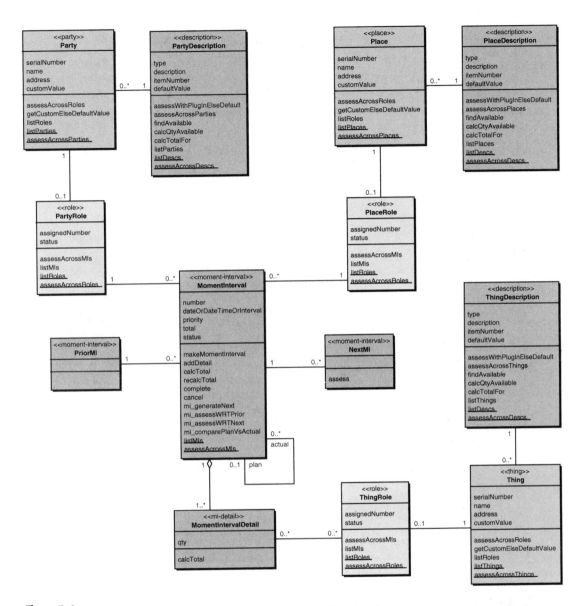

Figure 7–4
The domain neutral component (DNC).

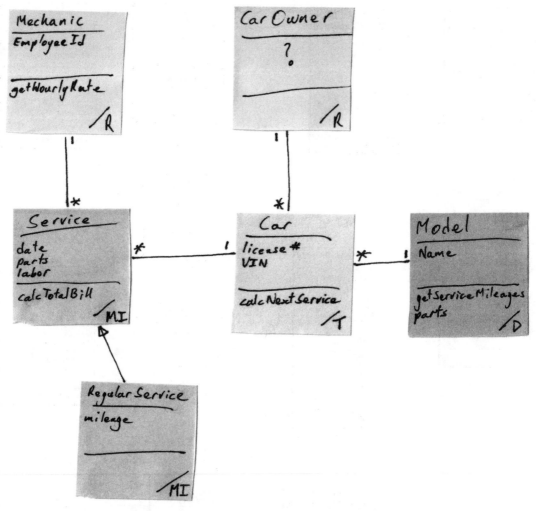

Figure 7–5
Drawing class diagrams using Post-It® notes and marker pens.

The *Develop a Team Model* Task

A *member from each small group presents that group's proposed model for the domain area. The Chief Architect may also propose further model alternatives. The modeling team selects one of the proposed models or composes a model by merging ideas from the proposed models.*

Expected Results

The output from this task is an agreed common object model for the area of the domain under consideration that is either consistent with and adds to the overall object model built so far or improves on the previous shape of the overall object model built so far.

Participation

The whole modeling team takes part in this task, listening to and commenting on the small group models as they are presented in turn. Again, the Chief Architect facilitates in the absence of a professional Facilitator.

Hints for the Modeling Team

1. One team may "get it," so choose that team's model to go forward with. Sometimes, multiple teams have good ideas, so pick one team's model and add the good bits of the others. Sometimes, it is clear that there is a difference of domain understanding; get clarification from the Domain Experts in the room and, if necessary, work in sub teams again to improve the small group models.

2. If the team is stuck, the Chief Architect makes the call or produces an alternative to try to progress the team.

3. It is not a sin to go back and work in small groups a couple of times to thrash out a particularly tricky area. Neither is it a sin to ask for a short, more in-depth domain walkthrough for a particular piece of the domain that is not clear. Small iterations are a hallmark of FDD and one of its sources of flexibility and power.

Hints for the Facilitator/Chief Architect

1. Ensure that everyone in the modeling team gets a chance to present—even the reluctant, quieter ones. Having presented a few times, the quieter ones grow in confidence, and the more extroverted people start to recognize the ability of the quieter ones and listen to them more carefully—the team starts to gel.

2. Ask the team to work to consensus. Define consensus for them as:

    A choice each person can live with, support, and help to implement.

    Reaching consensus means you are okay with a decision.

    It **DOES NOT** mean you like it or it is your ideal solution.

    It **DOES** mean you accept it, agree to support it, not quit over it or talk down about it.

You may want to do this as part of the introduction to the modeling activity or the first time a difference of opinion occurs.

3. You may also want to capture the small team presentations and team model on video or take photos of the diagrams with a digital camera (or a normal one if you can wait for the film to be developed and have access to a scanner so that the pictures can be loaded onto a shared file server or internal Web site).

4. After working on an especially tricky area of the domain, it is often wise to spend some time in the small groups creating a high-level sequence diagram for one or two of the complex requirements. This will test the object model to see whether it truly does stand up to what is required.

Mac and Steve are on a coffee break after the teams have agreed on a model of the car servicing area (Figure 7–6):

Mac: *I think that was a good result. I especially like the point from one of the other groups about adding the Person class as a role player for the Mechanic and CarOwner classes. Now the garage can distinguish between cars that belong to their own mechanics and those that belong to customers. Customers can be given higher priority, and mechanics can be given a discount.*

Steve: *Yes, a nice example of the role-player/role pattern that we see in the domain neutral component. And the separation of the reminder and scheduling from the actual servicing to distinguish between regular services and ad hoc repairs was a good idea.*

The *Refine the Overall Object Model* Task

Refine the Overall Object Model	Chief Architect, Modeling Team	Required

Every so often, the team updates the overall object model with the new model shapes produced by the iterations of the previous two tasks.

Expected Results

At the end of this task, the overall object model should integrate and include all of the agreed object models for the areas of the problem domain modeled so far.

Participation

This task is normally performed by a subset of the modeling team, usually only one or two members who enter the results obtained so far into some electronic modeling or diagramming tool and print the results or who redraw the overall model manually on potentially multiple pieces

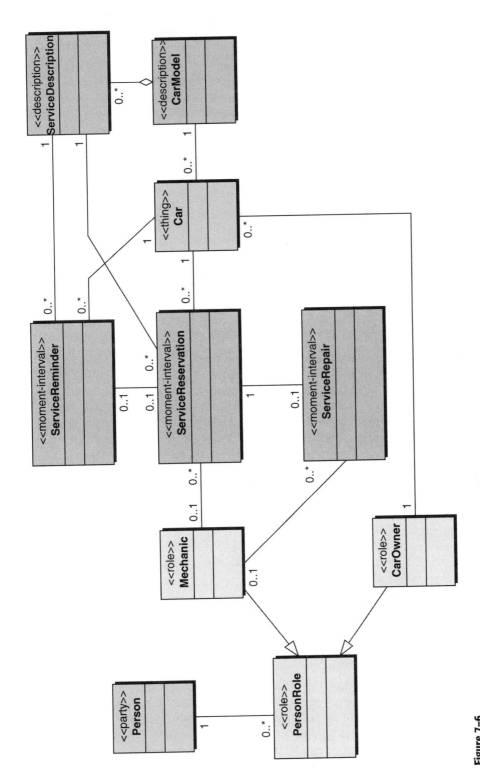

Figure 7-6

Team model for car servicing domain area.

127

of flipchart paper. The rest of the modeling team members informally check the result for errors when they next reconvene to consider the next problem domain area.

Note

The authors strongly recommend TogetherSoft's Together product for this activity, but other tools that can be used include Rational Rose and Microsoft's Visio diagramming tool.

Hints for the Modeling Team

1. The aim is to produce a consistent overall object model. If you do not integrate every now and then, the models you produce from each walkthrough may become inconsistent with each other.

Hints for Together Users

1. Manually producing an overall model diagram for a large system is a time-consuming, laborious task. It is something that we would like technology to help us with. Users of Together-Soft's Together platform can build overview diagrams from multiple detailed diagrams. At this stage, we are really using Together only as a sketching tool, so run it either in Object Modeler mode or switch off the text editor pane. Many variations exist but one approach is to:

   - Create a package called *analysis*.
   - For each domain walkthrough, create a sub-package and draw the class diagram for the team model. Create shortcuts to classes used from previous domain walkthroughs.
   - Record the alternatives in sub-packages underneath the chosen one.
   - In the analysis package, create a new class diagram called *overview* and add all the classes from the chosen packages as shortcuts.
   - Play with the layout of the overview diagram until happy and print.

2. Depending on your situation, edition of Together, and the capabilities of your version control system, it may be preferable to generate gif or wmf picture files from each of the packages and diagrams and put those under version control or export the diagrams as XMI files and version control those or version control the source code and diagram files as usual.

Hints for Those without Together or Equivalent

1. If you do not have Together or something remotely equivalent available, it is best to volunteer a couple of people to spend some time laying out the overall object model on multiple flipchart sheets as best they can. If the model becomes too large to manage, split the model into subject areas and build overview models for those, taking care to avoid inconsistencies between the models.

Steve: *Hey, Mac, we've just finished adding the servicing model into the overall model [Figure 7–7]. Do you want to take a look?*

Mac: *Okay.*

Steve: *It's really starting to take shape now. We still have a few areas to cover but it's looking good. By the way, I'm not showing the important operations or attributes that we have identified on this overview so that it does not get too cluttered.*

Mac: *I think I'm spoiled for life! Now that I've used the color modeling approach, it's going to be really hard to go back to modeling in black and white. The colors stand out so much better than the UML stereotype tags.*

Steve: *Yes, and another nice thing about working with the colors and in the small groups is that the Domain Experts actually do understand this model enough to hold intelligent conversations with the developers about it.*

Mac: *Just having all the developers that are in the modeling team agree on and understand the structure of the model is a huge step in the right direction, as far as I'm concerned. It should really help cut down on the number of miscommunications and misunderstandings later into the project.*

Write Model Notes	Chief Architect, Chief Programmers	Required

Notes on detailed or complex model shapes and on significant model alternatives are made for future reference by the project.

The *Write Model Notes* Task

Expected Results

The output from this task is a set of consolidated notes describing the major design and analysis decisions made by the team in each area of the problem domain modeled. These augment and annotate the overall object model produced by the team.

Participation

This activity is performed by a subset of the modeling team at convenient intervals throughout the modeling sessions.

Develop an Overall
Object Model

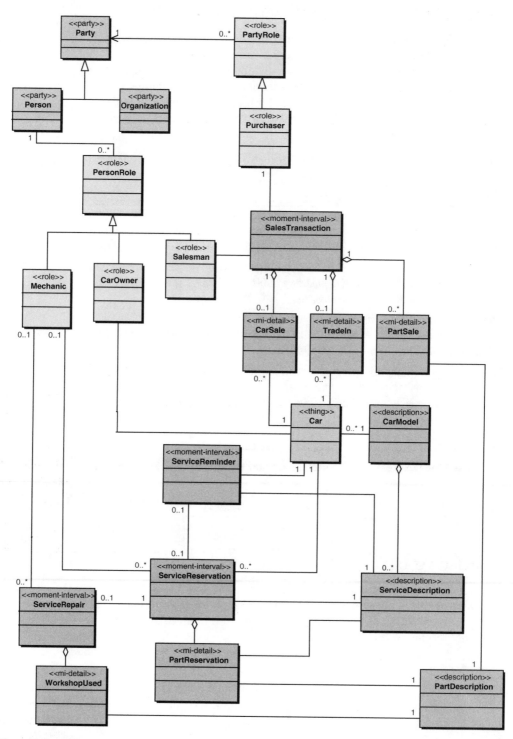

Figure 7-7

Overall object model so far.

Hints for the Facilitator/Chief Architect

1. Ask the Chief Programmers and other developers in the modeling team to take notes during the walkthroughs and during the small group presentations. At the end of a modeling session, pick three to write up the notes, consolidate them, and if possible, store them electronically so they are available to everyone.

2. Sometimes, an organization insists that you record requirements as use cases and produce other supporting UML diagrams or Extreme Programming user stories. You can write up the domain walkthrough notes as use cases or user stories and, if necessary, produce the relevant UML use case model, activity, and state chart diagrams to capture this information.

   Enlist the help of the Domain Experts in doing this and review the results for completeness and accuracy. You'll need to allocate more time for this activity, but when it is a strict organizational policy or standard, it cannot be helped; it might even be a contractual obligation. However, you must also record the modeling decisions made to avoid revisiting them at a later date, especially when someone new joins the project.

Mac: *Okay, this session's elected note writers have typed up the notes. We used Together ControlCenter to publish them as HTML [Figure 7–8].*

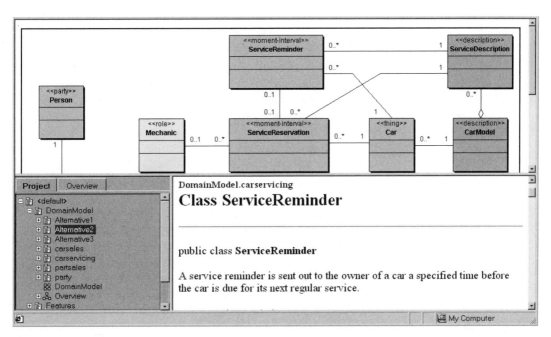

Figure 7–8
Object model and notes in HTML, courtesy of Together ControlCenter.

Develop an Overall
Object Model

Steve: How did you capture the various alternatives and design designs?

Mac: *We created a UML package for each alternative and used a combination of UML notes and diagram element properties to capture the decisions. The results are up on our new project intranet that Lisa the Project Manager had the support team create while we were modeling last week.*

Steve: *Excellent! I'll take a look after lunch.*

Verification

Domain Experts actively participating in the process provide internal or self-assessment. External assessment is made on an as-needed basis by referring back to the business (users) for ratification or clarification of issues that affect the model.

Participation

Note

This is not a task but a summary of how verification is performed throughout this process.

Hints for the Project Manager/Chief Architect

1. Many organizations have a process in place for seeking confirmation or clarification from users, clients, or sponsors. Unless completely unworkable, use it. You can always suggest improvements to the process but you are more likely to get a response quickly if you talk to the users, clients, or sponsors in a way in which they are already familiar.

2. Plus/Deltas are a great continual feedback and improvement technique. At the end of each session, draw a vertical line down the middle of large piece of paper to make two columns. Put a Plus sign at the top of one column; put a Delta symbol (triangle) at the top of the other. On the Plus side, elicit from the team things that went well, things that worked, and significant results. On the Delta side, list suggestions for improvements. List things we can do to get better results, to make our next time together more effective. There is no minus side—the emphasis is on improving the way we work.

At the end, write the date on the piece of paper somewhere so you know when these Plus/Deltas were produced.

Review your performance against the previous sessions' Plus/Deltas. Did you do better this time?

Exit Criteria

To exit the process, the modeling team must produce an object model to the satisfaction of the Chief Architect. The object model consists of:

- Class diagrams focusing on model shape: the classes in the domain, how they are they connected to one another and under what constraints, plus any operations and attributes identified.
- Sequence diagram(s), if any.
- Notes capturing why a particular model shape was chosen and/or what alternatives were considered.

Expected Results

Examine the team dynamics now. Not only should you have a very good overall object model for your problem domain, but you should also have a team of developers and Domain Experts used to talking to and working with each other. The team will also share a very good common understanding of the problem domain, its issues, and its complexities. A wonderful position to be in!

Hints for the Chief Architect/Facilitator and Project Manager

1. Watch for diminishing returns from the modeling sessions. If little new is being added to the overall model, few issues are being raised, and you have covered much of the domain, it is probably time to stop.

2. A rule of thumb is that initial object modeling should take approximately 10% of a project's construction time. For example, a project estimated to take 10 months in development might expect to spend 1 month in initial object modeling. A 3-month project may require slightly more than a week's worth of initial object modeling.

3. It is definitely not a sin to reform the modeling team or part of it later in the project to revisit a piece of the domain where requirements have changed or a significant problem with the model has been discovered. This is a judgment call by the Chief Architect after consultation with the Chief Programmers and the Project Manager.

4. This is a significant milestone. There is a fifth stage in the team development cycle, called *Adjourning*, where the team disbands. Although the team will continue to work together, the intensity of the modeling stage is over. It is a good idea to celebrate the achievement with some social event or activity. Who's up for beer and a barbeque?

chapter 8

Feature-Driven Development—Build a Features List

After working together to build the initial object model, the modeling team is now in a position to create a list of features (Figure 8–1) for the system. This hierarchically organized list will be used to plan, track, and report the progress of the development team as they repeatedly work through Feature-Driven Development (FDD) processes 4 and 5.

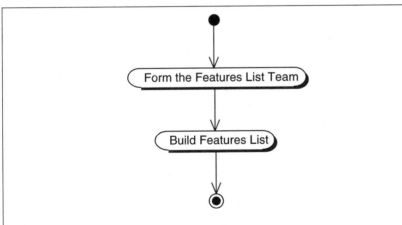

Figure 8–1
Build a Features List.

    An initial project-wide activity to identify all the features needed to support the requirements.

    A team usually comprising just the Chief Programmers from process 1 is formed to decompose the domain functionally. Based on the partitioning of the domain by the Domain Experts in process 1, the team breaks the domain into a number of areas (major feature sets). Each area is further broken into a number of activities (feature sets). Each step within an activity is identified as a feature. The result is a hierarchically categorized features list.

Of the five processes in FDD, this process causes the most confusion to those trying to learn FDD. The description of this process in the coloring book [Coad 99] muddied the waters by mentioning elements from both process 1 and process 3. For example, brainstorming about features is nearly all done in process 1, and prioritization is a planning activity best left to process 3.

This process is really no more than a functional decomposition of the problem domain, using the knowledge gained in process 1, and the focus is client-valued or business functionality, rather than system functionality. The end result is a formal, categorized list of features, where a feature is a small client-valued piece of function expressed in the form:

<action> <result> <object>

Each feature belongs to one and only one feature set (activity), and each feature set belongs to one and only one major feature set (area).

The other big problem people have with this process is the order—functional decomposition after object decomposition. This feels like it is the wrong way around. If this were a use case-driven process, it would sound as though we were advocating building the use case model after the domain class model, and this is wrong...isn't it?

First, we must not confuse the recording of results with the performance of the activity. The domain walkthroughs in process 1 provided a high-level, functional breakdown of the requirements of the system. From those, we identified the fundamental types of object involved and their interactions with each other as we built the domain object model. At that time, we clarified our understanding of the problem domain and the requirements, surfacing and resolving false assumptions, ambiguities, inconsistencies, and omissions.

Now we formally record the detailed functional requirements that were discussed in process 1.

Secondly, we are assuming that features or sets of features equate to use cases. This is a question and debate that recurs again and again. If use cases are equivalent to anything in FDD, it is that sets of use cases form a (poor, in our opinion) written form of a domain walkthrough. In a use case-driven process, the team identifies candidate objects and classes from use cases. In FDD, the modeling team identifies candidate objects and classes from domain walkthroughs. The same equivalence could be drawn for user stories in extreme programming. It should be noted that written instructions, no matter the form, format, or granularity, are never as good or as fast as having an instructor present in person. The modeling in process 1 puts domain experts in the same room as the developers; domain experts teach developers about the domain, and developers help the domain experts work through what is difficult and what is easy to automate.

Thirdly, it would seem to make sense that, in an object-oriented approach, we first identify the fundamental types of objects involved and their relationships, then examine how these objects support the detailed functional requirements of the system. Instead, we are often encouraged to define the functional details, then to use these to drive the construction of an object model. This nearly always leads to structural problems, inappropriate classes, and the need for a whole extra robustness activity designed to fix these problems (see [Jacobson 92] and, more recently, [Rosenberg]).

Mac: *To summarize what you are saying about the relationship between features and use cases*:

1. *If we have use cases, we use them to find features.*
2. *Depending on the level at which the use cases have been written, we may find whole feature sets within a use case or maybe even a whole feature area.*
3. *We may also find the same feature appearing in multiple use cases but a feature only ever belongs to one feature set.*

So if we draw it in Unified Modeling Language (UML), the relationship looks as shown in Figure 8–2.

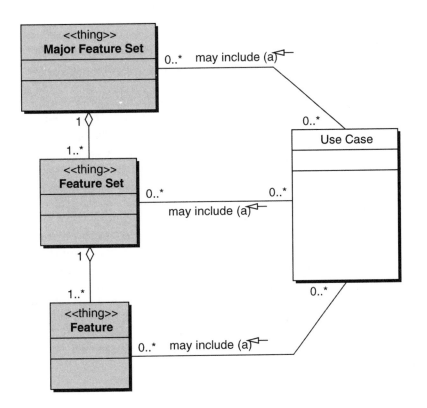

Figure 8–2
The relationship between use cases and features.

Steve: *I suppose so. I know this is an important issue to clarify. However, in no way do I want to imply that the use of use cases is mandatory or even usual when working on an FDD project. The F in FDD stands for Feature, after all.*

Mac: *Okay, I get the message. One last question and then I'll stop talking about them. If use cases do already exist and we have extracted features from them, when the business wants to change a requirement, should we update both the use cases and features to reflect that change?*

Steve: *I'd update just the features and treat the list of change requests as an addendum to the set of use cases. Updating use cases for every change request is a whole truckload of extra work for very little payback.*

Mac: *I thought you'd say that. Okay, let's set about building this features list…*

The *Form the Features List Team* Task

Form the Features List Team	Project Manager, Development Manager	Required

The team comprises the Chief Programmers from the modeling team in process 1.

Expected Results

The output from this task is obviously the list of names of the people chosen to form the features list team.

Participation

The Project Manager, together with the Development Manager and possibly the Chief Architect if the two roles are being played by different people, decide how many of the modeling team to devote to this task. Obviously, the more people working on the task, the faster it gets done. However, if developers are needed to complete other parallel activities, such as proving a technical architecture (see Chapter 12, "Technical Architecture"), it may be better to devote less resources to this task.

Hints for the Project Manager

1. The coloring book [Coad 99] says that the features list team consists of members from both domain and development. In practice, this job nearly always falls to a subset of the developers who were part of the modeling team. Domain members are usually on hand to help answer questions, provide clarification where needed, and review the results, but it is usually unnecessary to require all the Domain Experts from the modeling team to be present full time during this activity.

Lisa: How many people do you want working on the features list, and what sort of time do you need from the Domain Experts?

Mac: You are the Project Manager. How many can you spare? I'd like the whole modeling team if they are free but I know the Domain Experts also have to keep their business running, and there are some technical activities that need to get done in parallel. I really only need one or two of the Domain Experts available to look over the features list for each area to check that we have not missed anything obvious.

Lisa: I can probably ensure that one of the Domain Experts is available each afternoon this week. Will that be good enough?

Mac: Yes, that should be fine. So how many of the modelers can I have to do this task?

Lisa: I need two of the Chief Programmers on other tasks this week, so that leaves the other four plus yourself and Steve. Is that enough to get the features list process finished by the end of this week?

Mac: Yes, more than enough, I hope. We'll get started on it straight away.

Build the Features List	Features List Team	Required

The *Build the Features List* Task

Using the knowledge obtained from process 1, the features list team identifies features. The team may also use any existing reference or requirements documents, such as object models, functional requirements (traditional or use-case format), and user guides, noting the source document against any features identified in this way.

This task is a simple functional decomposition, starting with the partitioning of the domain used by the domain experts for their domain area walkthroughs in process 1. The domain is decomposed into areas (major feature sets) that comprise activities (feature sets) that comprise features, each of which represents a step in an activity.

Features are granular functions expressed in client-valued terms using the naming template:

$$<action> <result><object>$$

For *example*, calculate the total of a sale, and calculate the total quantity sold by a retail outlet for an item description.

Features are granular. A feature should take no more than two weeks to complete but not be so granular as to be at the level of simple getter and setter operations. Two weeks is an upper limit; most features take less than this time. When a step looks larger than two weeks, the team breaks the step into smaller steps that then become features.

Expected Results

At the end of this process, we should have a hierarchically organized list of all the features identified from the modeling session walkthroughs and discussions. For any nontrivial project, there will inevitably be redundant, duplicate features in the list, features that explode into three to four features on detailed examination, features that later disappear because of requirement clarification, and so on. This is okay because, in a reasonably large set of features, much of this will average itself out. Where a feature list starts to grow beyond 10% of its original size, the Project Manager needs to take action (see "Requirements Change Management" in Chapter 14).

Participation

There are a number of ways to organize the work, depending on the size of the team. One effective way to perform this task is to allocate two or three people to an area of the problem domain, have them individually list features from that area, then work together to combine their lists into a single list. Once the small group is happy with the list for an area, it moves on to build the feature list for another area of the problem domain.

Tips for the Features List Team

1. Use whatever inputs you can put your hands on. These will include domain walkthrough notes, sequence diagrams produced, and operations placed in classes during process 1. It may also include any existing requirements documents, such as functional specifications, use cases, policy manuals, etc. Remember to note the document that a feature came from so that there is a trail from the features back to the source document. This becomes important in process 4, and where a formal requirements activity took place before process 1, it enables someone to trace from a requirement to all the features supporting that requirement.

2. Use, as a starting point, the same breakdown as the domain experts used to present the domain during process 1. Within each of these domain areas or major feature sets, we want to list features grouped into named feature sets. In a business system, a feature set corresponds to some business activity, and features correspond to steps within that business activity. This is reflected in the coloring book's [Coad 99] relating of Moment Intervals archetype classes to feature sets. In non-business systems, such as a software development tool, a feature set is a logical grouping of features related to some client-valued activity. Sometimes, the feature sets or business activities are obvious, and they can be listed; then the features can be listed for each business activity. At other times (often in the case where existing requirements documents

exist), it is easier to spot individual features and group them up into feature sets. Of course, the most common scenario is a mix of the two approaches.

3. The feature-naming template is a powerful tool but on occasion it can be very hard to work a feature into that form. This is especially true of features for creating/deleting some of the most significant objects in a system. For example, we might have a feature called:

> Create *a* new mechanic *for . . . for what?*

We are creating the mechanic for our organization but the organization itself may not be explicitly represented in the class model. In these cases, we recommend expressing the feature as:

> Create *a* new mechanic *for a* Mechanic List.

This convention tells the developers that there was no domain concept identified that manages the list of Mechanics, and we may need to use a static or class operation as a factory method or introduce a factory class [Gamma].

4. The coloring book [Coad 99] suggests naming conventions for feature sets (activities) and major feature sets (areas). These are just a naming convention and not nearly as useful as the feature-naming template. In the current process descriptions, they have been omitted as an unnecessary distraction from the feature-naming template. If you want to use a naming convention for feature sets and major feature sets, we suggest but do not mandate:

> For feature sets: <action><-ing> a(n) <object>

> For major feature sets: <object> management

5. Concentrate on problem domain (PD) features. User interface (UI) features should be placed in a separate list. Likewise, system interaction (SI) features should go in a separate list. Part of the development of UI and SI features involves the linking of those features to the relevant supporting PD features. More on this topic in Chapter 12, "Technical Architecture in an FDD Project."

Steve: Hey Mac, we have come up with the list of features for the Car Service Management area. Here they are:

Scheduling a Service

1. Schedule a *service* for a car.

2. Add a *new customer* to a customer list.

3. ...

Performing a Service

14. Record a *service performed* for a car.

15. Record a *list of parts used* for a service.

16. Record a *total of labor expended* for a service.

17. ...

Billing a Service

26. Calculate a *total cost of parts used* for a service.

27. Calculate a *total cost of labor expended* for a service.

28. Calculate a *total cost of tax* of a service.

29. Create a *bill* for a service.

30. Send a *bill* to a customer.

31. Receive a *payment* for a service.

32. Print a *receipt* for a customer.

33. ...

Mac: Cool—I'll add it to the results from the other areas. We seem to have gotten over the initial temptation to put technical functions in the features list.

Steve: Yes, no more "features" like "serialize a class into an XML stream." When I showed that to Gary, he had a brief but confusing vision of a bunch of school kids marching into a small river in a straight line.☺

Mac: Amusing! It would've made a good feature if we were building a middleware tool. And using XML to serialize classes is a good idea; it will be a standard pattern or idiom on the project but the features have to be something a client can understand and put business value on.

Steve: Exactly!

Modeling team members actively participating in the process provide internal or self-assessment. External assessment is made on an as-needed basis by referring back to the Domain Experts from the modeling team or the business (users) for ratification or clarification of issues that affect the features list.

Participation

Note

This is not a task but a description of how verification is performed throughout this process.

Hints for the Features List Team

1. Again, it is important to record clarifications and confirmations from the business, and the organization's existing process should be used if one does exist. Otherwise, the project and the business will need to agree on a process. The definition of such a process lies outside the scope of the FDD processes because it is likely to differ dramatically between organizations.

Exit Criteria

To exit the process, the features list team must produce the features list to the satisfaction of the Project Manager and Development Manager. The features list consists of:

- A list of major feature sets (areas)
- For each major feature set, a list of feature sets (activities) within that major feature set
- A list of features for each feature set (activity), each representing a step in the activity of that feature set

Expected Results

We should now have a features list reflecting the scope of the project with maybe one or two areas missing or incomplete because they are waiting on clarifications of scope and requirements from sponsors,

Feature-Driven
Development—Build
a Features List

143

Table 8–1
Sample Features Database Table

Feature #	Major Feature Set	Feature Set	Feature Name	Requirements Cross-ref
4	Service Management	Scheduling a Service	Schedule a *service* for a car	Dealership Policy Doc
5	Service Management	Scheduling a Service	Add a *new customer* to a customer list	Domain notes 10a
…	…	…	…	…
18	Service Management	Performing a Service	Record a *service performed* for a car	
19	Service Management	Performing a Service	Record a *list of parts used* for a service	Mechanics Handbook
20	Service Management	Performing a Service	Record a *total of labor time* for a service	Mechanics Handbook
21	…	…	…	…

clients, or management. As strongly implied by the Feature-Driven Development name of the process, this list is used to plan, track, and drive the rest of the software development activities in the project. It is definitely worth spending enough time to ensure a quality result from this process. However, that must also be balanced by not delving into intricate, detailed discussion on how each feature will work; that task is reserved for process 4. This is actually more of a risk if the Domain Experts are available full time for this task, rather than on an as-needed basis.

Hints for the Features List Team

1. Features can be recorded in a spreadsheet, a simple database, formal requirements tool, or with a blatant abuse of the use case diagram in Together ControlCenter.

A spreadsheet or database table needs the columns shown in Table 8–1, as a minimum.

A more normalized database will, of course, factor out the Major Feature Set and Feature Set columns into separate tables, replacing them with a single foreign key column, but this is almost certainly overkill for a very basic tracking tool. Remember, we want to deliver a car dealership system, not the ultimate project-tracking tool.

chapter 9

Feature-Driven Development—Planning Feature Development

The last of the three project-wide processes in Feature-Driven Development (FDD) is the assignment and planning process. Having completed and recorded both an initial object decomposition and an initial functional decomposition of the problem domain, it is time to assign some responsibilities and priorities, and to produce an initial development plan (Figure 9–1).

At the end of this process, we should be ready to launch into the construction phase of the project represented by iterations of process 4 and 5.

The development plan provides a high-level view of the project, allowing the business to see the estimated release dates of sets of features to system test (see Chapter 13, "Testing: Failures, Faults, and Fixes," for more on formal system testing). Given a fixed amount of time planned for system testing after a set of features is released to system test, the business and deployment team have a date that they can plan to take delivery of those features.

Form the Planning Team	Project Manager	Required

The planning team consists of the Project Manager, the Development Manager, and the Chief Programmers.

The *Form the Planning Team* Task

Expected Results

Assuming that the developers playing the Chief Programmer roles have already been identified, this is a trivial task. If this assumption is false, then this role assignment needs to take place at this point and is

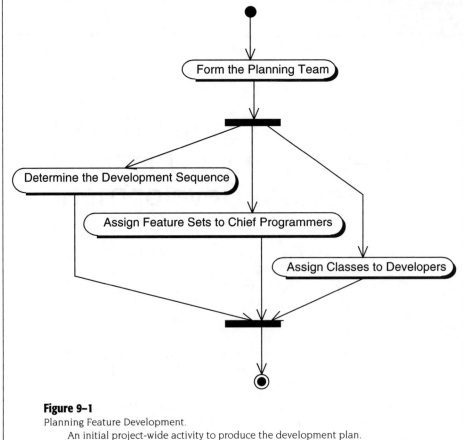

Figure 9-1

Planning Feature Development.

An initial project-wide activity to produce the development plan.

The Project Manager, Development Manager, and Chief Programmers plan the order that the features are to be implemented, based on feature dependencies, load across the development team, and the complexity of the features to be implemented. The main tasks in this process are not a strict sequence. Like many planning activities, they are considered together, with refinements made from one or more tasks, then the others are considered again. A typical scenario is to consider the development sequence, then consider the assignment of feature sets to Chief Programmers, and in doing so, consider which of the key classes (only) are assigned to which developers (remembering that a Chief Programmer is also a developer). When this balance is achieved and the development sequence and assignment of business activities to Chief Programmers is essentially completed, the class ownership is completed (beyond the key classes that were already considered for ownership).

performed by the Project Manager, aided by the Development Manager and Chief Architect.

Participation

Although the tasks in this process are largely performed without input from Domain Experts, it is not a sin to involve the Domain Experts, when required. They will certainly be needed to resolve debates about relative importance of feature sets or to help clarify any business dependencies between feature sets. Most of the priorities and dependencies should be clear from the modeling session but some may still need confirming. The domain experts will almost certainly want to review the plan with the Project Manager if it is to be presented to their managers or the project sponsors.

Mac: *Lisa wants to start the planning this afternoon. Can you let the four Chief Programmers know that they will be required to participate?*

Steve: *Okay, Gary is here this afternoon, too, if we need to ask questions of a Domain Expert.*

Mac: *Have you had any thoughts about who does what?*

Steve: *I think we should concentrate on making the problem domain classes safe first, so I think you, me, and two of the other CPs should work on that, with the other two CPs working on user interface and external system interfaces.*

Mac: *CPs?*

Steve: *Sorry! Chief Programmers.*

Mac: *Another acronym to recognize! The ideas sound reasonable. Once the problem domain is cracked, we can move more folks onto the user interface and external system interface features. I think Lisa will be happy with that arrangement. Have we selected the tool we are going to use for persistence yet?*

Steve: *The evaluation should be finished in the next couple of days. I'm keeping an eye on it; don't worry.*

Determine the Development Sequence	Planning Team	Required

The *Determine the Development Sequence* Task

The planning team assigns a date (month and year only) for completion of each feature set. The identification of the feature set and the completion date (and, thus, the development sequence) is based on:

- Dependencies between features in terms of classes involved
- Balancing load across class owners
- The complexity of the features to be implemented
- Bringing forward high-risk or complex feature sets
- Consideration of any external (visible) milestones, such as betas, previews, feedback checkpoints, and the "whole products" that satisfy such milestones

Expected Results

At the end of this task, each feature set within the feature list will have an estimated completion month. Listing the feature sets in order of completion provides an overall development plan for the project onto which additional milestones can be overlaid. Additional milestones might include formal demonstrations of progress to a senior management group or releases to an independent testing department, or may simply mark the completion of the minimum set of features that comprise a system that is truly useful to the business and could, theoretically, be deployed.

Participation

The Project Manager facilitates this activity. The Development Manager, Chief Architect, and Chief Programmers, using their knowledge from the modeling sessions in process 1, point out major dependency issues between feature sets and indicate which feature sets they consider to be of high risk or complex.

Hints for the Planning Team

There are many techniques for prioritizing and sizing requirements, including those in the form of features.

1. We could weight each feature as simple, medium, or complex and use this weighting to adjust progress reports. However, for anything more than a nontrivial project, we have found this to be an unnecessary level of detail. Features are granular, and each feature is tracked using six milestones. In the end, the varying complexities of features average themselves out in any but very small projects. The time required to do the weighting costs more than the dubious benefit of the result.

2. We can assign a priority to features, giving each feature either (A) Must have, (B) Nice to have, (C) Add it if we can, and (D) Future, in two categories: how satisfied the client would be if we delivered the feature and how dissatisfied the client would be if we did not deliver the feature. However, the client should guide this sort of valuation, and it is a time-consuming task at the feature level. This technique is probably best used at a feature set level and only when questions of scope arise. There is also the problem of users looking at history and realizing that, in their organization, if a feature is not rated (A), then it never sees the light of day. Users then refuse to rate any feature at anything other than a "Must have," ensuring that the project is delivered late and over budget, and phase two is shelved, so the vicious cycle repeats.

3. A less threatening prioritization scheme asks, "What do you want first?" Ask the client what feature sets they would like delivered first, then which features sets after that, and so on. Obviously, any strong dependencies between feature sets

must be taken into account but because these are normally domain dependencies understood by the client, it is hard for them to argue against them. This can be done in a short session with the Domain Experts before embarking on the detail of this process.

4. Another useful approach is to ask which feature sets make up the minimum product of value to the business. What is the minimum set of features that is worth deploying as a system? Then aim to develop those features first. This allows the business to deploy something of value as quickly as possible. It also enables the system test, data-conversion, and deployment teams to get involved as early as possible.

5. What about new features found or requested later? There is a rule of thumb called the 10% Slippage Rule. This says that anything that puts the project (as it was baselined at the end of this process) beyond 10% in any of its dimensions (cost, scope, quality, or time) cannot be recovered from without something else compromising by 10% (e.g., more time, more money, less features, less quality). So adding new features up to about 10% can usually be absorbed into the project without too much problem. Once over 10%, something else has to give, and that is normally scope or schedule because quality is normally not negotiable, and more money does not often fix anything, as Brooks' law describes:

Adding manpower to a late software project makes it later.
F. Brooks [Brooks]

6. It is useful to plan formal review points with stakeholders and upper management for projects lasting longer than two or three months. The frequency and format of the reviews are likely to be dictated by the existing process and structures in an organization. For example, in Singapore (discussed in the Introduction for this book), all major projects had a short monthly status meeting with the President or Deputy President and a longer quarterly progress meeting with upper management that often included a formal demonstration of the system in its current state of completion. Other teams have placed feature sets into six-week time boxes and reported progress to stakeholders and upper management at the end of each time box. These review points provide an opportunity to reset the plan if scope has grown significantly or the schedule has slipped significantly. In development of a shrink-wrapped product, the time box is likely to coincide with the regular release cycle of the product and becomes the point where the feature sets for the next release are confirmed.

Lisa: *Gary wants the car sales feature sets done first because they are the crucial part of the business. And it is the area suffering worst from the lack of a good computer system at the moment. The next priority after that is the servicing feature sets.*

Steve: *Hmm. Some of the servicing features rely on features from both the sales and parts management areas. Sales features will not be a problem if they are done first but we'll need to do a few of the features from the parts management area with the servicing features. For example, the parts area has the spare parts inventory features, and servicing needs to book out the spares needed for a service.*

Mac: *We could stub those features for now.*

Steve: *For some features that might be an option but if we want a servicing system that works as soon as possible, we will have to build the features that the servicing area depends on.*

Mac: *I see what you are saying. If we stub every feature we are dependent on, we will end up always waiting for the next set of features to be completed and integrated before we can release to system test; it'll be a big-bang delivery. Not what we want at all! So we have to order the feature sets so that the car models catalog features and parts inventory features are developed at the same time as the servicing features.*

Lisa: *While I remember, the CTO holds a major project status meeting once every two months. We will need to report at that, so I suggest setting three reporting milestones to coincide with those meetings. I'll get the exact dates from the CTO's secretary.*

Mac: *Okay, that will give us a chance to review progress with the CTO. Which feature sets will have completed by the date of the first one, do you think? Would it be worth demo'ing the system at that point? I would like to get some feedback from management on things like user interface style as early as possible . . .*

Steve: *According to our new plan, we should have enough to show a short demo; certainly enough to get that feedback anyway and demonstrate real progress.*

Lisa: *Good idea. I'll set it up. Okay, back to putting these feature sets in order, then we'll tackle the assignment of responsibilities . . .*

The *Assign Feature Sets to Chief Programmers* Task

Assign Feature Sets to Chief Programmers   Planning Team   Required

The planning team assigns Chief Programmers as owners of feature sets. The assignment is based on:

- The development sequence
- Dependencies between features in terms of classes involved
- Balancing load across class owners (remembering that Chief Programmers are also class owners)
- The complexity of the features to be implemented

Expected Results

After this activity, each Chief Programmer will have a collection of feature sets and will be responsible for their development. The completion dates of a Chief Programmer's feature sets should obviously be spread as evenly across the project duration as possible. This goal is one of the reasons why the planning team may need to revisit the previous task and adjust the order in which the feature sets are developed.

Participation

In this task, the Chief Programmers get to fight over who gets the responsibility to develop which feature sets, with the Project Manager and Development Manager trying to maintain order and achieve a sensible result. Having survived working closely together during the object modeling sessions of process 1, this task is not nearly as intense as it might otherwise be; in fact, it is often a good deal of fun.

Hints for the Planning Team

1. Look to balance the assignments so that a Chief Programmer has feature sets from no more than three major feature sets but has a spread of complex and simpler feature sets. Also, watch for bunching of a particular Chief Programmer's assignments in a certain time frame. Some Chief Programmers will be able to handle two or three feature teams running concurrently in different areas of the system. Others will not be able to manage the constant switching between these areas and will work better on one area at a time. Even the best Chief Programmer is unlikely to be able to handle much more than three different areas concurrently without losing significant time reimmersing him or herself in each area.

2. It is not a sin to reassign feature sets on occasion. It is much less disruptive to make a few small reassignments early than attempt a major reshuffle at a later date. However, assignments of feature sets are visible to upper management, clients, and sponsors in the suggested progress reports. A frequent, large number of reassignments should quite rightly ring alarm bells at that level suggesting that some Chief Programmers are not delivering for some reason or a particular set of features is causing big problems.

Mac: *What feature sets did you end up with?*

Steve: *I got all the feature sets in the Service Management major feature set; lots of fun scheduling and billing stuff. Then there were a couple of others to do with financing* and reporting, and the financing one is the highest priority because it contributes to the sales. How about you?

Mac: I got most of the Sales Management stuff. The approved car stuff has got some complexity in it I'm a little concerned about but it should be okay. I also got some reporting feature sets but I think those will be reasonably straightforward.

Steve: Well, once Lisa gets final approval from management, we can get cracking on iterating through processes 4 and 5.

Mac: Should be fun!

The *Assign Classes to Developers Task*

Assign Classes to Developers	Planning Team	Required

The planning team assigns developers as class owners. Developers own multiple classes. The assignment of classes to developers is based on:

- *Balancing load across developers*
- *The complexity of the classes*
- *The usage (e.g., high-use) of the classes*
- *The development sequence*

Expected Results

The output from this task is a list of the classes identified in the modeling sessions of process 1, together with the name of a developer who will own the responsibility for developing each particular class. Remember that Chief Programmers are developers, too, and need to be assigned ownership of some of the classes.

Participation

This is the third task in the triangle of planning tasks that the planning team needs to add to the planning equation. Again facilitated by the Project Manager, the Chief Programmers use their knowledge from the modeling sessions in process 1 to identify high-risk, high-use, and complex classes to assign to the more experienced or able developers. Obviously, the Chief Programmers will have a good idea which classes will be involved in the development of the feature sets for which they are responsible and will each be looking to get their preferred developers assigned ownership of those classes. Again, the Project Manager and Development Manager play a refereeing role to ensure fair play.

Hints for the Planning Team

1. Assigning too many closely related classes to one person overloads that person during development of features involv-

ing that cluster of classes. Far too often, failure to spread out the assignment of classes will result in feature teams consisting of only one or two developers.

2. Conversely, assigning too many classes from distinct parts of the model can cause task-switching delays as the person tries to remember details of each area.

3. When assigning classes, we need to balance these two opposing forces. We also need to be aware of people's abilities and assign more significant classes to more able or more experienced developers. An ideal assignment is probably two to three significant classes from each of two to three areas per person, depending on the person's ability and the number of developers on the team. Less significant classes can also be added to the developer's load.

4. If the developers are well known to the Chief Programmers, personality traits can be taken into consideration to avoid known personality clashes by ensuring that the classes of the two developers concerned are not closely associated with each other. A little like trying to arrange the seating at a wedding dinner to avoid offending any member of the couple's family, this can be worried about only so much, but occasionally it can be the difference between the success and failure of a crucial area of the development. Conversely, developers who work well together can be assigned classes closely associated with each other so that these developers frequently end up in the same feature teams.

5. On a day-to-day basis, Chief Programmers manage contention for a particular person (the need for a person to be in too many feature teams at one time). However, too much contention on a particular person is a hint that either:

   - Class assignments are not well balanced and they need a tweak.
   - One of the classes assigned to that person is too "big" and needs refactoring into smaller classes that can be assigned to others.

It is not a sin to reassign classes occasionally; in fact, it is good management. New people joining the project, someone leaving the project, and new classes being introduced over time are all factors that require small adjustments to be made to class ownerships. Another dynamic that encourages ownership adjustments occurs as the team starts to finish subject areas (major feature sets); classes in those areas cease to be involved in feature development, and their owners can take on ownership of other classes. Obviously, a series of small adjustments to class ownership over time is far less disruptive than a major reshuffle.

Lisa: *Suggestions for class ownership assignments, anyone?*

Steve: *I need someone good on the ServiceRepair class. It is going to take a lot of the weight in this system. I think we should put Larry on that and the ServiceReservation class because it's so closely related. I'm tempted to give the ServiceReminder class to Carrie because giving all three to Larry would probably overload him.*

Mac: *I agree. I think Harry should own the Mechanic class. That should mean that he will be on the same feature teams as Larry and Carrie a good deal of the time; those three work well together.*

Steve: *Barry has worked on the old Model catalog system before. He's a natural for the Model and Car classes . . .*

Verification

Self-Assessment	Planning Team	Required

The planning is a team activity, so self-assessment is achieved by the active participation of Project Manager, Development Manager, and the Chief Programmers, who use the knowledge they gained from process 1 to help make better-informed decisions.

Participation

Note

This is not a task but summarizes the way in which the tasks in the process are verified as being completed.

Hints for the Project Manager

1. The sequence of feature sets and their assignment to Chief Programmers allows us to construct and present a Gantt chart to upper management for its approval. However, before doing, so it is worth checking that this is a format they appreciate. If not, we are likely to be better received if we use whatever format they are used to seeing.

Exit Criteria

To exit the process, the planning team must produce the development plan to the satisfaction of the Project Manager and Development Manager. The development plan consists of:

*   Feature sets with completion dates (month and year)
*   Major feature sets with completion dates (month and year) derived from the last completion date of their respective feature sets

- Chief Programmers assigned to feature sets
- The list of classes and the developers who own them (the class owner list)

Expected Results

After the completion of this third process of FDD, we have an overall object model providing a conceptual framework within which to add features to the system, as comprehensive a list of features as possible at this stage, an overall plan for the development of those features, and responsible owners for both the features in the list and the classes in the overall model.

This point also provides an ideal time to review the situation with management, clients, or sponsors and to decide whether to continue with the project unchanged, modify the scope, or even drop the project as unviable economically.

Hints for the Planning Team

1. We can add an owning Chief Programmer (CP) column to our spreadsheet or simple database table (Table 9–1) from the previous process. We can also either add another column to hold the completion date for the major feature set or factor that out into a separate table. . .

Table 9–1
Updated Sample Features Database Table

#	Major Feature Set	Feature Set	Feature Name	CP	Date	Requirements Cross-ref
4	Service Management	Scheduling a Service	Schedule a *service* for a car	SRP	9/01	Dealership Policy Doc
5	Service Management	Scheduling a Service	*Add a* new customer to *a customer list*	SRP	9/01	Domain notes 10a
...	...	...	...		...	...
18	Service Management	Performing a Service	*Record* a service performed for *a car*	SRP	9/01	
19	Service Management	Performing a Service	*Record* a list of parts used for *a service*	SRP	9/01	Mechanics Handbook
20	Service Management	Performing a Service	*Record* a total of labor time for *a service*	SRP	9/01	Mechanics Handbook
21	...	...	...			...

. . . and create a new table to hold the list of classes with their class owners (Table 9–2).

Table 9–2

Classes and Class Owners

Class Name	Class Owner
Car	*Barry*
CarOrder	*Harry*
CarOwner	*Steve*
Mechanic	*Harry*
Model	*Barry*
ServiceReminder	*Carrie*
ServiceRepair	*Larry*
ServiceReservation	*Larry*
...	...

2. Then we need a script to generate the parking lot report (Figure 9–2), which is no more than a carefully arranged set of nested tables. Figure 9–2 shows the initial state of a parking lot report that would result from the completion of process 3. The initials of the assigned Chief Programmers are shown in the top right-hand corner of each feature set icon, and the completion month for each feature set is shown in the bottom compartment of each feature set icon. A snapshot of this report from later in the project is shown in Chapter 5, "Reporting to Sponsors and Upper Management," Figures 5–3 and 5–4.

3. If management is expecting to see a Gantt chart, we can create one by adding each feature set as a task assigned to a Chief Programmer, with the relevant completion date. The start date is a problem because in FDD, we do not really care when a feature set is started; we need only measure how much of a feature set is completed. You can either show the feature sets starting at the same time and produce a very strange-looking Gantt chart or you can use the number of features in each feature set and the estimated feature completion rate to produce an artificial start date for each feature set but a more conventional-looking Gantt chart.

Assuming that we gain management approval to proceed and the technical architecture is in place (see Chapter 12, "Technical Architecture"), the project is now ready to move into the highly iterative development of features through the repeated application of processes 4 and 5 by the Chief Programmers.

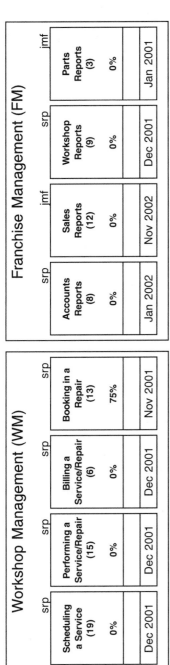

Figure 9–2
Initial parking lot progress report for Gary's Garage.

chapter 10

Feature-Driven Development—Designing by Feature

After processes 1 to 3 have been completed, the Chief Programmers each start iterations of processes 4 and 5. This is the engine-room phase of the project where real client-valued function is delivered. At the end of process 4, all of the low-level design activities for the features being implemented in that iteration will have been completed. Any notes, sequence diagrams, inspection reports, etc., produced during this process are bundled together to form the design package for this group of features (Figure 10–1).

To perform a *Design by Feature* and *Build by Feature* iteration, a Chief Programmer must select a handful of features to develop from the feature sets assigned to him or her. Generally, a Chief Programmer will select the next few features from a particular feature set that makes sense to develop at this point and can be completed in a few days, certainly within two weeks. This may mean that, for a small feature set, the whole feature set can be developed in a single iteration. More likely, it will mean a sensible handful of features within a feature set.

Hints for the Chief Programmer

1. Some features may not be ready for development because they are waiting for a requirements clarification, the completion of other features on which they depend, or a fix to a technology component bug.

    When some features are not ready to be started, we have a choice. We can leave them not started or we can start them as part of an iteration and allow them to go late. If there is plenty of work to do within a feature set, the block is not serious and likely to be resolved in a matter of a few days, and the completion date of the feature set assigned in process 3 is not at risk, then leaving the features not started is better.

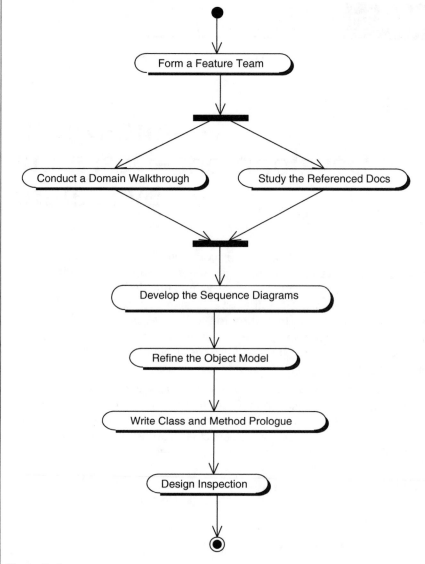

Figure 10-1

Designing by Feature.

A per-feature activity to produce the feature(s) design package.

A number of features are scheduled for development by assigning them to a Chief Programmer. The Chief Programmer selects features for development from his or her "inbox" of assigned features. Operationally, it is often the case that the Chief Programmer schedules small groups of features at a time for development. He or she may choose multiple features that happen to use the same classes (hence developers). Such a group of features forms a Chief Programmer work package.

The Chief Programmer then forms a feature team by identifying the owners of the classes (developers) likely to be involved in the development of the selected feature(s). This team produces the detailed sequence diagram(s) for the selected feature(s). The Chief Programmer then refines the object model based on the content of the sequence diagram(s). The developers write class and method prologues. A design inspection is held.

If, however, the blocked features are stopping the feature set from being completed, putting its completion date at risk, or the block is a serious issue requiring management attention, then it is wise to start the features and let them go late. The features show up in red in the progress reports, and the Project Manager has the visibility he or she needs to take action to clear the block.

2. A handful of features in one feature set may depend on one or two features from another of the Chief Programmer's feature sets so the Chief Programmer may choose to do them all in the same iteration.

3. It is faster to eat a large amount in many small bites than in huge mouthfuls. Do not bite off more than you can chew in a single iteration. If in doubt, do a small chunk, rather than a large chunk of features in an iteration.

Form a Feature Team	Chief Programmer	Required

The *Form a Feature Team* Task

The Chief Programmer identifies the classes likely to be involved in the design of this group of features. From the class ownership list, the Chief Programmer identifies the developers needed to form the feature team. As part of this step, the Chief Programmer starts a new design package for the feature(s) as part of the work package.

Expected Results

The result of this task is a small list of features (sometimes only one) that the Chief Programmer wants to implement next, plus a list of developers who own classes that the Chief Programmer believes will be involved in the development of that list of features.

Participation

This is an activity performed by the Chief Programmer on his or her own. However, he or she may need to check with individual developers and other Chief Programmers to determine availability and current workload of potential feature team members.

Hints for the Chief Programmer

1. Although this task describes the forming of a feature team, in practice, you cannot separate this task from the selection of the features to be developed during the iteration. If a particu-

lar class owner is currently heavily loaded, it is not wise to start more features requiring their participation. Postpone those features until that class owner is more available. If a class owner is never available, then either the class ownership list needs a tweak or a particular class owned by that developer is becoming too big. Raise the problem with the Development Manager, the Chief Architect, and/or the Project Manager. If necessary, start the features and let them go late so that the issue is visible in the progress reports.

2. Once we start working on the sequence diagrams, we may find that a class we thought would be involved is not, and another we did not consider is involved. It is not a sin to drop a person from a feature team or add one if the Chief Programmer finds that the initial selection was inaccurate. However, make a note of it so that others understand what has happened because it normally means an alternative design has been found that uses some different classes.

3. Start to build your work package for the iteration by listing the features you are going to implement and assigning planned dates (see Chapter 6, "Chief Programmer Work Packages," for details and alternatives for work packages and design packages). The planned dates should normally be the same for all the features being implemented in this iteration.

Then list the classes estimated to be involved and their owners (a custom-built, automated tool should populate the owner column for you). This records who is in the feature team and which classes are involved. We can also add the version of the updated class at the end of the iteration. The result should look something like Figure 10–2 (depending on the exact format chosen for the work package).

Work Package: Car Servicing 1

Form a Feature Team	Chief Programmer: Steve	Required

Feature#	Feature Set	Feature Name
0004	Scheduling a Service	Schedule a service for a car
0005	Scheduling a Service	Add a *new customer* to a customer list
0018	Performing a Service	Record a *service performed* for a car
...	...	...

Feature ID	Walkthrough		Design		Design Review		Development		Code Inspection		Promote To Build	
	Planned	Actual	Planned	Actual	Planned	Actual	Planned	Actual	Planned	Actual	Planned	Actual
0004	6/10/2001		8/10/2001		10/10/2001		14/10/2001		16/10/2001		17/10/2001	
0005	6/10/2001		8/10/2001		10/10/2001		14/10/2001		16/10/2001		17/10/2001	
0018	6/10/2001		8/10/2001		10/10/2001		14/10/2001		16/10/2001		17/10/2001	
...	...		...		...		...		...		...	

Package	Class	Class Owner	Class Version	Unit Test Results
com...servicing.	ServiceReminder	Carrie		
com... servicing.	ServiceRepair	Larry		
com... servicing.	ServiceReservation	Larry		
com... servicing.	Mechanic	Harry		
...	...	...		

Conduct a Domain Walkthrough	Domain Expert:	Optional
Study the Referenced Documents	Feature Team	Required
Develop the Sequence Diagram(s)	Feature Team	Required
Refine the Object Model	Chief Programmer	Required
Write Class and Method Prologue	Feature Team	Required
Design Inspection	Feature Team	Required

...

Figure 10–2
Car Servicing 1 work package—form a feature team.

Mac: Hey Steve! Can I check this with you, please? I'm about to start my first iteration through process 4. I am thinking of starting with some of the features from the Ordering a New Car feature set. From the overall object model, I think it's clear that the CarModel, CarOrder, and Car classes will be involved. Harry owns the CarOrder class, and Barry owns the other two. So am I right in thinking that makes the feature team Harry, Barry, and myself?

Steve: You got it. You may also find that the CarOwner class gets involved in a small way. That is the one class that I own, so if you do find you need me I'll join the team, too.

Mac: So I might get the Chief Architect playing his developer role in my feature team. Bargain! I get an experienced developer on my feature team . . . and you get to keep an eye on me to make sure I'm doing it right, I suppose. ☺

Steve: You said it! We may not own as many classes as the other developers but owning one or two keeps us close to the work and helps transfer knowledge between the Chief Programmers, including the Chief Architect and Development Manager.

Mac: What are you working on at the moment?

Steve: I'm just about to hold a domain walkthrough for a handful of the servicing features. Harry, Larry, Carrie, and myself are the feature team for this set of features; Larry and Carrie own the main car servicing classes, and Larry owns the Mechanic class. I think Larry and Carrie will get the weight of the work in this iteration, so Harry should be able to cope with being in both of our feature teams at the same time.

Mac: Great! Enjoy your domain walkthrough. . . .

The *Conduct a Domain Walkthrough Task*

Conduct a Domain Walkthrough	Domain Expert	Optional

At the request of the Chief Programmer, a Domain Expert walks the feature team through details of algorithms, rules, formulas, and data elements needed for the feature to be designed. This is an optional task based on the complexity of the feature and/or its interactions.

Expected Results

The Chief Programmer has a good, high-level idea from participating in the object modeling of how the features will work. However, after this task, the feature team will have a low-level understanding of the exact data items, algorithms, and minor objects involved. If there is little data or algorithmic complexity, this task can be skipped; the Chief Programmer decides whether the task should be performed.

Participation

The feature team members are all present in a suitable collaborative work area for the domain walkthrough.

Hints for the Chief Programmer

1. Where the domain is not so complex or there is plenty of supporting documentation, you might find it worthwhile to start work on the sequence diagrams with the team and build a list of specific questions for the Domain Expert. This can be especially useful if the Domain Experts are busy at the time you want them. Give the questions to the Domain Experts and ask them to walk the team through the answers, once ready.

2. If your organization requires the use of use cases or other particular forms of functional specification, record the domain walkthrough in that format but be wary of losing information; most use-case formats allow notes to be added; use them. Otherwise, a walkthrough can be recorded as a set of informal notes, as a series of questions and answers, or as meeting minutes. Be careful to record any actions or clarifications required as a result of the walkthrough.

3. Facilitate the walkthrough, helping the team to observe agreed norms for communication.

Hints for the Domain Expert

1. Be honest. It is far better to say you do not know the answer to a question and go and find out than to guess and be proven wrong after the feature team has completed the features. They will not be very appreciative!

2. Follow up on any outstanding questions or issues quickly so that the team does not block for longer than necessary.

Hints for the Feature Team

1. Remember to treat the Domain Expert as a team member and not as a defendant on trial for crimes against your sanity; the Domain Expert is not usually the guilty party.

2. Ask questions. If it is not clear to you, it probably is not clear to someone else.

3. Reference the notes taken or supporting memos, etc., in the domain walkthrough section of the work package (Figure 10–3). If publishing the work packages on a project intranet (recommended), hyperlink the references to an electronic version of the documents.

Steve: *Welcome to the first meeting of this feature team. Mike, our mechanic friend, is our Domain Expert today, and he's going to take us through the details of the features of the car servicing process. Feel free to ask questions; we want to get as much informa-*

Work Package: Car Servicing 1

Form a Feature Team	**Chief Programmer: Steve**	**Required**

...

Conduct a Domain Walkthrough	**Domain Expert: Mike the Mechanic**	**Optional**

Walkthrough Meeting Notes (Document: CS1 Walkthrough Notes)
Follow-up Questions and Answers (Document: CS1 Q&A)

Study the Referenced Documents	**Feature Team**	**Required**
Develop the Sequence Diagram(s)	**Feature Team**	**Required**
Refine the Object Model	**Chief Programmer**	**Required**
Write Class and Method Prologue	**Feature Team**	**Required**
Design Inspection	**Feature Team**	**Required**

...

Figure 10–3
Car Servicing 1 work package—conduct a domain walkthrough.

tion out of Mike as we possibly can. Oh, and please take notes, too. Okay, it's all yours, Mike.

Mike: Thanks, Steve. All of the mechanics are assigned to service a car by the reception manager . . .

The *Study the Referenced Documents* Task

Study the Referenced Documents	**Feature Team**	**Optional**

The feature team studies the documents referenced in the features list for the feature(s) to be designed and any other pertinent documents, including any confirmation memos, screen designs, and external system interface specifications. This is an optional task, based on the complexity of the feature and/or its interactions and the existence of such documents.

Expected Results

This task is very applicable where complex calculations or algorithms are involved. In process 2, we noted documents describing the details of particular features in the requirements cross-reference column of our feature list. Now it's time to dig out the relevant documents again and dust them off (or print them out from the project intranet site).

The only result from this task is increased understanding and more detailed knowledge for the feature team members of the data items and algorithms required to be implemented for the features under consideration.

Participation

This task can be performed as a group exercise or the team members can break to study the documents at their own desks/offices/cubicles. However, it is always more productive to have an instructor in person, i.e., a Domain Expert, than written instructions. If possible, have a Domain Expert walk the team through any documents produced by the business that describe formulas, rules, and equations.

Hints for the Feature Team

1. If a Domain Expert is not available immediately to conduct a walkthrough with the team, this task can be performed first by the team and a list of questions compiled for the Domain Expert to answer when he or she does become available.

2. Add the list of referenced documents to the work package to show that they have been taken into consideration (Figure 10–4). A custom-built, automated tool could very easily extract the list of documents from the features list built into process 2.

Steve: *Okay, the only relevant documents we have are the Mechanics Handbook provided by the car manufacturer and the old franchise's policy document. I suggest we take 40 minutes to go read through the sections on servicing, and we'll get back together after lunch to work on some sequence diagrams. . . .*

Work Package: Car Servicing 1

| Form a Feature Team | Chief Programmer: Steve | Required |

•••

Feature ID	Walkthrough		Design		Design Review		Development		Code Inspection		Promote To Build	
	Planned	Actual	Planned	Actual	Planned	Actual	Planned	Actual	Planned	Actual	Planned	Actual
0004	6/10/2001	6/10/2001	8/10/2001		10/10/2001		14/10/2001		16/10/2001		17/10/2001	
0005	6/10/2001	6/10/2001	8/10/2001		10/10/2001		14/10/2001		16/10/2001		17/10/2001	
0018	6/10/2001	6/10/2001	8/10/2001		10/10/2001		14/10/2001		16/10/2001		17/10/2001	
0018	6/10/2001	6/10/2001	8/10/2001		10/10/2001		14/10/2001		16/10/2001		17/10/2001	
...	...		...		...		...		...		...	

•••

| Conduct a Domain Walkthrough | Domain Expert: Mike the Mechanic | Optional |

Walkthrough Meeting Notes (Document: CS1 Walkthrough Notes)

Follow-up Questions and Answers (Document: CS1 Q&A)

| Study the Referenced Documents | Feature Team | Required |

| Manufacturers Handbook for Mechanics | 2001 |
| Franchise Policy Manual | 2000 |

| Develop the Sequence Diagram(s) | Feature Team | Required |

| Refine the Object Model | Chief Programmer | Required |

| Write Class and Method Prologue | Feature Team | Required |

| Design Inspection | Feature Team | Required |

•••

Figure 10–4
Car Servicing 1 work package—study the referenced documents.

168

The *Develop the Sequence Diagram(s) Task*

The feature team develops the detailed sequence diagram(s) required for each feature being designed. The team writes up and records any alternative designs, design decisions, assumptions, requirements clarifications, and notes in the design alternatives or notes section of the design package.

Expected Results

It is time to decide exactly how a feature is going to be implemented. The feature team members work together to design the optimal set of object interactions required to fulfill the requirements of each feature being developed in this iteration of processes 4 and 5.

Unified Modeling Language (UML) sequences are used to record this design and any significant alternative design alternatives.

Participation

The feature team members all contribute during the design session. Each member represents the responsibilities required of the classes that he or she owns, offering options that maintain the conceptual integrity of those classes and opportunities to refactor them, and pointing out flaws in the design. The ultimate decision is that of the Chief Programmer but combining multiple minds helps to improve the quality of the design of individual classes and reduce the need to refactor in order to support features in subsequent iterations.

Hints for the Chief Programmer

1. Normally, a team working around a whiteboard is the best way to facilitate this. For very complex areas requiring serious algorithms, it can be beneficial to send the team away to work in ones or twos for a few hours and come back together to compare and contrast designs.

2. UML defines two types of diagrams that show how a group of objects interacts to fulfill the requirements of a particular feature. These diagrams are the sequence diagram and the collaboration diagram. The two diagrams are semantically equivalent, and most UML modeling tools can derive one representation from the other. Therefore, although this task discusses sequence diagrams, it is just as valid to work with collaboration diagrams if the feature team members prefer that representation.

3. The sequence diagrams should be detailed and include parameters, returns, and notes on where exceptions are thrown (these are hard to represent in standard UML sequence diagrams but don't let this stop you from doing it—use UML note symbols on the diagram, if necessary). When working with a complex technical architecture, first work out the object interactions, ignoring technical architecture constraints. Then work on translating that set of object interaction onto the technical architecture. This prevents the team from becoming bogged down, trying to battle with technical constraints and detailed functional requirements at the same time.

Steve: *Let's tackle feature 4, the "Schedule a service for a car" feature.*

Larry: *Steve, there seem to be two scenarios here. In one case, there is a reminder sent out to a customer telling them their car is due for a service, and we need to link the new ServiceReservation object to the relevant ServiceReminder object. In the second case, the customer has asked for a service, and no reminder object exists for that service.*

Steve: *Okay. Let's work on a sequence diagram for the first case, then we'll do another one for the second case and try to use the same operations in both cases, as much as possible* (Figure 10–5).

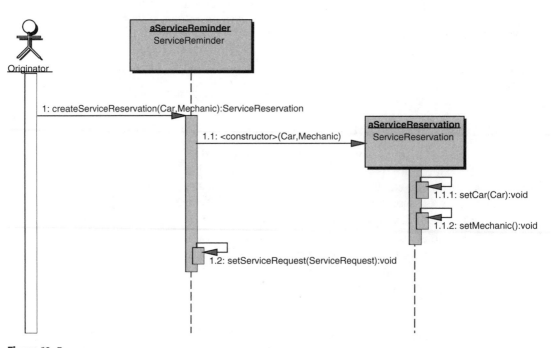

Figure 10–5
One of the sequence diagrams for the "Schedule a service for a car" feature.

Steve: *Larry, can you help me put these sequence diagrams in electronic form? Then we can put them on the project intranet and add links to each of them from the work package* [Figure 10–6].

Refine the Object Model	Chief Programmer	Required

The *Refine the Object Model* Task

The Chief Programmer creates a feature team area for the feature(s). This area is either a directory on a file server or a directory on his or her personal computer (backed up by the Chief Programmer as required), or it utilizes work area support in the project's version control system. The feature team uses the feature team area to share work in progress and make it visible among the feature team but not to the rest of the project.

The Chief Programmer refines the model to add additional classes, operations, and attributes, and/or to make changes to existing classes, operations, or attributes, based on the sequence diagram(s) defined for the feature(s). The associated implementation language source files are updated (either manually or automatically by some tool) in the feature team area. The Chief Programmer creates model diagrams in a publishable format.

Expected Results

The object model produced in process 1 concentrated on overall shape by identifying the major classes and their important responsibilities and relationships. In this task, the Chief Programmer adds to that overall model the detailed classes, attributes, and operations discovered during the previous task of producing the UML sequence diagrams for the features under consideration (Figure 10–7).

Participation

This is a task performed by the Chief Programmer, using his or her personal computer/terminal.

Hints for the Chief Programmer

1. If you are particularly busy, nominate a currently less loaded member of the feature team to do this for you. Do, however, check that they have done it correctly.

Work Package: Car Servicing 1

Form a Feature Team   Chief Programmer: Steve   Required

...

Feature ID	Walkthrough		Design		Design Review		Development		Code Inspection		Promote To Build	
	Planned	Actual	Planned	Actual	Planned	Actual	Planned	Actual	Planned	Actual	Planned	Actual
0004	6/10/2001	6/10/2001	8/10/2001		10/10/2001		14/10/2001		16/10/2001		17/10/2001	
0005	6/10/2001	6/10/2001	8/10/2001		10/10/2001		14/10/2001		16/10/2001		17/10/2001	
0018	6/10/2001	6/10/2001	8/10/2001		10/10/2001		14/10/2001		16/10/2001		17/10/2001	
...	...		...		...		...		...		...	

Conduct a Domain Walkthrough   Domain Expert: Mike the Mechanic   Optional

Walkthrough Meeting Notes (Document: CS1 Walkthrough Notes)
Follow-up Questions and Answers (Document: CS1 Q&A)

Study the Referenced Documents   Feature Team   Required

Manufacturers Handbook for Mechanics	2001
Franchise Policy Manual	2000

Develop the Sequence Diagram(s)   Feature Team   Required

Sequence Diagram Name	Feature
Schedule a Service (Case 1)	0004
Schedule a Service (Case 2)	0004
...	

Refine the Object Model   Chief Programmer   Required

Write Class and Method Prologue   Feature Team   Required

Design Inspection   Feature Team   Required

...

Figure 10–6
Car Servicing 1 work package—develop the sequence diagram(s).

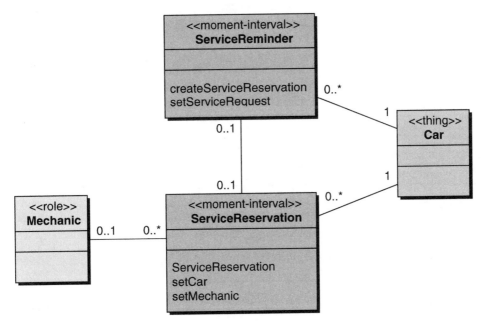

Figure 10-7
Updated classes in the object model.

The *Write Class and Method Prologue Task*

Using the updated implementation language source files from the Refine the Object Model task in the feature team area, each Class Owner writes the class and method prologues for each item defined by the feature and sequence diagram(s). This includes parameter types, return types, exceptions, and messages.

Expected Results

Each feature team member updates his or her classes, adding the project standard documentation comments to the new classes, attributes, and operations required for the implementation of the features under consideration. These comments will form part of the material used in the review of the design (the next task).

Participation

Each feature team member performs this task at his or her own personal computer or computer terminal.

Work Package: Car Servicing 1

Form a Feature Team	Chief Programmer: Steve	Required

...

Feature ID	Walkthrough		Design		Design Review		Development		Code Inspection		Promote To Build	
	Planned	Actual	Planned	Actual	Planned	Actual	Planned	Actual	Planned	Actual	Planned	Actual
0004	6/10/2001	6/10/2001	8/10/2001	8/10/2001	10/10/2001		14/10/2001		16/10/2001		17/10/2001	
0005	6/10/2001	6/10/2001	8/10/2001	8/10/2001	10/10/2001		14/10/2001		16/10/2001		17/10/2001	
0018	6/10/2001	6/10/2001	8/10/2001	8/10/2001	10/10/2001		14/10/2001		16/10/2001		17/10/2001	
...	...		...		...		...		...		...	

...

Conduct a Domain Walkthrough	Domain Expert: Mike the Mechanic	Optional

...

Study the Referenced Documents	Feature Team	Required

...

Develop the Sequence Diagram(s)	Feature Team	Required

...

Refine the Object Model	Chief Programmer	Required

...

ClassDiagram Name	Feature
ServiceReservation	0004
...	

Write Class and Method Prologue	Feature Team	Required

Click on the class names in Class and Class Owners section to view this documentation for each class

Design Inspection	Feature Team	Required

...

Figure 10–8

Car Servicing 1 work package—write class and method prologue.

Hints for the Chief Programmer

1. This takes a good deal of discipline on the part of the developers and can be one of the hardest parts of Feature-Driven Development (FDD) to get developers to accept. It requires that a truly thorough job has been done on the design steps so that it does not change too often during the *Build by Feature* process.

2. Tools such as Javadoc or Together ControlCenter can be used to generate a more human-readable form of the class and method prologues. This can be included in the work package as an attachment, if the work package is being maintained manually, or as hyperlinks from the list of class names in the work package, if it is available on an intranet Web site. Once this task is complete, the feature team has reached the next milestone in the feature's development, and the plan section of the work package can be updated again (Figure 10–8).

Design Inspection	Feature Team	Required

The feature team conducts a design inspection, either before or after the unit test task. Other project members may participate; the Chief Programmer makes the decision to inspect within the feature team or with other project team members. On acceptance, a To-Do list is created per affected class, and each team member adds their tasks to their To-Do list.

Verification: Design Inspection

Expected Results

Once members have completed this task, the feature team will have everything it needs to actually code its classes for the features in this iteration of processes 4 and 5.

Participation

The whole feature team participates in the design inspection, checking that the sequence diagrams, class diagram updates, and domain walkthrough notes have been correctly transferred to electronic format. In many cases, this is enough. However, for more complex or significant features, the Chief Programmer should invite other members of the development team to the inspection, as described below.

Hints for the Chief Programmer

1. If a design is going to impact the work of other feature teams, widen the design inspection to include the other Chief Programmers. This is likely to occur when:

- The feature team is advocating a new standard idiom for doing things.

- The feature team is advocating the refactoring of previously completed features to simplify the design of their features.

- The feature team is advocating the addition of a significant new class or classes to the object model.

- The feature team is advocating a significant change to the object model.

- The features are of sufficient complexity that the Chief Programmer wants some more experienced eyes to check the design before proceeding.

The bottom line is that a significant change requires a significant design review.

2. Experience has shown that an inspection's effectiveness deteriorates after about two hours. Therefore, large slabs of design should be split into chunks that can be inspected within two hours. This is unlikely to be required too often, given the granular size of features and iterations.

3. As Chief Programmer, you moderate the review or ask another of the Chief Programmers to do it if you feel that you may be too emotionally attached to the design.

4. Concentrate on defect detection and do not spend time on defect resolution because the right people and information may not be in the room. Discussions on improving processes and improving checklists should be stopped, noted, and discussed in a follow-up session.

5. At the first few inspections, remind people of the purpose and agreed norms (see Chapter 7, "Develop an Overall Object Model—Norms"). Stick the norms up on a wall in the inspection room, if necessary.

6. Personal criticism of any sort should not be tolerated.

7. Nominate one attendee to be the scribe. During lengthy inspections, rotate this duty between the attendees.

8. Do not allow the Project Manager in the room. If developers feel their performance is under review in any way, they will become defensive. Having the whole feature team on the hot seat does help alleviate this problem a good deal, however.

9. Remember to book a place in advance in which to hold the inspection and ensure that a whiteboard is available. Scheduling an inspection before lunch or before home time increases the likelihood of finishing on time.

10. It is imperative that reviewers do actually check the material before the inspection meeting. If the moderator finds that more than one of the reviewers has failed to check the code/design, he or she should postpone the inspection. The reviewers can then use the meeting time to check the material in preparation for the rescheduled inspection. Do not let the reviewers off the hook, because this will start a vicious cycle that will undermine the usefulness of inspections.

Hints for the Inspectors

1. Schedule preparation time in your personal calendar/work plan for an inspection. Otherwise, you will find yourself preparing over lunch or on the bus/train to/from work—not normally very good environments for effectively detecting defects. For a two-hour inspection meeting, reserve about 1.5 hours for preparation. Less experienced reviewers may need a little more time to begin with. Scheduling the time into the calendar/plan also enables the time taken by inspections and preparation to be measured.

2. The result of the inspection should be recorded as part of the feature team's work package (an example template can be found in the next chapter) and should describe:

- What was inspected
- Who attended
- The location, date, and start and end times
- The list of all defects, suggestions, and comments
- Overall result
- Signatures, if required by the organization or for legal reasons

3. The suggested options for the overall result of an inspection are:

- Accept as is
- Accept with minor revisions
- Reject with major changes
- Reject requiring a total rework

A rejection requires another inspection. The Chief Programmer can sign off modifications required by an "accept with minor changes."

Exit Criteria

To exit the process, the feature team must produce a successfully inspected design package. The design package comprises:

- A covering memo, or paper, that integrates and describes the design package so that it stands on its own for reviewers
- The referenced requirements (if any) in the form of documents and all related confirmation memos and supporting documentation
- The sequence diagram(s)
- Design alternatives (if any)
- The object model with new/updated classes, methods, and attributes
- The <your tool>-generated output for the class and method prologues created or modified by this design
- To-Do task-list entries for action items on affected classes for each team member

Expected Results

The work package is updated to reflect the completion of the design inspection (Figure 10–9).

Work Package: Car Servicing 1

Form a Feature Team   Chief Programmer: Steve   Required

...

Feature ID	Walkthrough		Design		Design Review		Development		Code Inspection		Promote To Build	
	Planned	Actual	Planned	Actual	Planned	Actual	Planned	Actual	Planned	Actual	Planned	Actual
0004	6/10/2001	6/10/2001	8/10/2001	8/10/2001	10/10/2001	10/10/2001	14/10/2001		16/10/2001		17/10/2001	
0005	6/10/2001	6/10/2001	8/10/2001	8/10/2001	10/10/2001	10/10/2001	14/10/2001		16/10/2001		17/10/2001	
0018	6/10/2001	6/10/2001	8/10/2001	8/10/2001	10/10/2001		14/10/2001		16/10/2001		17/10/2001	
...	...		...		...		...		...		...	

...

Conduct Domain Walkthrough   Domain Expert: Mike the Mechanic   Optional

...

Study the Referenced Documents   Feature Team   Required

...

Develop the Sequence Diagram(s)   Feature Team   Required

...

Refine the Object Model   Chief Programmer   Required

ClassDiagram Name	Feature
ServiceReservation	0004
...	

Write Class and Method Prologue   Feature Team   Required

Click on the class names in Class and Class Owners section for this documentation

Design Inspection   Feature Team   Required

Design Inspection Reports	Result
Report 1	Rejected: Major Change
Report 2	Accepted: As is

...

Figure 10–9
Car Servicing 1 work package—design inspection.

On occasion, the feature team may bump into an issue that blocks the development of one or more of the features. When this happens, that feature's line in the plan section of the work package may slip behind the other features and may go red, indicating that it is behind schedule. The Chief Programmer decides whether to carry on with the other features in the iteration or to hold the whole iteration, pending the resolution of the issue (the Chief Programmer would kick off another set of features while waiting). The resulting work package might look something like Figure 10–9.

chapter 11

Feature-Driven Development— Build by Feature

The fifth and final process in Feature-Driven Development (FDD), *Build by Feature* (Figure 11–1), follows straight on from process 4.

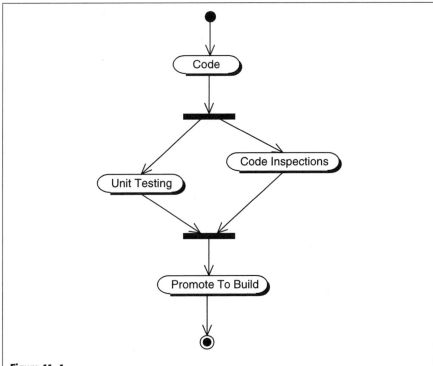

Figure 11–1

Build by Feature.

    A per-feature activity to produce a completed client-valued function (feature).

    Working from the design package produced during the *Design by Feature* process, the class owners implement the items necessary for their class to support the design for the feature(s) in the work package. The code developed is then unit tested and code inspected, the order of which is determined by the Chief Programmer. After a successful code inspection, the code is promoted to the build.

181

The two processes could have been written as a single process; it would be highly unusual not to do process 5 immediately after process 4 for a group of features. The main reason for the split is psychological; process 4 is about design, and process 5 is about implementation. Ideally, one follows the other for each feature. To say that a team will never bump into anything in process 5 that requires a reworking of tasks in process 4 is, of course, ludicrous. However, it should be the exception and not the norm. If it becomes the norm, there is not enough work being done in process 4.

When a team reaches process 5, it has designed in detail the implementation of each feature within the group being developed within the iteration. Now all that should be left is for each member of the team to code up his or her classes, unit test, and submit that code to inspection before the Chief Programmer promotes the completed features into the build.

The Implement Classes and Methods Task

Implement Classes and Methods	Feature Team	Required

The class owners implement the items necessary to satisfy the requirements on their classes for the feature(s) in the work package. This includes the development of any unit-testing code needed.

Expected Results

The result of this task is a set of source code modifications to existing classes and the possible addition of some subordinate classes. Also produced is any unit-testing code and data required to unit test each class and each feature.

Participation

Class owners normally work alone on their classes. However, it is not a sin to combine pair programming with FDD if a team finds it beneficial. The Chief Programmer is often found working with another member of the feature team when that member is struggling with a problem. Also, a team member who has completed his or her work on that group of features often helps other members of the team so that the features are completed on time.

Hints for the Feature Team

1. By the time we reach here, with all the hard brainwork done, the implementing should be little more than a typing exercise. However, if an unforeseen snag does occur, the Chief

Programmer decides what action to take. Anything affecting multiple classes is going to need the feature team to get together and agree on an appropriate action. Anything of significance is going to need a drop back to the *Design by Feature* process and modification to the work package as required. The Chief Programmer and the Class Owner can often sort out a minor issue within one class or one developer's classes without involving the rest of the team.

2. Once the work has been inspected, the resulting source code files can be attached or hyperlinked to the work package (Figure 11–2).

Steve: *How are we linking the source code files to the work package cover page?*

Mac: *The support team that created the work package template decided to reuse the table of classes in the first section. The version numbers of the classes have hyperlinks to the relevant source code file.*

Steve: *So we enter the version number and link that to the relevant version of the source code files?*

Mac: *Yes, it sort of makes sense but it could have been made a bit more obvious, I agree. They did put a note in the relevant section to explain . . .*

Work Package: Car Servicing 1

Form the Feature Team   Chief Programmer: Steve   Required

Feature ID	Walkthrough		Design		Design Review		Development		Code Inspection		Promote To Build	
	Planned	Actual	Planned	Actual	Planned	Actual	Planned	Actual	Planned	Actual	Planned	Actual
0004	6/10/2001	6/10/2001	8/10/2001	8/10/2001	10/10/2001	10/10/2001	14/10/2001	14/10/2001	16/10/2001		17/10/2001	
0005	6/10/2001	6/10/2001	8/10/2001	8/10/2001	10/10/2001	10/10/2001	14/10/2001	14/10/2001	16/10/2001		17/10/2001	
0018	6/10/2001	6/10/2001	8/10/2001	8/10/2001	10/10/2001	14/10/2001	14/10/2001	15/10/2001	16/10/2001		17/10/2001	
...	...		...		...		...		...		...	

Package	Class	Class Owner	Class Version	Unit Test Results
com...servicing.	ServiceReminder	Carrie	0.1	
com... servicing.	ServiceRepair	Larry	0.1	
com... servicing.	ServiceReservation	Larry	0.1	
com... servicing.	Mechanic	Harry	0.2	
...	...	...		

Domain Walkthrough   Domain Expert: Mike the Mechanic   Optional
...

Study the Referenced Documents   Feature Team   Required
...

Develop the Sequence Diagram(s)   Feature Team   Required
...

Refine the Object Model   Chief Programmer   Required
...

Write Class and Method Prologue   Feature Team   Required
Click on the class names in Class and Class Owners section to view this documentation for each class

Design Inspection   Feature Team   Required
...

Implement Classes and Methods   Feature Team   Required
Click on **version numbers** in Class and Class Owners to view the source code files and change history for each class

Figure 11–2
Car Servicing 1 work package—implement classes and methods.

The *Conduct a Code Inspection* Task

The feature team conducts a code inspection either before or after the unit test task. The Chief Programmer decides whether to inspect within the feature team or with other project team members. The decision to inspect before or after unit test is also that of the Chief Programmer.

Expected Results

The result of a code inspection is a short report listing the defects found and an overall result for the inspection.

Participation

Normally, the feature team members review each other's code. Other members of the wider development team are invited for a particularly significant or complex feature.

Hints for the Feature Team

1. Many of the hints about performing design inspections that were discussed in the previous chapter are just as relevant for code inspections. For example, as with the design inspection, the Chief Programmer decides on the level of formality required for the sections of source code to inspect, who is invited to be a reviewer, etc.

2. It is not usually necessary to inspect all code written during a project. For example, where the same simple scenarios are repeated throughout a piece of code, inspecting only a representative sample is sufficient to find the majority of defects; the Class Owner can be left responsible for fixing similar defects in similar code.

3. Agree on a checklist of criteria for code to enter inspection. For example:

   - Unit tests should be run and results included (if unit testing is being done before inspection). This proves that the code compiles and runs correctly for the scenarios tested.

   - Javadoc or equivalent should be run and should not report any errors. This proves that attention has been given to the commenting.

   - The source code should be printed using an agreed common tool and format so that it is easier to read because the format is familiar.

4. Do not turn up to the code inspection with a different version of the code than the one distributed. The reviewers will have made notes on their copies, and a good deal of time will be wasted trying to ensure that everyone is on the same page at the same time.

5. An example code inspection report is shown in Figure 11–3.

   The report should be included in the work package (Figure 11–4). If there are multiple inspections needed before the code passes, include the reports from the inspection failures, as well as the final successful inspection.

6. As with the design inspection, a rejection would require another inspection to be held. The Chief Programmer can approve any modifications to code identified with an "Accept with minor revisions" (see Chapter 10, "Verification: A Design Inspection-Hints for the Inspectors").

7. Remember the code inspection milestone can be considered complete only if the unit-testing task has been completed, as well. Often, this is done before code inspection but it is just as valid to do it afterward. The unit testing should certainly be repeated if any noncosmetic changes are made to the source code.

Code Inspection for Work Package: Car Service 1		

Reviewers: Steve, Harry, Larry, Carrie

Location: Meeting room 3

Date: 16/10/2001　　Time Started: 3:00pm　　Time Finished: 5:00pm

Result:

Accepted:	**Rejected:**
As is	With Major Changes
With Minor Modifications　　**X**	Total Rework

Defects Found

Severity	Location	Description
Minor	ServiceReservation class line 47	Comment is incorrect
Minor	ServiceReservation class line 55	Confusing use of ? operator
Minor	Mechanic class line 68	Check for null parameter needed
...	...	...
...	...	...

...

Figure 11–3
Example code inspection report.

Work Package: Car Servicing 1

Form the Feature Team — Chief Programmer: Steve — Required

Feature ID	Walkthrough		Design		Design Review		Development		Code Inspection		Promote To Build	
	Planned	Actual	Planned	Actual	Planned	Actual	Planned	Actual	Planned	Actual	Planned	Actual
0004	6/10/2001	6/10/2001	8/10/2001	8/10/2001	10/10/2001	10/10/2001	14/10/2001	14/10/2001	16/10/2001		17/10/2001	
0005	6/10/2001	6/10/2001	8/10/2001	8/10/2001	10/10/2001	10/10/2001	14/10/2001	14/10/2001	16/10/2001		17/10/2001	
0018	6/10/2001	6/10/2001	8/10/2001	8/10/2001	10/10/2001	14/10/2001	14/10/2001	15/10/2001	16/10/2001		17/10/2001	
...	...		...	...		...		...		...		

Package	Class	Class Owner	Class Version	Unit Test Results
com...servicing.	ServiceReminder	Carrie	0.1	
com... servicing.	ServiceRepair	Larry	0.1	
com... servicing.	ServiceReservation	Larry	0.1	
com... servicing.	Mechanic	Harry	0.2	
...	...		...	

Domain Walkthrough — Domain Expert: Mike the Mechanic — Optional

...

...

...

Write Class and Method Prologue — Feature Team — Required

Click on the class names in Class and Class Owners section to view this documentation for each class

Design Inspection — Feature Team — Required

...

Implement Classes and Methods — Feature Team — Required

Click on **version numbers** in Class and Class Owners to view the source code files and change history for each class

Code Inspection — Feature Team — Required

Design Inspection Reports	Result
Report 1	Accepted: With Minor Changes

Figure 11–4

Car Servicing 1 work package—conduct a code inspection.

The *Unit Test* Task

Each Class Owner tests their code to ensure that all requirements on their classes for the feature(s) in the work package are satisfied. The Chief Programmer determines what, if any, feature team-level unit testing is required—in other words, what testing across the classes developed for the feature(s) is required.

Expected Results

The unit testing demonstrates that each new operation of a class produces the expected results.

Participation

In the first task of this process, individual team members write the test code for their classes. In this task, the test code is run to demonstrate that the code executes the test cases correctly.

Hints for the Feature Team

1. FDD takes unit testing almost for granted as part of the *Build by Feature* process. FDD does not define the mechanisms or level of formality for unit testing; it leaves that to the Chief Programmer to determine what is appropriate.

2. It is quite acceptable, for instance, to use the unit-testing techniques promoted by Extreme Programming in an FDD environment. FDD does not specify this because technology and resources differ so much between projects. In some circumstances, it is very difficult to produce the set of completely isolated, independent tests that run in a reasonable amount of time that Extreme Programming demands.

3. Where continuous or regular system builds are performed, it certainly makes sense to have a growing set of tests that can be run against a new build.

4. Although the description talks about the Chief Programmer determining the amount of end-to-end class testing to be done, this is often done by default. Each feature has one or two operations that start the feature. The unit tests for these operations should cover most if not all of the testing requirements for the feature as a whole. The Chief Programmer must decide whether extra feature-wide testing is required, and this will again be based on the complexity and impact of the features being developed.

5. If applicable, the unit test results can be attached or hyperlinked to the work package (Figure 11–5). At a minimum, the work package should indicate that the unit tests have been run and passed.

Feature-Driven Development— Build by Feature

189

Work Package: Car Servicing 1

Form the Feature Team	Chief Programmer: Steve	Required

...

Feature ID	Walkthrough		Design		Design Review		Development		Code Inspection		Promote To Build	
	Planned	Actual	Planned	Actual	Planned	Actual	Planned	Actual	Planned	Actual	Planned	Actual
0004	6/10/2001	6/10/2001	8/10/2001	8/10/2001	10/10/2001	10/10/2001	14/10/2001	14/10/2001	16/10/2001	16/10/2001	17/10/2001	
0005	6/10/2001	6/10/2001	8/10/2001	8/10/2001	10/10/2001	10/10/2001	14/10/2001	14/10/2001	16/10/2001	16/10/2001	17/10/2001	
0018	6/10/2001	6/10/2001	8/10/2001	8/10/2001	10/10/2001	14/10/2001	14/10/2001	15/10/2001	16/10/2001	16/10/2001	17/10/2001	
...	...		...		...		...		...		...	

Package	Class	Class Owner	Class Version	Unit Test Results
com...servicing.	ServiceReminder	Carrie	0.1	Passed
com... servicing.	ServiceRepair	Larry	0.1	Passed
com... servicing.	ServiceReservation	Larry	0.1	Passed
com... servicing.	Mechanic	Harry	0.2	Passed
...	...	...		

Domain Walkthrough	Domain Expert: Mike the Mechanic	Optional

...

...

...

Write Class and Method Prologue	Feature Team	Required

Click on the class names in Class and Class Owners section to view this documentation for each class

Design Inspection	Feature Team	Required

...

Implement Classes and Methods	Feature Team	Required

Click on **version numbers** in Class and Class Owners to view the source code files and change history for each class

Code Inspection	Feature Team	Required

Design Inspection Reports	Result
Report 1	Accepted: With Minor Changes

Figure 11–5

Car Servicing 1 work package—unit test results.

The *Promote to the Build* Task

Classes can be promoted to the build only after a successful code inspection and unit test. The Chief Programmer is the integration point for the entire feature(s) and responsible for tracking the promotion of the classes involved (either by personally promoting them or through feedback from the developers in the feature team).

Expected Results

This is the final step of the process and results in a set of new versions of source code files being made available to the build process.

Participation

Once the Chief Programmer is convinced that the features have been completed, he or she signs off on the features by promoting them to the build. The next time the build process is run, the newly completed features are included and are available for formal system testing, demonstration to clients, inclusion in user manuals, etc.

Hints for the Chief Programmer

1. Some developers have a problem with the definition of the word *finished*. You ask them if they are finished, and they say, "Yes." You ask why the code is not yet in the build, and they reply, "I just have such and such to do first." The developer's definition of *finished* is obviously different from that of the Chief Programmer or Project Manager. Making *Promote to the Build* a formal task enables everyone to define *finished* as "promoted to the build." No feature is complete or feature team finished until the code is in the build—a clean compile is not finished; unit testing is not finished, passed code inspection is not finished. Only the *Promote to the Build* task is finished.

Chief Programmer Work Areas

The use of feature teams requires two levels of version control and check-in:

- At one level, only code for completed features gets checked in. This level supplies the source code for the build.
- At another level, each feature team member needs to add his or her completed code to the rest of the feature team's code for

testing and inspecting before it is checked into the build system. This intermediate stage must also be isolated from other feature team's work.

Where the configuration management systems (CMS) or version control system (VCS) does not provide a team working area, one can be synthesized using a shared directory or folder. Depending on the technology available and organizational constraints, this could be a folder on a mapped network drive, a directory on an FTP server, a shared folder on the Chief Programmer's machine, or any other file-sharing mechanism. It is, of course, important that its contents are backed up reliably.

When the feature team starts, the classes involved are checked out of the "build" version control system into a new Chief Programmer's work area for that feature team. Each team member works in their personal space, updating their code, and when finished, puts that code back into the Chief Programmer's work area.

What about branching? On occasion—and it must be reiterated that this is an exception and definitely not the norm—a developer can find themselves in two feature teams at the same time, both of which require changes to the same class. If there are no dependencies between the two sets of changes, both teams can continue in parallel. When this happens, the class owner, in collaboration with the Chief Programmers, is responsible for ensuring that both sets of changes are correctly integrated by the time the second feature team promotes its work to the build.

Branching at the build level results in multiple versions of the desired system. This may be a temporary expediency or it may be planned. This is business as usual, and FDD adds nothing new to the challenges and opportunities available where this level of branching is used.

Verification

| Code Inspection and Unit Test | Chief Programmer, Feature Team | Required |

A successful code inspection plus the successful completion of unit testing is the verification of the output of this process. The code inspection and unit test tasks are described above.

Participation

Note

This is not a task. It is a summary of the way that the tasks of the process are verified as being complete.

To exit the process, the feature team must complete the development of one or more whole features (client-valued functions). To do this, they must have promoted to the build the set of new and enhanced classes that support those features, and those classes must have been successfully code inspected and unit tested.

Expected Results

A set of features has been added to the build. An iteration of processes 4 and 5 has been completed, and the work package contains a comprehensive record of the work done, put together as the work was done (Figure 11–6).

The feature team is now disbanded, and the Chief Programmer goes away to pick the next set of features to develop; the Chief Programmer starts process 4 for that new set of features, and the cycle repeats until all the features required by the project are completed.

Mac: *I see you finished that last set of features. Well done.*

Steve: *Cheers! Larry was great help. I think we might have struggled if he hadn't spotted a couple of gaps in our designs early on.*

Mac: *I like this process; we get many people contributing to the design, reinforcing each other's abilities. However, we still maintain the conceptual integrity from having the Chief Programmers' relatively few, experienced minds steer the whole thing.*

Steve: *Yes, and the developers are learning from the Chief Programmers and each other all the time....Hey, do you want to see my team's latest completed work package? It's a perfect blend of genius, elegance, and efficiency, believe me!* ☺

Mac: *At 5:00 p.m. on a Friday evening? You have got to be kidding! I'm meeting the other guys at the bar in about an hour or so; I heard you were buying.* ☺

Steve: *Only if you agree that my latest work package is the best you have ever seen.* ☺

Mac: *Oh, all right! Where is it? . . .*

Work Package: Car Servicing 1

| Form the Feature Team | Chief Programmer: Steve | Required |

Feature#	Feature Set	Feature Name
0004	*Scheduling a Service*	*Schedule a service for a car*
0005	*Scheduling a Service*	*Add a new customer to a customer list*
0018	*Performing a Service*	*Record a service performed for a car*
...	...	...
...	...	...

Feature ID	Walkthrough		Design		Design Review		Development		Code Inspection		Promote To Build	
	Planned	Actual	Planned	Actual	Planned	Actual	Planned	Actual	Planned	Actual	Planned	Actual
0004	6/10/2001	6/10/2001	8/10/2001	8/10/2001	10/10/2001	10/10/2001	14/10/2001	14/10/2001	16/10/2001	16/10/2001	17/10/2001	17/10/2001
0005	6/10/2001	6/10/2001	8/10/2001	8/10/2001	10/10/2001	10/10/2001	14/10/2001	14/10/2001	16/10/2001	16/10/2001	17/10/2001	17/10/2001
0018	6/10/2001	6/10/2001	8/10/2001	8/10/2001	10/10/2001	14/10/2001	14/10/2001	15/10/2001	16/10/2001	16/10/2001	17/10/2001	17/10/2001
...	...	...	...	...	...	...	...	...	...	...	...	...
...	...	...	...	...	...	...	...	...	...	...	...	...

Package	Class	Class Owner	Class Version	Unit Test Results
com...servicing.	ServiceReminder	Carrie	0.1	Passed
com... servicing.	ServiceRepair	Larry	0.1	Passed
com... servicing.	ServiceReservation	Larry	0.1	Passed
com... servicing.	Mechanic	Harry	0.2	Passed
...	...		...	

| Domain Walkthrough | Domain Expert: Mike the Mechanic | Optional |

| Walkthrough Meeting Notes (Document: CS1 Walkthrough Notes) |
| Follow-up Questions and Answers (Document: CS1 Q&A) |

| Study the Referenced Documents | Feature Team | Required |

| Manufacturers Handbook for Mechanics | 2001 |
| Franchise Policy Manual | 2000 |

Figure 11–6

Car Servicing 1 completed work package.

Develop the Sequence Diagram(s)   Feature Team   Required

Sequence Diagram Name	Feature
Schedule a Service (Case 1)	0004
Schedule a Service (Case 2)	0004
...	

Refine the Object Model   Chief Programmer   Required

ClassDiagram Name	Feature
ServiceReservation	0004
...	

Write Class and Method Prologue   Feature Team   Required

Click on the class names in Class and Class Owners section to view this documentation for each class

Design Inspection   Feature Team   Required

Design Inspection Reports	Result
Report 1	Rejected: Major Change
Report 2	Accepted: As is

Implement Classes and Methods   Feature Team   Required

Click on **version numbers** in Class and Class Owners to view the source code files and change history for each class

Unit Test   Feature Team   Required

Click on **unit test** column in Class and Class Owners section for unit tests and results for each class

Code Inspection   Feature Team   Required

Design Inspection Reports	Result
Report 1	Accepted: With Minor Changes

Promote to the Build   Chief Programmer, Feature Team   Required

Click on **version numbers** in Class and Class Owners to view the source code files and change history for each class

Figure 11–6
Car Servicing 1 completed work package (*continued*).

part 3

Feature-Driven Development— Additional Topics

Having learned about Feature-Driven Development (FDD), a number of questions come to mind. This section answers the most frequently asked questions about FDD. These questions are:

- What about technical architecture?
- What about system test and defect fixing?
- What about managing changes in requirements?
- What about user documentation?
- What about data cleaning and conversion?
- What about deployment?
- How do we introduce FDD to our organization?

All of these are very good questions and an entire book could be written about each of them (for some of the topics, several books have been written, some of them very good). We concentrate on the opportunities and challenges that the use of FDD brings in these areas and leave the detailed justifications, theories, and principles to books that can do them more justice.

Chapter 12 discusses when and how a technical architecture is defined for an FDD project.

Chapter 13 addresses the issue of system testing; that is, the formal testing of the new system's functionality and performance.

Chapter 14 briefly introduces the topics of managing requirement changes, writing user documentation, data cleaning and conversion, and deployment of the finished system.

Chapter 15 looks at the effects of change on people, process, and technology and how that affects the adoption of new processes such as FDD. We wrap things up by talking about making change possible in an organization, and we look at some strategies for adopting and adapting FDD to work within your organization.

chapter 12

Feature-Driven Development— Technical Architecture

Successful projects rarely concentrate on building all layers of the architecture at the same time. Instead, they focus first on the domain, for it represents the heart of the system. Get the domain right and it is far easier to get the rest of the architecture right. Get the domain wrong and very little can save the project.

Luke Hohmann [Hohmann]

Driving a project using client-valued features is all very well, as is developing by feature, based on a problem domain object model—but what about the technical architecture? Where, when, and how is this defined? When is it built, and is this task part of the FDD process? What comprises a technical architecture, anyway?

There are very few software projects that would be considered viable if the development team had to write all the software components needed to make the various pieces of computer hardware perform the functions that the clients of the project required. Instead, nearly all software development projects will make use of existing software products, platforms, or components, such as:

Technical Architecture

- Operating Systems
- Database Management Systems
- Network and Communication Software
- Transaction Processing Monitors
- Security Subsystems
- World Wide Web Servers
- Application Servers

199

- Directory Servers
- User Interface Toolkits and Graphical Control Libraries
- Business Components

We could define the technical architecture of a system as the set of such software products or components used in the implementation of that system. However, that definition is too simplistic.

There are always new and better technology products appearing on the market, and we want to be able to make use of those better products without having to rewrite large amounts of our system. Also, if you look at a particular business or functional area and the systems built to support that area, you will find that technology changes far more frequently than the fundamental business or functional rules of that area. Isolating business logic and business rules from specific technology components is the *key* to developing a robust solution.

For example, consider a large corporate account management application. The fundamental rules of accounting have remained unchanged in the last 10 years, yet the preferred user interface technology could have changed four times. Possibly written with a Customer Information Control System (CICS) user interface originally, such applications might have been upgraded to use a graphical user interface running on a PC, then upgraded to use Web browser technology, and finally upgraded again so that handheld wireless devices can access accounts. So, although a few new business features may have been added to the system, this is a relatively small amount of change, compared with that of the user interface technology used.

A good development team will want to write "wrappers" for technology components. The team can then write code that uses the interface provided by a wrapper, rather than the interface provided by a particular vendor's product. Replacing or upgrading the vendor's product means updating the wrapper code, but as long as the interface provided by the wrapper does not change, there is no impact on the rest of the system; the amount of work required to support the new technology product is minimized.

The technical architecture of a system, therefore, consists of a set of interfaces used to invoke the services of general-purpose software products (such as those listed above), together with the wrapper software and a set of general-purpose software products that provide implementations of those interfaces.

Defining interfaces, selecting components, and writing wrapper code to produce a technical architecture for a system can be a complex and time-consuming task. Many organizations involved in software development try to define an architecture that is both comprehensive enough and flexible enough to be used for the vast majority of their software development efforts. If this can be done, it eliminates or at least minimizes the effort required to perform this task for each new project. If as many projects and systems as possible use the same technical architecture, it also means that less training and learning are required for the organization's developers, and there is a higher chance that the systems will integrate easily with each other. Therefore, in many organizations, you will find an architecture group responsible for researching and defining the organization's standard technical architecture to be used on software development projects. Other organizations outsource this task to a large software development consultancy or adopt an architecture defined by a particular computer hardware or software vendor on whose products they have decide to standardize.

Some of the most complicated technical architectures are those for enterprise systems. Typically, these systems consist of a number of logical layers distributed across multiple physical machines. They require distributed transactions and security services and support for hundreds or thousands of concurrent users, while providing reliable, persistent storage of large amounts of data. In contrast, some of the simplest technical architectures are those for a single-user, stand-alone application for a PC of some sort.

At the time of writing, one of the most popular, comprehensive, and flexible technical architectures for enterprise systems is the Java 2 Enterprise Edition (J2EE) defined by Sun Microsystems and its partners for developers working in the Java programming language. The J2EE architecture (Figure 12–1) combines a large number of Java application program interfaces (APIs) into a cohesive whole, enabling a large number of different vendors to compete in the production, selling, and marketing of software products that implement and support those APIs. In the meantime, Microsoft and its partners are readying their new .NET architecture, aimed primarily at users of Microsoft Windows operating systems.

Strategies, Idioms, and Patterns

Defining and, if necessary, implementing the architecture is only a part of the picture. We also need to put in place the strategies, idioms, and patterns that enable a development team efficiently and correctly to translate high-level analysis and design results onto the technical architecture. The technical architecture includes the definition of the patterns, strategies, and idioms used to translate:

- The domain object model classes into the technical architecture
- Objects in memory into persistent objects, database tables, or files on disk and vice versa
- Data in problem domain objects into network protocol messages or batch file records and vice versa

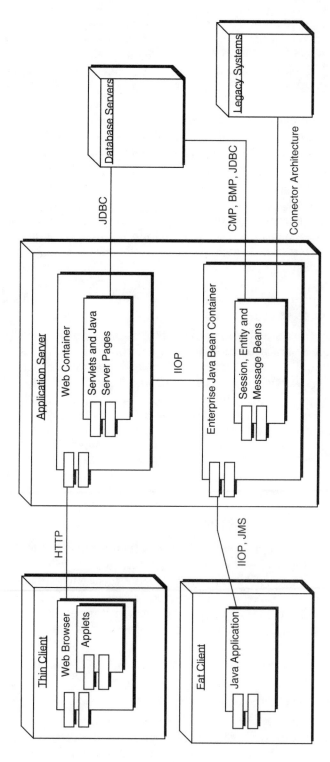

Figure 12-1
J2EE architecture example.

- Changes in problem domain objects into updates in user interface displays

Programming language idioms are often included within an organization's or project's coding standards for a particular programming language.

Depending on the architecture, we may also have help in identifying the patterns we need to use. For example, in the case of Sun Microsystem's J2EE architecture, Sun's engineers have put together a catalog of design patterns commonly found in J2EE-based systems [Alur] and an example application illustrating common J2EE techniques [Kassem].

Of course, there is still the task of picking the subset of patterns that are applicable to a project and proving that the vendor's products selected do, indeed, live up to their marketing statements but at least we have a head start on those who have to discover their own design patterns.

Technical Architecture in an FDD Project

We know that evaluating, defining, and proving the technical architecture, as well as producing a set of patterns and strategies for translating the problem domain model onto that technical architecture are critical activities if a project is to succeed.

If we have to do it ourselves, when does this work get done in FDD? Is it part of the overall FDD project? Is it a separate project? When does it get completed?

From the above discussion, we can see that, at the start of any software development project, we have a number of different possible scenarios:

1. We may have a technical architecture that we can reuse from a previous project. Genuine reuse! Rare, but occasionally pleasantly true!

2. We may have a technical architecture defined by an organization's central architecture group or an external consultant.

3. We may be faced with the results of a high-level decision to standardize on a particular vendor's technical architecture or software products.

4. We may be starting with a blank sheet of paper and need to choose or define our own technical architecture.

5. The technical architecture required might be complex or relatively simple, depending on the type of software being developed.

6. Our team may be big enough to be able to devote some developers solely to the task of defining and building the technical architecture. Other teams may be too small to do this.

When defining a process where we have a number of widely differing scenarios, we have two choices. We can choose to define in detail the process for each scenario, hoping that we cover all the possible variations. The result is a large amount of process documentation for developers to wade through.

Alternatively, we can choose to leave the task largely undefined so that the development team is free to adapt the process to its own particular situation. This is the approach taken in FDD when it comes to defining a technical architecture. That is not to say that a properly defined technical architecture is not important. It is critical! What it means is that the possible variations make it impossible to provide a concise, one-fits-all answer.

On an FDD project, there are several possibilities to choose from when it comes to planning the definition and building a technical architecture for the project. Much of the decision depends on the size of the development team, the complexity of the architecture required, and the amount of knowledge already collected about the proposed new system. Much of the work in defining a technical architecture can be done in parallel with the object modeling, feature list building, and feature-planning activities. Of course, if the whole team is involved in the modeling, the architecture needs to be defined before or after the modeling. It could be part of a project startup phase that happens before the object modeling and in parallel with a more formal requirements-gathering process or feasibility study. Or it could be done in parallel with processes 2 and 3. It could also be done between process 3 and process 4 while we seek approval from upper management to proceed with the construction phase of the project. The bottom line is that we need to have enough of the technical architecture in place to start iterating through the *Design by Feature* and *Build by Feature* processes (4 and 5).

Setting up a new technical architecture can be highly technical, vendor specific, and require in-depth knowledge of the system. Therefore, this task is best assigned to senior, experienced people, often working under the guidance of a consultant who has proven experience with that sort of technical architecture. We have even seen the task of producing a proof of concept prototype for a technical architecture run a little like a small Extreme Programming subproject within the main project.

If the project is using new technologies in its architecture, we can expect our technical architecture to evolve as we proceed through the project and learn better ways to translate our analysis and high-level designs into the architecture. We may make an initial effort at defining and proving the architecture before or in parallel to processes 1 to 3. We may make adjustments after the initial object modeling, while the features list is being built and planned. However, we can still expect to learn a good deal about a new technical architecture during the first iterations through the processes 4 and 5. This should be considered as a factor when planning and estimating in process 3 because it will slow down the

Design by Feature and *Build by Feature* cycles of the project for the first two or three iterations.

Four Logical Layers

There are some general guidelines about technical architecture that do impact the way in which a project applies FDD. Most modern projects will result in partitioning technical architectures into a number of logical layers or tiers. Each layer provides a different set of technical services to the other layers.

In older books, these layers or tiers are often called *domains*, only one of which is the problem or application domain. However, the term *domain* has more recently been commonly used as a short equivalent of *application domain* or *problem domain*, and the term *different domains* is now more commonly used to talk about different application areas (e.g., manufacturing, lending, travel planning, etc.). Another term commonly used in discussions of layered architectures is *separation of concerns*. Each layer in the architecture is *concerned* with one and only one technical aspect of the system.

The idea of splitting a technical architecture into logical layers has become widely accepted and practiced in the software industry. Single-tier, two-tier, three-tier, and *n*-tier architectures abound. The details of the exact split differ widely between architectures, and there are many different mappings of the logical layers to physical machines.

However, in general, we can talk about four layers (Figure 12–2).

| User Interface (UI) Layer |
| Human Interaction, User Interaction, Man-machine Interface, Presentation Logic |

| Problem Domain (PD) Layer |
| Business Logic Layer |

| Data Management (DM) Layer | System Interaction (SI) Layer |
| Persistence Layer, Data Storage Logic | System Interface, External Interface Layer |

Figure 12–2
Four layers of technical architecture.

The technical architecture also defines how the various layers communicate with each other. Where a logical layer is distributed across more than one machine, the technical architecture also defines how components in that layer communicate with each other.

The User Interface (UI) layer interacts with the Problem Domain (PD) layer to provide useful views of data and enable users to easily invoke the problem domain features they need to get their desired results. The

PD layer is responsible for notifying the UI layer of relevant changes that occur to business objects.

The PD layer uses the Data Management (DM) layer services to store and retrieve objects from disk.

The PD layer uses the System Interaction (SI) layer services to communicate with external systems. The SI layer notifies the PD layer of changes at external systems and enables external systems to invoke problem domain features.

Another way of looking at this is representing each of the layers as a package in Unified Modeling Language (UML) (Figure 12–3). Notice the dependencies. The UI, DM, and SI layers are all dependent on the PD layer. If engineered correctly, the problem domain layer will not be dependent on the other layers.

Figure 12–3
Layers as UML packages.

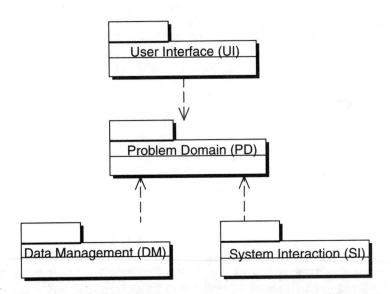

Obviously, not all systems require all four layers. An embedded system may not have a UI or a DM layer. A personal computer application may not need an SI layer.

Teams, Layers, and Feature Lists

A big side benefit of separating out into layers is that these layers form natural boundaries for development teams. The skills required by the developers of each layer are different. The user interface development team needs to know the user interface toolkit being used. The data management development team needs to be intimate with the relevant database, persistence tools, or file system being used. The system interaction development team needs an understanding of the communication protocols and middleware products used. The problem domain team needs none of this knowledge; it needs the most in-depth domain knowledge and, where appropriate, the distributed object or component technology being used.

If we choose to split our development team into teams responsible for each technical architecture layer, then we need to provide a features list for each team and a means of integrating the results from each team with those from the other teams.

The PD Layer

The most important layer in any system is the PD or Business Logic layer. If analyzed correctly, the PD layer is the most stable of the four layers; the way a business works does not change fundamentally very often. If this layer is poor, the system will be inflexible—too complicated in places, too simplistic in others, and very hard to change and enhance. The long-term investment in a significant software development project is, therefore, the analysis, design, and code of the problem domain. In other words, the long-term investment in a software development project is in the development of mechanisms for structuring and manipulating our business data. A development team needs to invest the majority of its time on ensuring that this layer is well structured, which is why this layer should be independent of the other layers. The other layers are fully dependent on this layer.

The features list first produced in process 3 contains problem domain features.

The UI layer is the layer most likely to change. As we said previously, a green screen terminal was good enough last week; yesterday, a GUI on a PC was required; today, everyone wants a World-Wide-Web-based user interface; and tomorrow, they will all want to use wireless, handheld devices.

The DM layer is more stable but still subject to change. Last year, it was an indexed file system; this year, it's a relational database; next year, it will be an application server-managed persistence mechanism.

The SI layer is also subject to change because the external systems that we need to talk to may be replaced over time or differs according to the sites where we deploy our system.

The SI Layer

The system interaction team's features are the subset of features from process 3 that require interaction with external systems. External systems are typically existing legacy systems. We make a copy of these features to produce the feature list for the system interaction team. The development of these features is now split into a problem domain section and a system interaction section. The problem domain does as much as it can without involving itself in specifics of the external systems. The system interaction team takes it from there.

Where an external system requires a service from our system or is notifying us of changes in data values, the system interaction team is responsible for decoding the data sent by the other system and invoking the appropriate problem domain operations. If necessary, the system interaction team also needs to format any results and send them back to the requesting system.

Where our system needs to invoke a service of an external system or inform it of changes in data values, the problem domain team defines a generic interface for that operation, and the system interaction team provides a wrapper or proxy class that provides an external system-specific implementation of that interface (Figure 12–4). This enables the SI layer to be changed without affecting the PD layer. All dependencies between the two layers are from the SI layer into the PD layer.

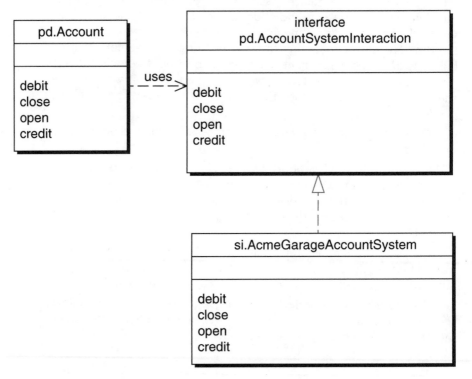

Figure 12–4
A generic account interface defined in the problem domain implemented by a specific system interaction class.

Hints for the System Interaction Team

1. Much of the work in the system interaction team involves liaising with the owners of the external system. If another team within our organization supports the external system, it is enormously beneficial if one or more of those owners become an official part of our project team. If not, there is little incen-

tive for the owners of that external system to help us; we are just making more work for them. Their attitude will be to minimize the work they need to do, even at the cost of a less appropriate solution. Making some of the external system owners an official part of the project team gives them a greater sense of purpose and includes them in any project bonus or incentive scheme. We are more likely to achieve a good result and to achieve it more quickly.

2. Communications between our system and the external system could take one of three basic forms:

   - Synchronous call
   - Asynchronous message
   - Batch file (Although this could be viewed as a set of asynchronous messages held until a certain time and all sent at once, the "queuing" mechanism is very different.)

   If not already in place, the technical architecture needed to support these three types of interaction can be developed and tested while the problem domain team is producing its part of the system interaction features.

3. Include in the system interaction feature teams the problem domain developers who own the classes on which the system interaction features need to invoke operations and the problem domain developers who defined the interfaces through which operations on system interaction classes are invoked. The problem domain developers may need to participate only in the domain walkthrough but it is often useful to call them back for the design inspection, too.

4. Produce a simple test harness to represent the external system and hook up and test to that before testing to the actual external system. This reduces the amount of often-expensive time needed to test with the actual external system by eliminating simple errors first.

Hints for the Problem Domain Team

1. Produce a set of simple classes that implement the interfaces to the SI layer. Use these classes to do unit testing to prove the problem domain part of the feature before including the system interaction part.

Hints for the Project Manager

1. Concentrate on constructing the PD layer first. Once the PD layer is safe, transfer some of the problem domain developers to the boost the system interaction team. Look for problem domain developers who have worked on the problem domain side of the system interaction features.

The UI Layer

The UI layer can be split into two sublayers:

- Navigation and Look and Feel
- Presentation Logic

Navigation and Look and Feel

The navigation and look and feel sub-layer defines the ways in which a user:

- Sees data retrieved from the PD layer
- Enters data to be used by the PD layer
- Invokes problem domain features
- Moves from one part of the user interface to another

Much of the usability of the system comes from the work done in this layer. These days, with GUIs and World-Wide-Web-based user interfaces, the design of this sublayer is much more about graphical design than about programming.

The overall design of navigation and look and feel is part of the definition of the technical architecture and needs to be worked on before the building of the user interface by feature can really be started. Again, this can overlap with the building of the problem domain if the resources exist to do so. The work done in the initial object modeling and building of the features list provides valuable input to this task. Just like the rest of the technical architecture, this may have been done for us by a previous team, a central user interface standards team, or a user interaction consultant hired to do the job.

Hints for the Project Manager

1. The expense of a good graphical artist and good user interface designer can be repaid by much faster user acceptance of the system. Users encountering a polished, professional user interface that is easy to navigate are more likely to start with an attitude of wanting to like the system. Users encountering an ugly, clumsy, and awkward user interface start with a negative attitude. For example, after a graphical artist had worked on one of our user interfaces, a user seeing the system for the first time was so impressed that he would not believe it was developed in-house; he thought we must have bought the system.

2. Hiring a good graphic artist should also help to avoid the less able amateur graphic artists in the user interface team, wast-

ing enormous amounts of time fiddling with pixels and colors when they should designing and coding the objects to link the user interface to the problem domain.

Presentation Logic

The presentation logic sublayer handles the connecting of each element in the user interface to the relevant problem domain objects, the management of the user session, and the population of data for the various graphical elements in the user interface.

The architectural pattern most often associated with user interfaces is the Model-View-Controller (MVC) pattern. Most popular GUI toolkits combine the View and the Controller in graphical components and use an event notification mechanism (publish/subscribe) to keep the problem domain independent of the user interface [Coad 96]. World-Wide-Web-based user interfaces separate the View and Controller again, putting the View on the client machine inside a Web browser and the controller on the server machine implemented, using technologies such as Java Servlets and Java Server Pages.

A similar process to that used to identify the system interaction team's features is used to identify the user interface team's features. Take the subset of features that are invoked by users and copy them to make the user interface features list. User interface feature sets are often related directly to a specific Web page or GUI panel that forms part of the user interface.

Hints for the User Interface Team

1. State charts and low-fidelity panel/screen/window designs are often a more useful alternative when it comes to the design step of the *Design by Feature* process (process 4). The sequence diagrams showing how a user interface element connects to the relevant problem domain object are all very similar after the first few.

2. It is not a sin to rework the user interface features list to better fit the navigation and look and feel but do keep a reference to the problem domain features invoked by each user interface feature. User interface features are often clearer if the action part is something such as display, start, stop, or select.

3. Domain walkthroughs provide information about the fundamental sequences of features that is useful when designing a user interface but beware of domain experts making business processes too sequential where parallel or different ordering of tasks is valid.

4. Designing and building user interfaces is fun. Writing the code is a real pain. It seems that we need three times the lines of code to create a decent user interface than we do to build the problem domain code. GUI-building tools should be the answer but most produce poorly factored code. GUI-builder tools can be used to rapidly prototype a user interface but be prepared to rework and heavily refactor to get decent performance and maintainability.

5. A big problem when building user interfaces is the temptation to waste time optimizing the look of individual elements. There is a great temptation to tweak that placement, adjust that color, better align those two components, sharpen that image, or improve that icon. This is analogous to optimizing performance of some small part of the problem domain with little idea whether the optimization will improve the performance noticeably for the users.

6. Beware of over concentrating on the look and feel of individual pages, panels, and screens at the cost to the navigation. The result is a super-looking user interface that feels awkward to use.

7. Do not be afraid to rework a user interface. Expect it and plan for it. If built well, it is quick to move user interface components around. If not built as components and if business logic has been allowed to creep into the user interface layer, then it all becomes much, much harder to change.

8. Review the user interface regularly with real users at different levels in the organization. Do not forget to review with the project sponsors and upper management because if they hate it, it does not matter how much the other users like it.

9. Beware of becoming unit testers for the problem domain team. If the user interface team starts finding large numbers of simple errors in the problem domain, examine the thoroughness of the inspections and unit testing in the problem domain team.

Hints for the Problem Domain Team

1. Try as hard as possible to build the problem domain so that it is independent of the user interface. If the separation is done correctly, there should be few if any changes in the PD layer needed to support different user interfaces. Of course, a new user interface is always an opportunity for users to demand new problem domain features so there is likely to be some problem domain enhancement work. Beware of feature creep in the name of features to support user interface design.

2. A rule of thumb for problem domain development is to make the user interface team's job as easy as possible but do not trust them.

Make problem domain services as general as possible. Offer alternative versions of operations to allow the user interface team the choice. For example, provide a check operation that throws a detailed exception explaining why an operation may not be performed. Provide an alternative that simply returns true or false to indicate whether an operation can be performed (writing one in terms of the other). Let the user interface team choose which one is most appropriate to use in a given context.

Do not trust the user interface to pass the problem domain valid data. One style of user interface may validate data before passing it across; a different user interface may not be able to do so. Do not trust the user interface to invoke any set of operations in a specific order. One style of user interface may enforce a certain sequence of actions; another may allow the users to perform actions in any order they like.

Hints for the Project Manager

1. Concentrate on constructing the PD layer first. Once the PD layer is safe, transfer some of the problem domain developers to the boost the user interface team. Look for the problem domain developers who have worked on the problem domain side of the user interface features.

The DM Layer

Although it is more stable than the user interface and system interaction layers, it is a good idea to separate the specifics of persistence from the problem domain code. Doing this allows the storage approach to change without impacting the PD layer. An example might be a decision by an organization to standardize on a particular relational database management system (RDBMS) or a decision to improve performance by storing read-only reference data as serialized objects or text files on a client machine instead of in a central database server.

Obviously, if you are using an object-oriented persistent storage mechanism, the need for this architectural layer disappears (or at least becomes trivial).

Where an RDBMS is selected as the persistence store, many projects have opted to use data mapping tools that generate the object to schema mapping and the necessary persistence code. The cost is varying amounts of invasion of the problem domain by persistence code, depending on the tool being used. Varying amounts of control over the database schema are also lost. The benefit is much quicker production of persistent objects and an enormous reduction in the work of the data management team.

One example of persistence tools are those provided by vendors of application server products conforming to Sun Microsystem's J2EE architecture. These provide a declarative mechanism called *Container-Managed Persistence*, where the mapping between a class's (entity bean's) instance variables and table columns in a relational database is described in an XML file called a *deployment descriptor*. When the class is deployed in the application server, the server reads the deployment descriptor and generates the extra code needed to read and write data between the objects and the database. This approach has the advantage that the mapping can be changed without modifying any code; only the deployment descriptor is modified.

Where the data management layer must be hand-coded, this is the one layer that cannot be feature driven; the PD layer completely drives the need for persistence. Each persistent class in the problem domain needs to be mapped to the data storage mechanism and save and restore operations created for the objects themselves and related objects. The work involved, once the patterns for persistence are established, is very repetitive work, ideal for a good tool to automate.

Some data management teams provide generic persistence services and leave the actual specific work for a class to the problem domain class owners. Other handcrafted persistence frameworks create a partner class for each problem domain class that performs the object to relational mapping and handles the specifics of talking to the database. In this case, the problem domain class owners need to inform their counterparts who own the data management classes when a change in the persistence of a class is required [Coad 97].

Layers and the Build

As mentioned earlier, from a dependency point of view, we want the UI, DM, and SI layers dependent on the PD layer but no dependencies from the PD layer to the other layers. These dependencies between the layers and the splitting of development teams by architectural layer also have an impact on the build order. The problem domain team can produce builds that the other teams can use as baselines to add their services.

Often, user interface and system interaction will require an unforeseen change or a fix for a bug in the problem domain code to complete their work. This change is added to the problem domain and becomes available to the user interface and system interaction at the next regular build.

Hints for the Project Manager

1. As deadline crunch takes hold, the latency time between a request for change/addition to problem domain and its availability to user interface and system interaction becomes unacceptable. At this point, the pressure and temptation to

combine user interface and system interaction code dependent on the change/fix into the same build as the problem domain change/fix is often overwhelming. However, if for some reason the problem domain change/fix does not make it into the build (last-minute defect, a missing file, etc.), the build fails when it comes to make the user interface/system interaction. The correct solution is to reduce the time between builds so that the problem domain service becomes available to user interface and system interaction quickly but still in a controlled manner.

Reducing Dependencies between Components

We said way back in Chapter 1 that, if we could decompose our problem into smaller independent problems, we could do more in parallel by adding more developers.

One way to do this is to enhance the technical architecture wrappers and interfaces so that they provide a powerful, standard API that other developers can build on. This core engine provides useful generic services on top of which more specific functions are built. Communication between these blocks of functions is handled by the architecture. As the system matures, more sophisticated layers of architecture can be added. These, in turn, make adding more function in that area easier and quicker. TogetherSoft's Together ControlCenter product is a great example of this sort of technical architecture.

This sort of approach is more appropriate for product development than enterprise system development because it takes considerable time and effort and often-repeated attempts to build this sort of advanced architecture. It normally takes at least three attempts at building a product before it becomes acceptable to mainstream users—before the combination of architecture, requirements, and user interface are sophisticated enough for general use. A product that reaches this stage often seems to take off suddenly in the marketplace. Again, the history of TogetherSoft's Together ControlCenter product is a good example; demand really took off with the release of version 3.0 in 1999. The J2EE architecture is another example of a technical architecture that has taken three or four releases to mature to a point where it is genuinely and generally useful.

Enterprise system builders are rarely given the time by their clients or project sponsors to build three versions of a system so that they can develop an advanced architecture. Enterprise system domains also tend to be more connected and harder to break into independent components than software tools or stand-alone application products. Few enterprises want their developers working on building infrastructure, anyway, when they could be delivering business function. Most enterprises would rather purchase technical architecture and infrastructure components from product vendors who do have the time and incentive to develop powerful technical architectures.

FDD can be applied well to both circumstances. When looking to build a powerful technical architecture, the object modeling needs to produce more generic classes that can be configured by data or subclassed to provide the specific problem domain services required. It is here that the line between what is technical architecture and what is conceptual object model starts to blur.

chapter 13

Feature-Driven Development—Testing: Failures, Faults, and Fixes

First of all, it pays to distinguish between failures
(the symptoms) and faults (the diseases).
Gerald Weinberg [Weinberg 92]

The five processes defined within Feature-Driven Development (FDD) say very little about testing. Other processes, such as Extreme Programming, list testing as one of their core best practices. So why does testing take such a low profile within FDD?

When most people point out that FDD does not cover testing, they are talking about what the authors know as system testing. System testing corresponds to the activity labeled as testing in many traditional "waterfall" process outlines. This is formal testing of the whole system by a team of specialized testers. In incremental and iterative processes, system test is much the same as the waterfall equivalent, except that the system, as completed so far, is tested after each increment or after a certain number of iterations.

One of the reasons FDD does not say much about testing is because, in many cases, the processes used for testing are not the main process issues with which a team or organization are struggling. Usually, the core development processes—the designing and constructing of the software in a timely and cost-effective manner—are the main problem.

In other words, we need to ensure that we are able to produce a system worth testing before we spend too much time worrying about the details of the processes to follow when testing.

Entire books have been written on testing, and most organizations already have reasonable testing processes in place. Therefore, once we establish a good set of development processes and begin regularly to deliver software worth testing, the testing processes usually need only minor adjustments, if any.

As we said in the beginning of Chapter 4, FDD is specifically targeted at the core activities of software design and construction. The emphasis in FDD is also on constructing high-quality, working code to make system testing as much a formality as possible.

None of this is intended to belittle the importance of testing. Passing a set of specified tests is still the ultimate criteria used for demonstrating to stakeholders that the software operates as desired.

The nature of FDD projects and the emphasis on the frequent delivery of working features do provide some opportunities and suggest certain ways to structure the testing of a system better. In the rest of this chapter, we will look at some of these ideas.

Different organizations have very different ways of dealing with testing, so these ideas are merely an optional set of tools that may help to streamline some of the testing processes and help them integrate more coherently with the core FDD processes.

Kinds of Testing

In traditional testing practice, system testing is just one of a number of kinds of testing. Although the terminology differs considerably in this area, most developers broadly understand the terms:

- Unit testing
- Integration testing
- System testing
- Customer/user acceptance testing

Testing is such a broad subject that, in a single chapter, we can hope only to introduce the topic. Therefore, we do not go into too much detail but do try to point you in the right direction. We examine each kind of testing briefly in the light of the five FDD processes, concentrating mainly on system testing. However, first we need to step back and take a quick look at some testing fundamentals and define some terms.

Failures, Faults, and Fixes

When we talk about testing, we are really talking about the processes of finding and reporting failures of a software system. A software failure is a specific test and its result, where the result was not that expected by the testers of the software. However, discovering and communicating software failures is useless unless there is also a means to have the software modified so that the failures no longer occur. Therefore, we also have to talk about the processes we use to fix the faults (defects) in the software that are causing the failures. Software failures need to be diagnosed to locate the fault in the documentation, code, design, analysis, or the test itself that is causing the failure and to determine the nature of that fault. If necessary, the software must then be modified to fix the fault.

Note

Although the use of the term fault *makes for great alliteration in literature, we have found it to be too easily confused with the term* failure*. For this reason, we prefer to use the term* defect *instead and have done so throughout the rest of this chapter and book.*

So we need processes for:

1. Finding failures
2. Reporting failures
3. Diagnosing defects
4. Fixing defects

Testers are concerned with only the first two processes; the latter two are the responsibility of the developers.

In an ideal world, all defects would be fixed, but in the real world, we also need to determine whether the work of diagnosing or fixing a defect is worthwhile. Therefore, there is a decision point between both processes 2 and 3 and processes 3 and 4.

Figure 13–1 summarizes the four processes and their interactions:

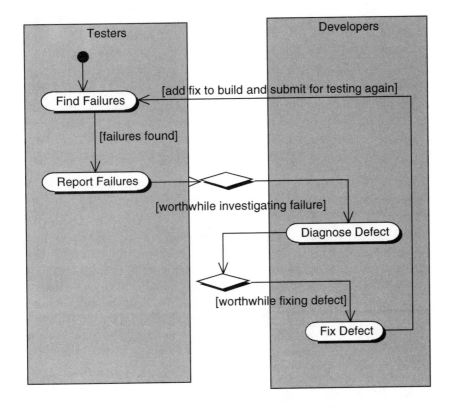

Figure 13–1
The four processes and two decision points in formal testing.

Feature-Driven Development— Testing: Failures, Faults, and Fixes

219

Figure 13–1 is obviously overly simplistic. In real life, there is far more feedback and communication going on between the developers and testers, and each process expands into a number of subactivities. For example, the first three processes are likely to expand to include activities such as those shown in Figure 13–2. The *Fix Defect* process is likely to include similar activities to those described in the *Design by Feature* and *Build by Feature* processes.

Also, to add to the complexity:

- Some failures may be the result of multiple defects.
- Some defects may cause multiple failures.
- Some defects may require multiple modifications to the software before they are fully fixed.
- Some defects may be only partially fixed because the remaining failures they cause are not significant enough to warrant the effort needed to fix the defects completely.
- Some defects may not be fixed at all.
- Some failures may not be the result of a defect in the code, design, or analysis but in the test data or the test cases themselves, or they may be just a misunderstanding of what is required or desired.

Figure 13–3 shows the many-to-many relationships between failures, defects, and fixes as a Unified Modeling Language (UML) class diagram.

FDD and Unit Testing

Unit testing is the testing of the smallest granularity of function that is meaningful to test. In object-oriented programming, this consists of the nonprivate methods of a class. In unit testing, finding and reporting failures and diagnosing and fixing of defects is most often performed by individual developers, without formal intervention by others. The processes for reporting failures, diagnosing defects, and fixing defects, therefore, are trivial, informal, and largely uninteresting. However, they are efficient, and it is much quicker and cheaper for a developer to diagnose and fix a defect during development than it is for the same defect to lay hidden until system testing.

Effective unit testing is certainly worthwhile but the only interesting process in unit testing is the process used to find software failures—the exact mechanisms used and the levels of formality of the testing. This was discussed in Chapter 11, "The Unit Test Task," because process 5, *Build by Feature*, mandates unit testing. We shall say no more about it here except to remind ourselves also that, in FDD projects, unit testing is complemented by design and code inspections; inspections have been proven to find more defects than testing alone and have been proven to find different types of defects, as well.

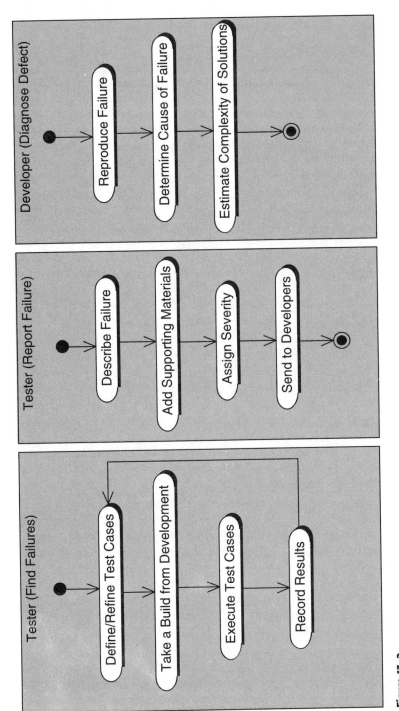

Figure 13–2
Simplistic test processes.

Figure 13–3

The relationship between failures, defects, and fixes.

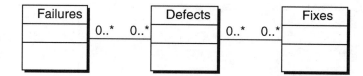

Failures		Defects		Fixes
	0..* 0..*		0..* 0..*	

FDD and Integration Testing

Integration testing, or "end-to-end" testing is the testing of meaningful sequences of function. In FDD, this could be described as *Testing by Feature* because features are, by definition, meaningful sequences of object interactions. As stated in process 5, *Build by Feature*, the Chief Programmer who owns the feature is responsible for ensuring that enough end-to-end testing is performed to verify that the feature functions correctly. Within projects where teams and features are split according to architectural layers, the Chief Programmer is responsible for testing within his or her architectural layer. The Chief Programmers of each layer must also work together to test features across the various layers. This often falls to the user interface or system interface Chief Programmers to coordinate because a problem domain feature usually starts as a result of a user interface event or a system interface event.

There are some options here. Depending on the workload and number of Chief Programmers involved in the project, the Chief Programmer can create and run the tests for the feature or, if preferred and if resources and project complexity warrant it, a Tester can be assigned a number of features and becomes a member of feature teams developing those features. The Chief Programmer remains responsible for ensuring that the testing is done to his or her satisfaction but the Tester does much of the low-level work of preparing the test harnesses and test data, executing the tests, and recording the results.

As in unit testing, the communication of failures can remain informal. However, there is ample scope to formalize the communication, if that is found to be necessary. This may be because the project team is too large or the team is distributed across multiple geographical locations, and informal communication is not working. Formalized communication for integration testing across architectural layers looks very similar to that used in system testing, the topic of the next section. The downside to making the process more formalized is the added overhead from the additional "paperwork."

The regular build process also provides an opportunity to do some integration testing by running the growing number of unit tests against the latest build to ensure that things still work when all the pieces are fitted together. However, this is only practical if the tests can be made to be independent of each other and relatively short in duration, when compared with the frequency of the build. For some applications, this is just not feasible but where it is, it is very useful in smoking out bugs before the software goes into formal system testing.

As we said earlier, system testing is the formal testing by a specialized team of testers of the software system, as completed so far. The test team prepares a set of test cases describing the tests to be performed, executes the tests they describe against the latest version of the software, records the results, and reports any failures.

Test cases are prepared from requirements. This means that the input for test cases in an FDD project comes from the features list and domain walkthroughs in whatever form they were recorded. Input may also be taken from anything used as requirements during the development, such as existing use cases, screen mockups or prototypes, functional specifications, user manuals, business policy documents, etc.

It is important that the test team and the development team have a separate reporting structure to avoid any conflicts of interest between shipping earlier and delivering higher quality code. However, it can also be important that the test team members feel part of the project so that they feel that they are providing a valuable service—that of helping to ensure a quality product.

Mac: *Some organizations use completely separate and independent quality assurance teams to do formal testing of their software products. In other organizations, the testing team is part of the project team. On this project, we used a separate subteam within the project, with the Test Manager reporting directly to the Project Manager. What's the official FDD way of doing formal system testing?*

Steve: *FDD is silent on the matter. Much of the choice depends on the type of software being developed and the experience and size of the teams involved. Independent testing teams are often used to test shrink-wrapped products because they are the last quality assurance check before a product is released to the public. Separating the test team from the project team avoids a conflict of interest for the Project Manager between shipping earlier and delivering higher quality. Custom and in-house software usually has another layer of testing done by the client before it is deployed. Therefore, system testing is often performed by a part of the project team to assure itself or its management that the software is ready for customer/user acceptance testing.*

Mac: *When completely separating testing and development teams, I've observed that it often isolates the testing team from the development efforts, slows down the flow of critical information, and reinforces the project team's view that the formal testing group is working against it, rather than providing a valuable service to the project team. I personally prefer the way we did it for Gary's Garage, with the testers part of the project team but reporting to the Project Manager and not the Development Manager. However, even this arrangement can be problematic, especially in larger teams. Ideally, the development team and testing team should work together to reduce the defects in the software. Often, however, it seems that, instead of being best of friends, the teams are the worst of enemies. The testers take delight in pointing out errors made by developers, and developers take offense at testers repeatedly criticizing their work.*

Steve: *I think the key to persuading testers and developers to work together is putting in place a reward system that encourages them to work together instead of against each other. Most project incentive and bonus schemes are aimed at delivery of the system and* *send the message that delivery is the thing that management is most concerned about and by which it is measuring success. Unfortunately, this is often true. Despite evidence of poor quality costing so much more to fix later rather than sooner, this message still prevails. A reward system for both developers and testers that measures feature delivery and measures the lack of defects shipped encourages developers and testers to work together to remove defects quickly.*

Mac: *I see! It's the same principle that is applied to the feature team. The feature team member's job isn't finished until the whole feature is complete, functional, and verified. In this case, both the development and test team activities for a feature or group of features must be complete before the job is done. They have to rely on each other to deliver in order to be successful!*

Steve: *Exactly! Establishing the right measurements and rewards system will really help to unify the teams and, ultimately, contribute to delivery of higher quality systems!*

Where to Start

In systems using a layered technical architecture, the system test team has the choice of testing the problem domain (PD) layer directly, then testing the user interface (UI) layer or testing only from the UI layer. The decision often comes down to the amount of time the test team is allowed; it is always possible to do more testing when given more time. Testing the PD layer directly means any failures found are known to be caused by defects within that layer. Testing only from the UI layer immediately begs the question, "Is the defect in the UI or PD layer?" whenever a failure is detected. This can obviously significantly increase the amount of time required to locate the defect or defects causing the failure.

Testing to the problem domain is akin to unit-level testing, and regression testing can be largely automated by testing tools such as the popular JUnit test framework. Testing at the user interface level is much harder because automated tools at this level will usually fail if the user interface layout changes significantly between releases to the test team.

Starting System Test Early

FDD completes client-valued features early. This is a real advantage when it comes to system testing. A list of completed client-valued features is always available from the features list. The system test team can start running test cases as soon as the first features are completed. Testing early provides early feedback, and that enables early fixes to be made. The test cases can also grow and improve as the system is developed, and by the time the system is complete, the system test should be a formality.

Having system testing start early in a project also encourages a greater sense of belonging to the project team for the testers. They can get more involved working with the developers when scheduled milestones are not so pressing, and the developers are not under as much pressure as they might be toward the end of a project or large increment or iteration. The testers are verifying the system, identifying and communicating problems early, and tangibly adding to the quality of the delivered system. This is a critical business issue for many software development organizations! This is in stark contrast to a waterfall approach or even iterative and incremental approaches that use large-grain increments and iterations. System tests started at the end of construction is rarely a formality in these cases, and the cost of fixing the defects found is larger because they are found later.

Which Builds to Test

The test team is unlikely to be able to complete the running of all of its test cases on every build produced by the development team. The test team needs to determine at what intervals it wants to take on a new build. Testers could choose to take a new build every week, every month, or at each significant milestone; they may choose to take a new build whenever they finish a run of the current set of test cases and have updated the test cases, based on that experience and on the newly completed features in the next build.

One idea that has been suggested but not tried by the authors is to have testers split into test case writers and test case runners. Test case writers attend the domain walkthroughs of process 4, *Design by Feature*, as observers and produce test cases that are reviewed by the relevant domain expert and other testers. Test runners continually run and rerun the tests, reporting any failures discovered. The theory is that the test case writers can be preparing new test cases while test case executers are running existing test cases on previously completed features.

The focus of customer acceptance testing is to verify to the customer's or users' satisfaction that the system does, indeed, meet the agreed requirements. The test cases are either prepared by the customer or signed off by the customer as being the criteria upon which the system will be accepted.

Although very similar in form to system testing, customer acceptance testing should be performed in a setting that is as close to the customer's production environment as possible. This helps the client to verify that what was built meets expectations and is usable.

In contrast, system testing may be conducted in a slightly more generic environment to allow for testing of options or features designed to work in another customer's environments or in an expected future variation of the customer's environment.

Customer/ User Acceptance Testing

Feature-Driven Development— Testing: Failures, Faults, and Fixes

Finding Failures

In all testing, preparing and organizing the test cases is a critical activity. There are some key characteristics that need to be considered when preparing to run a set of test cases:

1. *A clearly defined environment.* Technology components, such as operating system version, versions of test tools used, and any other network or environmental requirements, such as specific domains, access to the Internet or intranet, etc., need to be specified. If the list of these components and settings covers a range of test cases, the environment needs to be defined only once and referenced from the test cases.

2. *Repeatable, Repeatable, Repeatable.* Ad hoc testing is fine for general discovery, but to be truly useful and provide consistent, verifiable results, test cases must be repeatable (preferably even by a client, customer, or end user). The test case must describe the test clearly enough so that someone without specific knowledge of the system could successfully run the test and achieve the same result. As always, common sense prevails in determining the detail provided, and consistency is essential. The Quality Assurance (QA) Manager and Project Manager should define the acceptable level of detail for test cases for the project as early as possible.

3. *Record the input values, the test result (pass, fail), and the program output (screen shots, file data, email messages, etc.).* A test is considered incomplete or nonrepeatable if the input, output, and test result are not present. If possible, these should be hyperlinked to the rest of the project information, such as the relevant build output and the features list for each run of the test cases.

4. *Traceable to features and/or requirements.* Ideally, each test case should be hyperlinked to a high-level requirement statement or feature on the feature list. Each successive level of testing can include regression tests from previous test levels. Only new tests at each level need to be traced. The level of traceability is an overall project requirement and should be established at the beginning of the project.

5. *Automated testing.* It is desirable but not mandatory that the tests at each level be automatically run, in the form of either programs or automated scripts. This will help to minimize the manual, repetitive tasks so that the testers can concentrate on their job of verifying the functionality of the system. At each level of testing, tests from the previous levels can be collected to form regression test suits. Running the regression test helps to ensure that new features and changes don't break the existing code.

If the tests are not automated as they are created, the quality of testing will become a function of the time and test resources available. This will have a major impact on the verifiable quality of the system. Usually, the test team runs out of time, and the project is postponed or delivered without complete testing.

6. *Defect tracking and retesting*. Each time a test is run and fails, the failure should be identified, dated, verified, and recorded. It is useful to keep a count of the number of consecutive times a test has been run and failed. This does two very important things:

- It provides measurable input into the defect tracking and software development process.
- It provides a measurement of how many times a feature fails a specific test. This can be used to identify especially complex areas of the system that may need additional attention.

Defect tracking is critical to providing measurements about the overall health and effectiveness of the software development process. Many organizations have difficulty in managing this effort, tracking test failures effectively, and retesting.

Organizing Test Cases

The features list provides a hierarchy in which features are organized. We can leverage the same hierarchy to organize our test cases.

1. Feature Testing

Ideally, each feature in the feature list should have one or more test cases that demonstrate that the feature functions as desired in both normal and unexpected circumstances. However, this is likely to be too much effort, given the granularity of features in the features list.

Because a feature is the smallest client-recognizable business activity, it could be argued that this is still a unit test of a business component. It could also be considered the first level of integration testing because it is testing a meaningful sequence of business functionality.

It is more likely, therefore, that some subset of the features in the features list will actually have test cases prepared for them. The testers should work with the domain experts to identify the most valuable subset of features to test.

2. Feature Set Testing

Rather than assign the testing of individual features to specific testers, it is better for the QA or Test Manager to assign ownership of whole feature sets to test personnel, in the same way that feature sets are assigned to Chief Programmers for development.

Where a project is using a layered technical architecture, the test cases for a feature set may be divided into groups reflecting the layers (e.g., PD, UI, data management (DM), and system interface (SI) layers), with a final set of tests involving all layers. This essentially reproduces traditional integration testing. The interaction between layers can be handled through interfaces with stub implementations that simulate the other layers to verify that the features for each layer behave correctly. Then, as the other layers become available, the interfaces can be turned on and the behavior tested and verified.

If a given layer has functionality for the feature set, test plans should be written to run that functionality independently of the other layers. The integrated testing of the features can be focused on the interfaces between features (common data, function, or component interactions).

This is obviously a considerable amount of extra work, when compared with the alternative of just testing from the UI or SI layers and may be feasible only if automated testing tools are available.

3. Major Feature Set or Domain Area Testing

Grouping test cases by feature set will automatically group test cases by major feature set. However, there may be a few more test cases that can be defined that span feature sets. These can be added if desired. For large projects, explicitly identifying the test cases for a major feature set allows regression tests to be run on a particular major feature set instead of the whole system, which might take more time than is available. Normally, the QA or Test Manager is responsible for scheduling such test runs. Of course, the major feature sets need only act as rough guides to grouping tests. Other high-level groupings of test cases may work as well or better, depending on the specific circumstances. We could, for instance, decide to deploy a group of features without necessarily completing all the features of any one major feature set or, indeed, of any one of the feature sets. Although this is highly unlikely, it is not impossible. There may be nonessential features in every single feature set (e.g., a print screen feature for each feature set that is awaiting an upgrade to a technology component before it can be completed).

Test Case Characteristics and Attributes

Table 13–1 summarizes the general characteristics of the different types of tests.

Table 13-1
Test Characteristics

Description	Unit Test	Feature Test	Feature Set Test	Major Feature Set Test
Defined environment	Part of design and code	Required	Required	Required
Repeatable	Required	Required	Required	Required
Record input, output, and test result	Inputs, expected results, and test results	Inputs, expected results, and test results	Inputs, expected results, and test results	Inputs, expected results, and test results
	Outputs can be reproduced	Outputs can be reproduced	Outputs can be reproduced	Outputs can be reproduced
Trace to features and/or requirements	Trace to feature	Tests trace directly to delivered feature	Tests trace to high-level requirements	Optional Testing is mostly regression tests
				Trace any new tests to high-level requirements
Tests are automated/run-able	Use third-party tool, such as JUnit, or write test program	Recommended	Recommended	Recommended
Track defects/ no. of times tested	N/A	Required	Required	Required

A complaint often heard from developers is, "Testers do not describe failures well enough. They do not provide enough information to replicate and locate the defect. Just saying that something does not work correctly is not good enough."

Good testers will capture screen shots, file and database contents, debug output, printouts, or any other pertinent information on tests and attach them to the failure report. However, there is nothing like showing someone in person the failure that has been found. A tool to record and replay a sequence of screen shots can be an invaluable tool in communicating the nature of failures to developers.

Reporting Failures

Severity

Each failure report should be assigned a severity to indicate the importance of the failure. Unless there is a good reason not to, a simple severity scheme is generally best. Three levels of severity are normally enough—high, medium, and low. Each level needs to be very clearly

Feature-Driven Development— Testing: Failures, Faults, and Fixes

229

defined so it is obvious for the vast majority of failures which severity should be assigned. Here is one set of possible definitions:

- Low severity is cosmetic or usability problems.
- Medium severity is the failure of a noncritical function under exceptional circumstances.
- High severity is certain failure of a function or failure of a critical function under exceptional circumstances.

The important point is to have understanding and agreement on the severity levels and their precise meanings across the whole project team before starting to use them in failure reports. Otherwise, considerable time can be lost in debates about which severity should be assigned to a failure.

Diagnosing Defects

Diagnosing defects is often much harder than fixing them. A Development Manager is likely to allocate defects to developers based on a best guess of the defect location. Developers add assigned defect diagnosis tasks to their list of tasks so that when not working on a feature team, they are diagnosing defects.

The Development Managers need to keep an eye on the number of unresolved failure reports and, if it starts to grow too high, ask for more time to be spent on diagnosing and fixing defects and less on new features.

If the rate of defects starts increasing without any obvious and adequate explanation, it is usually an indicator that something in the *Design by Feature* and *Build by Feature* processes is getting skipped or is not clearly understood. If this starts to happen, the Development Manager should review the performance of the process steps, especially the design and code inspection steps.

Not all failures are a result of a defect in the low-level design or code of a system. Sometimes, a diagnosis will conclude that a failure is, in fact, an error in the test case or requirements. Changing the requirements is managed by a separate process and is discussed in Chapter 14, "Requirements Change Management."

Once diagnosed as a defect in the low-level design or implementation of the system, a decision needs to be made by weighing the cost of fixing the defect against the significance of the failures it causes.

Fixing Faults

Once defects have been located, the Chief Programmer who owns the feature in which the defect has been found needs to decide what action to take. For simple fixes to one class, simply asking the Class Owner to make the fix and informally verifying that fix is usually good enough. For more severe defects, the Chief Programmer may need to reform the feature team and iterate through the *Design by Feature/Build by Feature* processes again to make a satisfactory fix.

Alternatively, the Chief Programmer can advise the Development Manager that a fix is not needed and it's the test case that is wrong, or that the cost of fixing the defect significantly outweighs the cost of the failures it causes (i.e., the failures are not significant but the effort required to fix them is). This can lead to disagreement between the Domain Expert, Development Manager, and the Test Manager and may require a Defect Board for resolution.

The Defect Board

A Defect Board can be used to resolve situations where domain experts, developers, and testers cannot agree about the significance of a failure. The formation of a Defect Board is a technique that is useful and nicely complements FDD. Consisting of a representative from development (normally, the Development Manager) and testing or QA (normally, the Test Manager), and a Domain Expert (normally, the Domain Manager, in a large project), the Board is chaired by the project manager. The Board frequently reviews the list of contentious failure reports or difficult defects and decides on the appropriate action.

Summary

Although testing is not talked about much within the five FDD processes, it is a critical aspect of any software development project hoping to deliver frequent, tangible, working results. Also, FDD provides some wonderful opportunities for building synergy between the development and test teams.

There are no "silver bullets" in this area but there is a wide variety of options and choices. Some key points to remember are:

- FDD can work well with existing test processes and environments.
- There are ways to build or modify your test processes so that they align more closely with the FDD process, especially the short cycles and frequent deliverables of FDD.
- The levels of tests can be tailored to fit within the features, feature sets, and major feature sets, or other alternative groupings, based on similar functions and dependencies.
- The FDD process encourages the test team to be involved very early in the development cycle. This leads to increased effectiveness of the test process, early identification of defects, early validation of the levels of quality being delivered, and lowered development costs.
- It is important to understand that, for a software development process to produce high-quality working results frequently and consistently, frequent and effective communication and cooperation between the domain experts, developers, and the testers is an absolute requirement of the process.

Feature-Driven Development—Testing: Failures, Faults, and Fixes

chapter 14

Feature-Driven Development— Other Surroundings

It's not the strongest species that survive, nor the
most intelligent, but the most responsive to change.

Charles Darwin [Darwin]

In this chapter, we briefly touch on a number of other activities that take place in a software development project. Each topic is worthy of its own book, so again, we only introduce the subject here, pointing to where these activities and processes interface with the core Feature-Driven Development (FDD) processes.

First, we look at managing changes to requirements. Then we look at producing user documentation. Finally, we take data loading and conversion into consideration.

Requirements Change Management

They say that the only users who do not change requirements are dead users. So how does FDD handle new additional features and changes to existing features? First, let's be clear about what a change is and what it is not.

Clarifications of Requirements

Any statement of requirements made in English or other human language is going to suffer from ambiguities and vagueness.

A clarification is a request by developers for the domain experts to resolve some ambiguity or elaborate on some vague statement in the requirements. A clarification is not officially a change to the agreed functionality but can lead to some nasty surprises.

"OK, we have the doors in place, what color do you want them painted?"

"We want glass doors!"

"Hang on. It doesn't say that in the requirements."

"It does not say we want painted doors either; it's obvious that glass doors are needed."

"Not to us, it isn't" . . .

Thankfully, in FDD, the initial object modeling uncovers many of these assumptions that would lie undiscovered in use cases, functional specifications, or even user stories. Many of the smaller assumptions get caught during the domain walkthroughs in the *Design by Feature/Build by Feature* (DBF/BBF) processes.

Most organizations have a process through which developers can ask the business people questions about the requirements and record their answers. These vary greatly, depending on who the business people are and where they are located. Often, an informal telephone conversation is all that is needed and is then followed up by a written note to confirm the telephone conversation.

Defects in Requirements

Believe it or not, requirements can have inconsistencies, conflicting statements, and obvious omissions! Yes, even use cases have them!

Correcting such a defect in requirements is technically not a change to the agreed functionality of a system. However, it can be used as an excuse to sneak in a change.

"One part of the requirements says you want a window here and another says you want a second door. One of these statements is obviously wrong. Which is the right one?"

"It should be a door but we only want one door, the door you have already put in is wrong."

"But it clearly says to put that door in."

"That must be because the person who wrote that bit of the requirements thought there was a window going here when it really is a door" . . .

Again, the initial object modeling and domain walkthroughs in the DBF process (process 4) uncover many of these defects.

Changes in Requirements

Real changes in the agreed functionality of a system have numerous causes:

- A marketing decision emphasizes a different aspect of the product or takes the product in a new direction.
- A change in relevant regulations is announced by a governing body.

- A change in organizational policy is announced by upper management.

- Technology advances provide new business opportunities that cause a change in the business process or requirements.

- Users realize they can gain substantial benefit from doing something differently.

- User representatives misunderstood the requirements and got them wrong.

- Clarification requests or defects found in requirements documents uncover missing requirements.

- Developers spot a way to simplify greatly the business process and the new system or to apply a new technology or algorithmic solution.

The last cause is, unfortunately, a rare one; the majority of change requests are user- or client-initiated. Real changes add new features to a project and may also require modifications to features already completed or currently in progress. The easiest change requests replace only existing but not yet developed features. Regardless of the reason or complexity, the development process *must* allow for controlled changes, deletions, and additions to requirements and features or the resulting system will not meet expectations. On the other side of the coin, if changes are allowed without controls, the system will most likely never be completed and will usually fall far short of user expectations. One method we have found that helps to control project scope and changes is the 10% Slippage Rule.

The 10% Slippage Rule

As we mentioned in Chapters 8 and 9, the 10% Slippage Rule states that a project can absorb up to a 10% increase in features without affecting the project. Any changes to the project beyond 10% will force a 10% change in something else, usually time (schedule) or scope (delivered features). One reason this is possible in FDD is because the features are small and the duration of a single feature's development is relatively short (no more than two weeks).

Note that a new requirement may cause the addition or change of many features. Additions and changes to new features need to be tracked separately from the main features list. Only when the number of new features starts to approach 10% of the number of features on the original list is action really required. Up until that point, the new features can usually be absorbed by the project without significant impact on schedule. For anything above that level, the project manager needs to inform the project sponsors and upper management of the situation.

At this point, there are three basic options. Four, if you count canceling the project:

1. Cut scope by removing less important features.
2. Extend the schedule to allow for the new features.
3. Increase the capacity of the team to develop more features concurrently by adding a new chief programmer and more developers to the project.

These options are all about managing risk in a responsible and realistic manner. User and sponsor expectations must be managed. This is easier through use of frequent communication and the regular, timely delivery of features of the system, where the user and sponsors are seeing frequent delivery of quality solutions that can be measured and reported on—in other words, the techniques and results we have used and achieved with the FDD process.

Reducing the Scope of the Project

During the *Plan by Feature* process (process 3), we identified features that had to be delivered and features that, if present, would enhance the system's value to the client but would not render the system unusable if they were missed. These "nice-to-have" features are the first candidates to be trimmed from the project.

Mac: *That's easy to say, Steve, but what happens when we run out of nice-to-have features? According to the proverbial Murphy's Law, if we have 10 optional features, we will have 11 new ones that we need to add.*

Steve: *If you cannot reduce the scope affecting the core functionality of the system, the Project Manager must look at either extending the schedule or increasing the development capacity (more resources). If those options are not available, the Project Manager must work with the project sponsors and upper management to identify the features that have priority.*

Extending the Schedule

This option seems to be the anathema to upper management and sales and marketing departments. "We can't possibly extend the schedule!" or "The deadline is firm!" or "We have to deliver on the scheduled date, even if it doesn't work! Our reputation is at stake!" are cries that are all too often heard when new requirements are slipped in to a project and user and sponsor expectations are not managed. The fact is, sometimes an organization is its own worst enemy, settling for mediocrity in the face of a perceived embarrassing situation, rather than correctly managing expectations in order to deliver a quality system.

One way that a manager can successfully negotiate with upper management and the customer for extended schedules is to refer to some of the reports produced during FDD, which show delivery and user acceptance rates of features, then directly show the impact of the new features on the project. Being able to show that you have consistently averaged delivery of 18 new features every two weeks is a very powerful statement. If the changes result in needing to add 32 new features, this would mean an extension of only 4 weeks to the project, while still delivering the new functionality. It's hard to argue with accurate tracking of feature delivery rates.

This approach doesn't normally work with other process methods because the metrics are not available to back up the statements, and the argument becomes emotional. If the metrics are there, it is much easier for management to go to the client and say, "We can deliver these new features, but we will need 4 additional weeks. At that point, customers must decide what they can live with. The important thing is that management has the supported information that is needed to manage customer expectations.

Increasing the Capacity of the FDD Project Team

Adding more resources during the middle of the project dramatically increases the risk to the project. A larger team means additional communication overhead. To stand any chance of success, both a Chief Programmer and additional developers need to be introduced into the team. This allows more feature teams to work concurrently but requires that the new Chief Programmer get up to speed on the project very, very quickly. This is a key role. One way to minimize the risk is to pick the new Chief Programmer from the existing team so that ramp-up time is fast. The new developers should come up to speed rapidly under the influence of the Chief Programmers and through participating in feature team activities.

Steve: Hey Mac! I'm sorry. I know you wanted to talk about user documentation before we got this far into the project. We ought to discuss it. Are you free to do so at the moment?

Mac: Yes, certainly! In my experience, user documentation is often left as an afterthought in software development processes and projects.

Steve: I'm probably as guilty of doing this as the next person. Do you have any experience or tips in this area?

Mac: In general, my experiences have been similar. However, I've also had a few successes with it, as well. I think FDD provides some very useful possibilities in the area of developing user documentation.

Many project managers, systems designers, and developers think of user documentation, help fields, or even standardized error and warning messages as "nice-to-have" deliverables. All these are usually in a common language, so people tend to think it doesn't need to be developed. That's the trap! To say that online help and user manuals need thinking about early is a gross understatement! The absence of an adequate, usable help system and documentation can give users the perception that a system is unusable. Thinking about user guidance, help, and documentation functions throughout requirements analysis, design, and implementation is the only way to deliver a

User Documen- tation

Feature-Driven
Development—Other
Surroundings

237

user-helpful system and can be essential in ensuring user acceptance of the system being built.

Steve: *Ouch! This is obviously one of your "hot button" topics! What do you have in mind?*

User documentation, regardless of how and where it is presented, is help documentation. It contains information such as definitions of terms, tutorials on specific tasks, tips on how to correct problems, strategies explaining how best to use the system, and contact information for additional support. The ideal help system provides the users with exactly the information they need to perform a task at the point they need it.

Many traditional help systems fall very far short of this ideal in that they are little more than an electronic version of a large monolithic printed user guide with some additional hyperlinking and search functions. Even so-called context sensitive help systems usually require a user to start-up a whole new subsystem to view help text. This style of help encourages the infamous "When all else fails, read the instructions!" approach adopted by so many users.

Of course, system users differ in their levels of expertise, familiarity with the system, and preferred ways of having help presented to them. Also, systems differ in the levels of user interaction, user interface style, and user sophistication. However, thinking about user help early in the user interface design can significantly enhance the usability of a system.

For a system with a Web front end or more traditional graphical user interface (GUI), the types of help mechanisms that should be considered include:

1. *Embedded help*. Where space allows, displaying help documentation within a spare user interface panel or portion of a Web page provides immediate access to help for those who want it. Figure 14–1 shows such embedded help in TogetherSoft's Together ControlCenter. This sort of help is so easy to use that there are few excuses not to read it. However, advanced users wishing to squeeze every ounce of performance out of their computers appreciate being able to customize the amount of help displayed in this way or being able to turn it off altogether. Obviously, this sort of help needs to be considered in the design of the user interface, and its development can be included as a user interface feature in the features list. The text itself is best loaded from a file or database so that it can be refined by a technical author without the need to re-compile source code.

2. *Tool tips (flyover help)*. Having help text pop up as a mouse is moved around a user interface or panel is probably the second most widely read help mechanism. Flyover help can be used to explain the function of graphically depicted buttons

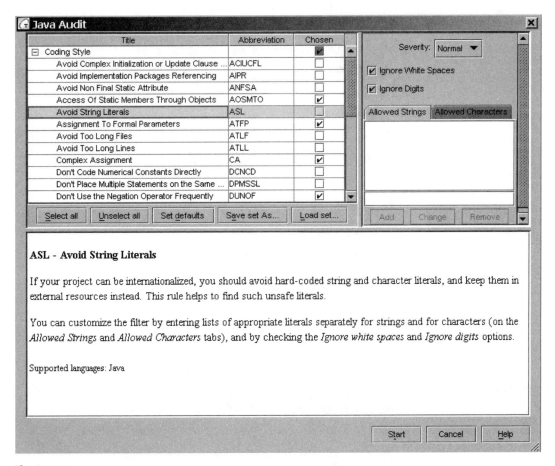

Figure 14–1
Together ControlCenter's audits panel with embedded help.

(Figure 14–2), display the full name or description where space restrictions have required the user interface to truncate a name or description (Figure 14–3), and provide more details of an item in a user interface panel or page. Again, conventions for flyover help should be set up as part of the user interface section of the technical architecture. In most GUI toolkits, the addition of flyover help is very easy. The hard part is supplying concise, useful text to display.

Figure 14–2
Together ControlCenter uses tool tips to explain toolbar button function.

239

Figure 14–3
Together ControlCenter
also uses tool tips to
expand and annotate
items truncated on the
user interface.

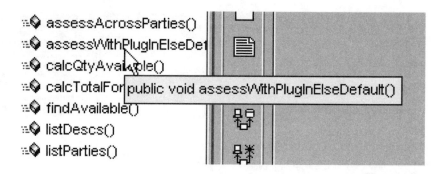

3. *Error and warning messages.* There is nothing worse than receiving a cryptic error or warning message and having to trudge through large amounts of user documentation, trying to find out what the message is attempting to communicate (see Figure 14–4). Error and warning messages should be considered part of the help documentation and should be standardized, edited, and reviewed for usability and understandability. An error or message dialog can also serve as an entry point into context-sensitive help documentation that expands on the meaning and implications of the error or warning message.

Figure 14–4
Not a particularly help-
ful error message from
Together ControlCenter
and no easy mecha-
nism to use to get fur-
ther explanation.

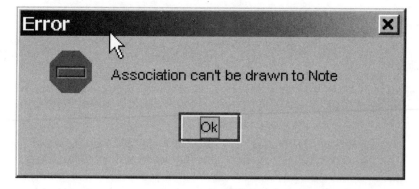

4. *Context sensitive help.* Normally accessed by pressing <F1> on a standard PC keyboard or a help button in a user interface panel, this type of help is generally displayed in its own panel or page (Figure 14–5). This is often little more than an online users guide "opened" at the most relevant page for the task being performed. In many systems, users are put off from using this type of help because it is slow to display and is often not particularly helpful because it is either not specific enough (i.e., the context is set as the whole user interface panel, rather than one particular control or field in that panel that the user is struggling with) or too specific, omitting the overall purpose and results of using the panel. User interface

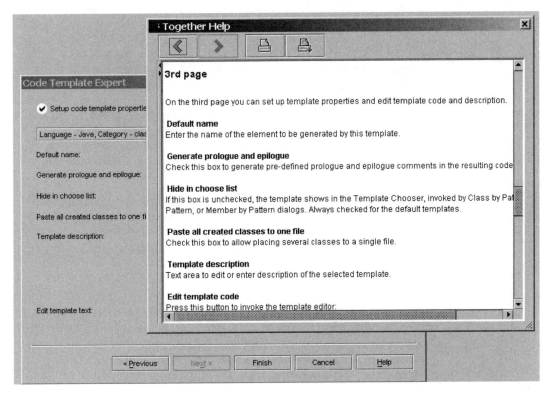

Figure 14–5
Context-sensitive help for a dialog in Together ControlCenter.

standards (part of the definition of the technical architecture) should define the mechanism for linking and displaying context-sensitive help. The help text itself can be developed independently of the user interface features, if so desired.

5. *Online manuals with user guides.* Consisting of tutorials and reference volumes, the main body of online help often seems to be read by users only as a last resort. This is usually because the documentation is hard to read and poorly organized, making it hard to find the relevant information when it is needed. This type of documentation requires good planning and structuring if it is going to add value to the system. Poorly planned and inaccurate user guides and manuals can damage a system more than most people realize. It is better to delay this as a deliverable for the system (set customer expectation early) and deliver quality manuals and user guides late than to throw something of limited use and poor quality to the users of the system. Some cultures demand printed manuals, so it is useful if the manuals and user guides can be delivered in both online and hardcopy output. Use a publishing tool to do this. Don't develop two deliverables!

Feature-Driven Development—Other Surroundings

6. *Magic help*. Intelligent help systems that monitor a user's action and suggest better ways to do things, auto-correct mistakes, or offer to perform some extra action on behalf of the user are often more a hindrance than a help. Customizable, animated figures (e.g., Microsoft Office's animated help figures) that can initiate interactive help sessions are a nice, flashy feature in product demonstrations but are very soon tiresome to work with. Most competent users will turn them off as soon as possible. The time spent developing these would probably be better spent developing a more intuitive user interface.

7. *Others*. Tips of the day, slide presentations, annotated and animated screenshot sequences, streaming video, examples and samples, and regular tips and tricks newsletters are all other ways of helping users learn to use a system without resorting to reading large documents.

The type of user documentation, the standards, and the patterns that are to be used for the help documentation should be considered and defined as part of the technical architecture of the project. Embedded help text, context-sensitive help, tool tips, etc., can be listed as user interface features. Standards on content style and presentation formats should be discussed at this time, also.

Planning the Development of User Documentation

As we have seen, there are enormous variations on the level, amount, and format of user documentation, even within a project with a traditional GUI. The exact means of incorporating user documentation development within an FDD project will depend on the type of system being developed. One of us (Mac) has seen three different ways that development of help documentation has been incorporated into an FDD project. There are, no doubt, many other variations on these themes:

1. Require all user documentation for a feature involving a user interface to be delivered as part of the DBF/BBF activities. The main drawback to this approach is that the effort involved is hidden.

2. Define an additional milestone(s) for each user interface feature that tracks the creation and verification of the documentation for each feature. Owners for this activity may be assigned to work with the other members of the feature team.

This method has the advantages of making the creation of documentation (and the owner) part of the feature development (part of the feature team). It facilitates communication between the designers, programmers, and technical writers, and insures that the documentation will be delivered with the system. This can also be coordinated with the delivery of user interface features. As soon as a user interface feature is finished, the documentation for it can be written.

3. Set up a separate project to manage the development of documentation. This may be done in addition to the first two options and can be done in parallel with the development of the system. This option works well for complete user manuals and guides. The producers of this type of documentation need access to all design and technical documents and notes, and should participate in reviews so that they are aware of any changes. This does have the drawback of sometimes creating a communications barrier between the technical writers and the rest of the project team. Manage this carefully.

Steve: *So basically what you are saying is plan the user documentation, in whatever form, to be delivered as part of the system.*

Mac: *Exactly. The most successful projects I've seen, in terms of producing good, usable user documentation, were projects that treated documentation as a real, tangible, and required deliverable of the working system! It goes through the same steps as the rest of the system—analyzing the needs, identifying the requirements, scheduling, developing, testing, and user acceptance.*

Steve: *So who should be responsible for producing the documentation? Who writes the online help? Most developers I know, hate doing this sort of documentation . . . and I certainly do not want to get lumbered with it.*☺

Mac: *Good question. It also tends to be the starting point of some very heated debates!*

Specialized technical authors are great, if available. The domain experts on the project also form a pool of possible writers because they know the domain well and can use that knowledge to structure the online help usefully. Developers do not often write good online documentation because they know the workings of the system too closely and find it hard to communicate in a nontechnical way to users of the system. Many lack the specific writing skills needed. And most programmers I've met, although they may see documentation as a requirement or necessary evil, hate to do any kind of additional documentation. It's difficult enough to get them to document at the code level, let alone to provide documentation for the users. However, because of their knowledge of the system, they do remain a primary source of information, and I would strongly recommend that they produce the initial content. It doesn't have to be pretty.

The most successful results are achieved by organizations that recognize technical writing skills as necessary and who hire the appropriate people to be part of the team. The next ingredient for success is that the writers have access to the developers, the technical documentation, and project notes through the life of the project. They need to be involved and valued members of the project team.

I like the idea that we could add a milestone to the user interface feature development so that a feature is not complete until the user documentation for a feature is complete. It does mean that those responsible for producing the documentation need to be part of the feature team. They also need to be involved in the navigation and look-and-feel design sessions for the user interface. Technical authors, if available, can sit in on these sessions as observers, then refine results to improve readability.

Steve: *Okay, let's try that and see whether it works for our team. If not, we'll have to think again but it would be great to spread the work of producing user documentation across the project and not leave it until it becomes a mountain of a task at the end of the project.*

Data Loading and Conversion

Many systems require various bits of data to be in place before they can "open for business." That data falls into three categories:

- Business data
- Reference data
- Configuration data

Business data includes such items as customer records and records of business transactions. These normally have to be converted from manually kept records or records stored in one or more older systems. This data is often dirty. It may be incomplete, inaccurate, and contain duplicates. It also may not contain all the data elements required by the new system. It is almost certainly in a different format.

Data should always be cleaned at its source, whenever possible. Loading a new system with dirty data only propagates the errors. This can be done in parallel with the development of the new system.

Converting data from one electronic format to another is certainly easier than converting from manual records to electronic. During the development of the new system, it may not be possible to convert manual data into the format to be used by the new system because it is not fully known. However, there is nothing stopping the entry of data into some intermediate, structured electronic format that can then be converted programmatically into the final format. The conversion to the intermediate format can take place in parallel with the construction of the new system. The conversion software can be used to load test data into the new system from the intermediate format, thus testing the data conversion code.

Reference data provides the user with lookup lists, catalogs of products, standard templates, etc. This data is likely to be a mix of new and existing data. This data can be treated in the same way as business data, with existing data cleaned at its source and new data entered into an intermediate format, ready for loading once the format required for the new system is confirmed.

For complex data, XML makes a great intermediate format. For simpler data, comma- or tab-separated files or simple property files (key-value pairs) are good enough, and XML is overkill.

Reconciling converted data with existing data is often a requirement, so converting the new systems data back to the intermediate format and comparing the results can become necessary. This is normally required where correct data is absolutely critical or where the data conversion programs have to be so complex that they are not fully trusted (not a preferable scenario; see Figure 14–6). Two-way conversion is obviously much more coding work than one way. However, if XML representations of objects are being used for other purposes, it may not be quite as horrific.

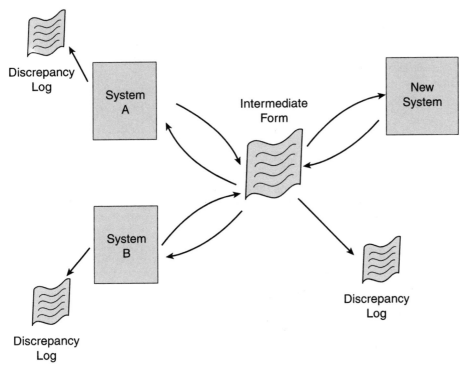

Figure 14–6
Untrusted data conversion programs.

Where the data conversion programs are more trustworthy, the reverse direction for data conversion can be dropped (Figure 14–7). Validation rules can be run against the data to provide a sanity check, both before and after loading into the new system.

For paranoid data converters, both techniques can be combined. The construction of data conversion programs can follow the same FDD process as the rest of the project but will often be reworked as the new system matures.

Configuration data is specific to the system and rarely needs converting. The deployment descriptors of an Enterprise Java Beans system are

Figure 14–7
Trusted data conver-
sion programs.

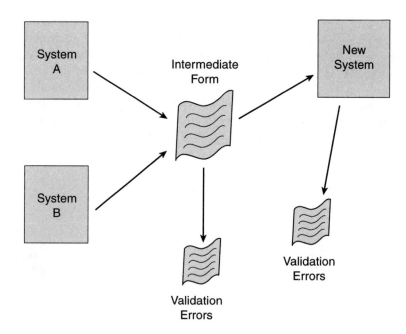

a good example of configuration data. Configuration data selects from the various runtime options available in the software. It includes such things as:

- Look-and-feel settings
- Localized information settings
- Performance settings
- Security and access permissions

Configuration data does not normally require data conversion of any sort. However, data loading utilities that make it easy to bulk-load configuration and reference data are extremely useful for testing and deployment.

Deployment

Deployment is the moving of the completed software and converted data from the development and testing environments into the production environment. It also often includes the training of users in the use of the new software.

Deployment teams need to know from development the requirements on machine sizes, the exact list of software components for each type of machine, and the procedures for initial loading of data. A large deployment can be a miniproject all its own.

Delivering features early allows the deployment team to practice deploying while the rest of the system is built. It allows pilot sites to be set up and users to be trained on actual software in an incremental fashion. FDD enables this but, again, just because we can does not mean we have to. Some organizations will already have well-defined deployment procedures in place that work well enough.

Summary

1. Projects can usually absorb up to a 10% increase in scope. For any more than 10%, something else, such as schedule or resources, has to give by 10%. Counting additional features enables projects to track that 10% accurately.

2. User documentation varies greatly, depending on the sort of system being built. FDD can be adapted to include the development of user documentation within feature development or the user help documentation can be tracked as a separate subproject.

3. Early and frequent delivery of features allows the data conversion and deployment teams to become active earlier in a project.

chapter 15

Feature-Driven Development— "All Change"

And it should be considered that nothing is more dif-
ficult to handle, more doubtful of success, nor more
dangerous to manage, than to put oneself at the head
of introducing new orders. For the introducer has all
those who benefit from the old orders as enemies, and
he has lukewarm defenders in all those who might
benefit from the new orders."

Niccolo Machiavelli [De Marco and Lister]

A long time ago in Chapter 2, we introduced the three main components in a software development project that form a "magic triangle"
(Figure 15–1): people, process, and technology. This book has been pre-
dominantly about process although, as we have seen, it is impossible
(and incredibly naïve to try) to talk about one side of the triangle without
discussing the other two sides. Managing the three sides of the triangle
is a constant balancing act.

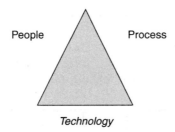

People / Process / Technology

Figure 15–1
The three components
of a software develop-
ment project.

Focusing on one side of the triangle or ignoring one side results in a
broken working environment, and changes to one component of the triangle will inevitably affect the other components. In this final chapter, we
briefly revisit each side of the triangle, looking at the impact of change
and some of the factors we need to consider when trying to introduce

change. In this way, we hope to be better equipped to introduce Feature-Driven Development (FDD) into a team or organization.

People and Change

As we discussed in Chapter 2, any nontrivial software development effort is really all about people because if we use good people, they will, by definition, pay proper attention to process and technology. If people on a software project or any project of any sort cannot or will not communicate, cannot or will not work together to achieve the goals of the project, or are not able to collaborate and work to make things better, nothing significant can be accomplished; the work environment is broken and dysfunctional. People are the cornerstone of the work environment!

Any time that an organization changes, people are affected. When we install a new system for customers to use in conducting their business, people are affected. When we adopt a new software development process, people are affected. When we adopt and acquire new tools to be used for software development, people are affected. When we act as change agents by introducing a new method or other change within the organization, we need to be aware of how people may react to the change and minimize any negative impact in order for it to be successfully adopted into the organization.

Many attempts at making a change to a software process or introducing a new technology fail because the people attempting the change have a naïve mental change model (Figure 15–2). They believe that announcing the change is all that is needed and that a team or organization will simply switch from doing what it used to do to doing the things the new way.

Figure 15–2
Naïve change model.

```
┌──────────┐                ┌──────────┐
│   OLD    │  A better way  │   NEW    │
│  STATUS  │ ─────────────▶ │  STATUS  │
│   QUO    │                │   QUO    │
└──────────┘                └──────────┘
```

Both Tom De Marco and Gerald Weinberg promote the work of Virginia Satir and her Satir Change model [Weinberg 92; De Marco]. This mental model (Figure 15–3) shows four stages to any significant change.

Figure 15–3
Satir change model.

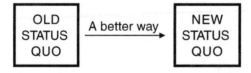

The Satir change model says that, while doing THIS happily and productively, some new, foreign element will be introduced that makes doing THIS an unhappy and unproductive experience. This catalyst for change could be a project failure, a more ambitious target than usual, a drop in profits for the company, the appearance of a new competitor, the release of a new product line, the desire to switch to object-oriented software development, or simply the introduction of new ideas about software process.

This new, foreign element causes the team to move from happy, productive work to a state of chaos, where things that used to work no longer do, and people flounder about, trying new ways to do things with little success.

A transforming idea is an idea that starts to move the team out of the chaos stage and into a stage of practice and integration of the new ways of doing things. The transforming idea could be a simple twist on the new process that makes it fit better in this context or it could be the idea to hire a consultant with proven experience in the area that is causing trouble to provide some training and guidance for a short time.

Eventually, the new ideas start to take hold, and through practice and integration, the team moves to a new status quo, where doing THAT is now as much a habit as doing THIS used to be.

People are very much creatures of habit. Some people like change if they are in control or instigators of that change. No one likes changes being forced upon them. Change forced upon us by others pushes us into the unknown, it's risky, it's exciting, it's challenging, and it's something we are not fully in control of. A person's fundamental response to such change is, therefore, not logical; it is always emotional. Knowing this when trying to introduce change is a huge help in managing that response. It is not personal. No amount of logical argument will make it any easier. The person is responding emotionally to the change. If we have ever been involved in the deployment of a new system, we will have seen the emotional responses from the users of the new system as they try to cope with an enormous change to the way they work. As developers, we rarely consider the impact our work has on our end users. However, we cause far more change to the way they work than they ever do with their changes to requirements.

The discipline of managing how change is introduced into an organization and how to manage the impact of change in an organization is known as *Organizational Change Management* (OCM) [E&Y; ODR].

One of the issues that OCM addresses is the effect of stress on the ability of an individual to accept and adapt to change, specifically within the organization. This can be a very important issue, particularly for a team that is implementing a new process for the first time.

Some Key Points to Remember:

- The effects of stress are additive. Each stressor contributes to an individual's stress level.

- Stress levels are dynamic, not static. Stressors are added and removed continually.

- Personal issues, such as financial pressures, personal relations, and personal and family health, can be significant and chronic or long-term stressors. They just don't go away overnight and will have the greatest affect on an individual's behavior in the workplace.

- Change is a stressor.

- Each individual has a *stress threshold* beyond which they are unable to cope with additional changes (see Figure 15–4).

- As an individual's stress level approaches the stress threshold, he or she will become more resistant to change. At this point, the individual can no longer assimilate change without displaying dysfunctional behavior, which can be exhibited in behaviors such as irritability, isolation, reluctance to participate, or in extreme cases, sabotage or permanent withdrawal (the "Take this job and shove it! I quit!" solution to stress management).

If an individual starts to display some of the above behaviors, encourage the person to talk about it. If necessary, encourage the individual to talk to his or her supervisor or project manager. Point out the ways that he or she benefits directly from the change. Listen to understand

Figure 15–4
Stress levels vs. ability to change.

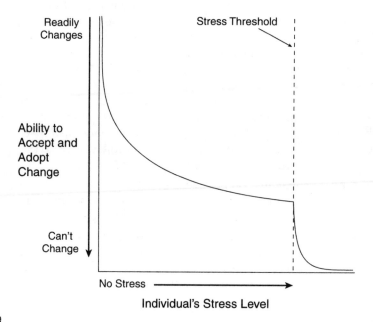

As stress levels increase the ability to change decreases. Once the threshold is reached, ability to change deteriorates quickly to zero.

what the problem is. Help the individual determine what it will take to remove the stressor and allow him or her to accept the change.

The ability of a group to help individual members of the group accept and adopt changes will have a directly proportional affect on the success of the changes being implemented by or in the group. Also, if the pain of the change is more than the pain of maintaining the status quo, the change will not be implemented successfully, and people will go back to the *old* way of doing things!

Stress can be a critical factor in a project's success, particularly when major changes are being implemented. The team's acceptance of change should be monitored as an indicator of the relative stress people are working under. The more major the change, the more stress should be managed as a risk item.

Technology and Change

Technology forms the next side of our triangle. The selection and appropriate use of technology is a key factor in any project. If not done well or ignored, a project is faced with far more tedious, repetitive, error-prone, time-consuming tasks to do, and work must be done to build from scratch at greater cost what could have been bought as a technology component. Over-emphasis on new technology at the cost of people and process results in overly complicated, low-quality systems that the end users find of little business value or too slow, difficult, or unreliable to use.

Technology should be used to avoid having to implement infrastructure when cost-effective to do so. However, many technologies claiming to replace the need for building infrastructure cause as many problems as they solve. This is especially true when a certain technology is selected as a *strategic direction* without considering whether the benefits it delivers matches the needs of the organization. Databases, application servers, middle-ware frameworks, and graphical user interface libraries can all severely reduce the effort involved in the development of an application if they can be made to work well and work well together.

Technology should be used to automate the repetitive and tedious. For instance, we can use development tools to translate from one representation to another and back again—translations that we would otherwise have to do manually or mentally. With more sophistication, we can do the translations in real time so that we have to keep only a single source, and the problem with maintaining multiple sources of information is eliminated. This is one of the big goals of products such as TogetherSoft's Together ControlCenter, with its LiveSource technology.

Preparing progress and status reports are jobs that few if any enjoy doing. It is a great place to employ technology to minimize the time and effort required to prepare them. As we have seen, such tools do not need to be highly sophisticated to provide accurate information about the state of a project with the minimum of manual effort.

Considering Technology Changes

One thing to remember is that, any time one side of the triangle changes, it is more than likely that all sides of the triangle will need to change. If you are the change agent or have to implement the change, it is important to be aware of this and, if possible, manage the change on all three sides.

Here are a few simple tips to help determine whether a technology change is needed and how to choose the "right" technology for your work environment.

1. Examine the current technology and processes you are using. Does it meet the requirements of the environment? Look for steps in the process or activities that the people have to do in order to make the technology work. For example, after writing source code in a specific text editor, does the programmer have to go through a conversion process to store it in a source code repository or can the editor interface with the repository directly? Manual processes and workarounds are indications that a technology change may be in order. Look at how much time a person has to spend doing the manual process and how often it is repeated during the day or week. This will give you a good idea of the cost of the manual process and also help to justify moving to a new technology that could automate or eliminate those steps.

2. List the various steps and activities of the current process. Determine/estimate the frequency of occurrence and normal duration of each activity. By accumulating each of the activities, the cost of the current process can be calculated, including those processes that are nonproductive or inefficient (candidates for automation). For example, consider the task of getting status from development teams. Let's assume that the frequency is daily, and the duration is 5 minutes per person. With a team size of 12, this is 1 hour per day, or 1/8 of the work day. That's 12.5% of your time spent collecting status! What would be the value of a technology that could automate that process?

3. Now list the changes in technology (mandated, proposed, or desired), which would either reduce cost or improve productivity. This will form the basis for comparing the effects of the new technology with the costs of the existing technology and processes (particularly the non- or counterproductive activities that have to be done to make the technology and process work). This usually becomes the requirements list and the cost justification for the new technology.

4. In considering how to maintain or increase profitability by reducing costs versus increasing productivity, remember that reducing costs does not increase your capability to reach goals such as decreasing time to market, maintaining quality, and meeting market opportunities. Measures aimed at reducing costs often not only fail to reduce costs as much as expected, but also usually decrease the organization's capability to meet its goals and miss market opportunities (lost opportunity cost). Successfully implementing technology that increases productivity and the ability to meet organizational goals using fewer resources is much more desirable and in the long run is more beneficial.

5. Research the capabilities and benefits of each technology. For each technology or tool set, consider:

   - Initial cost or licensing.

   - Maintenance cost.

   - Implementation cost (time, effort, internal support costs, maintenance).

   - Ease of acceptance: How well does it fit with corporate culture and environment? For example, are object-oriented tools in a traditionally COBOL/mainframe development organization a good fit?

   - Availability: How soon can you start incorporating the technology?

   - Ease of use.

   - Training: How much training is required to make the technology useful, and what is its availability? Include hourly cost of the resources and reduced productivity during training.

   - Existing customer references—successes and failures, direct interviews, lessons learned, things that worked from existing and former customers.

6. Compare the features of each technology to the current processes to see what will be changed or eliminated. Compare those costs (savings) with the acquisition, implementation, and ongoing maintenance costs of the technology. This will be the estimated return on investment and initial payback period (for those few brave accountants reading this book) for each technology. You now have a basis for choosing the technology or arguing against a change.

7. Manage the expectations of both the group and upper management to control bias and minimize any "deals" that vendors may try to make with upper management. Return on investment and bottom line financial costs often help. There

are times when the choice of a particular technology is mandated, regardless of impact. In this situation, steps 1 through 4 (for the specified technology or tool set) will help to identify the changes that will be needed on the people and process sides of the triangle to minimize the potentially negative impact of the change.

Steve: *Mac, another project wants to know why we selected the version control tool that we are using on this project. Do you know why we decided to go with that particular product? Did we just start using it or did we evaluate a number of other options first?*

Mac: *In fact, we specifically chose the one we are using. As you know, we have access to several source code control or configuration management tools. For the last project I worked on, we didn't have any source code management tools. We used that as the model to look at source code control tools. We didn't do a full ROI but just looked at the process, determined how we wanted to manage our environment on this project, and picked the tool. I have the list of the current process activities we were concerned with and the requirements we identified for the technology on this project. Here is the analysis we did on the original process used in "Project A." I also have one problem activity we identified and the requirements that came out of that analysis for our current project—"Project B."*

Project A's Environment

1. *22 Programmers on team; average salary—$25 per hour.*
2. *No source code control.*
3. *Running baseline—baseline programs constantly change. Cannot reliably construct previous versions of code unless programmer saved starting version.*
4. *Reasons for change often lost or poorly documented.*
5. *Concurrent development—no code owners. Multiple developers changing routines at the same time, overwriting each other's changes, having to redo code when test fails.*

Project A's Process

1. *Programmer assigned to make changes—either add new feature or fix existing defect.*
2. *Programmer "checks out code" from running baseline area.*
3. *Programmer researches change—if defect, attempts to recreate.*
4. *Programmer designs and codes solution.*
5. *Programmer tests solution.*
6. *Programmer documents solution.*
7. *Programmer submits change to QA test environment for testing.*

Project A's Activity Problems

1. Finding correct version of source—no way to consistently find out who is changing the running baseline code; may be multiple programmers.

   - Frequency—average three times per week per programmer (assume three routines or programs being modified per change).

   - Duration—average 20 minutes checking with programmers and testers.

   - Total 60 minutes/1 hour per programmer per week—22 hours per week for the team or 22 × $25 or $550 per week.

Failure rate of this activity to accomplish its purpose is 20%. This means that of an average 66 changes being worked on per week, 13 use the wrong source code. Test catches about 50% of these errors; the rest are released to production and discovered by the client. Average 13 hours for development + 1 hour to deploy to test + 2 hours to test, or 16 hours per error working on the wrong baseline. Assume that 6 are caught on average, that's 96 hours that are caught. Another 96 hours of effort goes into production. That's 24 days of wasted team effort, not counting the additional cost of the effort to deploy those changes to production and allowing the customer to catch them.

Project B Requirements

Activity 1 for Project A resulted in the following requirements for a technology solution for our project. Our project has a smaller team. Communication is not as great an issue, and because we are assigning code owners and working at teams on a feature, occurrences of concurrent development will be less likely.

1. Version Control System must prevent checkout for update by more than one person concurrently—Required.

2. Version Control System must show who has the version checked out—Required.

3. Version Control System should notify holder of checked-out version that someone is trying to use the code and identify that person—Optional.

4. Version Control System must allow access to check-out versions for view only. Prevent check-in unless checked out—Required.

Project B Technology Candidates

For these specific features, all four of the technology products met each of the requirements, either by setting options or because that was the only way they worked. With some of the other activities, however, two of the products were eliminated.

Steve: *You used an informal format to list the calculations. Couldn't this have been done better in a spreadsheet format? Or was that considered overkill?*

Mac: *The final presentation of information was in spreadsheet and graphical form. These are just the notes from the initial workup and information gathering that we did. The spreadsheet and graphs are sitting on one of the secretary's personal computers. I can find them later if you really need to.*

Steve: *The notes are probably good enough for the other team. They can ask for the spreadsheet if they need it.*

Avoiding Shelfware

One outcome that is desirable to avoid is the acquisition or delivery of "shelfware." This is a common and very costly outcome that we see over and over again. It happens when the technology purchased or the systems created do not meet the needs of an organization or when there is a failure in gaining acceptance of a new technology.

Indicators of a mismatch between technology and the working environment can be seen on both sides of the triangle. Extreme resistance to the change in the form of refusal to learn the new technology or even sabotage is not uncommon on the people side of the triangle. A champion (a respected individual, group, or outside expert) is needed to help the people see the transforming idea and accept/adopt the new technology. If this does not happen, the change will fail, and people will go back to the old, comfortable technology. A critical success factor is that the new technology must be easier to use (less painful) than the old technology. It is the job of the champion to demonstrate the benefits of the new technology and lead the group to the point where they can adopt the change.

The same is true for the process side of the triangle. Mismatches occur when the process is inflexible, slow to change, or just incapable of incorporating the new technology. Again, the champion must work to modify the process to use the new technology and help the people accept the new changes. The changes to both the people and process sides need to be coordinated. They can be concurrent or sequential, as long as the changes are visible and well communicated to the organization. Facilitated sessions are a good way to work with people to help identify the new process and achieve buy-in and support from the group. Achieving consensus within a group is always a more optimal solution and will help to ensure success in adopting new changes.

The use of development tools can be a religious issue with many developers, and imposing a standard toolset can be a nonproductive thing to do. Look for tools and technologies that interface with or work readily with other tools and technologies. Three useful criteria for selecting tools are:

1. Can it be used easily out of the box?
2. Will it work in the existing environment and adapt as the environment and processes change? (This is important when the

intent is to migrate from an existing technology and environment to a new one, and current products still need to be supported.)

3. Can it be modified, if necessary, to adapt and work with new tools and technologies or to work with specific tools critical to your environment?

Single-User-Oriented Tools

Be wary of single-user tools (even those with advertised, after-the-fact, bolted-on concurrency and versioning capabilities). They are useful only if concurrent update access is not required. In a team environment, it is unusual to have a tool used by only one member of the team or used to produce perfectly independent and isolated results. As soon as more than one person wants to edit a particular artifact, single-user tools become painfully frustrating to use, especially if each one is backed by a different proprietary repository or versioning system.

Traditional single-user tools aimed at fulfilling one project function or working at one level of abstraction, such as requirements managers, diagramming tools, traditional integrated development environments, etc., actually restrict the iterative nature of a process. It is hard to be highly iterative if the tools being used do not encourage easy and rapid movement from one activity to another; the artifacts that they produce need to be converted first, either manually or mentally, to the representation needed in the next activity. The work needed to do this translation encourages working longer at a particular task or level of abstraction than might be ideal; it encourages a more waterfall approach.

Process and Change

The third side of our triangle is process and has been the main subject of the preceding chapters. Because "all work is a process," if any goal is to be reached or product created, work has to be done. There is always a process, whether it is ad hoc, hidden, or well defined and publicly visible. If it is not working, if the process is not flexible, and if it is seen as being chiseled in stone ("That's the way we've always done it"), then the ability of the working environment to adapt to produce new desired results will be limited or nonexistent. The ability of the process to change and adapt to people, technology, and business issues is critical! If a process is not agile enough to adapt to the use of new development tools, new technical architectures, or a different programming language, it will very quickly find itself obsolete and quite literally left on the shelf.

Hints on Adopting FDD

Making small, frequent course adjustments is much easier than making large, infrequent course adjustments. Introducing small changes is easier than introducing large changes. No single practice in FDD is the real answer; it is the mix that makes the whole work so well. However, it can be introduced to the development team in smaller pieces as a project proceeds. In the end, a team will want to use all five of the core processes to enjoy all of the benefits of the process.

A team could adopt the workshop style domain object modeling without the rest of FDD. This would be beneficial in many ways but is not going to solve low-level design and coding process problems. A team could adopt all three of the first processes—building a features list and planning and developing in a feature-centric manner—but again, the actual code construction process is left untouched.

The ideal approach is to take the whole thing on board and practice on a noncritical project. However, in our experience, such a beast does not exist. If a noncritical project is identified, it is unlikely to prove anything because the pressures on the project are different. Also, at the first sign of trouble in an organization, the project is likely to be declared as no longer worthwhile and cancelled.

A good opportunity to introduce FDD is the first object-oriented project on which an organization embarks. The existing procedural development process is unlikely to be usable, and a new process is required; FDD can be that process. Another good opportunity to try out a new process is after a reorganization, where reporting lines and team structures have changed and new ways of working are needed, anyway.

FDD does have the advantage that it fits in between an existing requirements-gathering activity and the formal testing activity and, therefore, only really affects the core development team, who may be struggling with process issues already. A team can adopt FDD and still use the existing surrounding processes to communicate with parties external to the development team.

Once the five core processes of FDD are established, they can be used as a foundation to improve the processes around it. Having real working code delivered frequently opens the door to process improvements all through the project lifecycle.

A frequent objection to the introduction of FDD is that the system being built does not have many client-valued functions (features), when compared with the number of technical functions required. It is important to remember that "client" does not equal "user," even though in most business systems, a high percentage of client-valued function will be of direct use to some user of the system. A client is the person or organization paying or sponsoring the project; the people who have the ultimate say on requirements of the system. A client must be able to understand a feature. A client must be able to assign business value to a feature. Only then can a client help prioritize and steer the project. A real-time or heavyweight data storage project may need more time spent on the object model, more time spent in the design sessions and reviews, or more elaborate patterns for translating the object model onto the underlying technologies. However, somewhere there is a client paying for the capabilities and functions provided by the system, and that client has a right to be able to monitor progress of the project in terms that he or she understands.

As with any new endeavor, it is worthwhile partnering with others who have proven experience in the areas that are new to you.

If you are an Extreme Programming shop needing to scale to development teams of much larger than 10 people, FDD provides a great way to add the minimum additional structure needed to do this without losing many of the social benefits, sense of fun and achievement, and highly iterative nature of Extreme Programming practices.

Alternatively, if you are a unified process shop needing to work within much shorter project cycles, FDD provides the structure and well-defined processes needed to produce high-quality code with greatly reduced overhead. FDD provides a highly pragmatic, proven alternative for project teams experiencing analysis paralysis or "death by use cases."

However, remember FDD is just a process, a good process, but just a process all the same. Repeatable, quality results on time and within budget are what we want. So please, if you are struggling with process, take the ideas in this book, try them, modify them if necessary, but do not turn them into a 1,000-page process manual that no one will ever read (unless you are forced to by an external regulatory body). As we said in the Introduction, if there is one thing more boring than writing a book on software process, it is reading one; it is much more fun to actually use a process to develop high-quality, useful software in a timely manner without nearly killing the project team with exhaustion and stress.

Please take a careful look at your people and your development tools, and tailor FDD around their strengths and weaknesses.

Please use FDD to produce good software and not as more fuel for the discussion group debates . . .

. . . and above all, have fun delivering frequent, tangible, working results.

References

[Alexander] Alexander, et al. A *Pattern Language*. New York: Oxford University Press, 1977.

[Alur] Alur, Deepak, John Crupi, and Dan Malks. *Core J2EE Patterns: Best Practices and Design Strategies*. Upper Saddle River, NJ: Prentice Hall PTR, 2001.

[Astels] Astels, Dave, Granville Miller, and Miroslav Novack. *Practical Guide to Extreme Programming*. Upper Saddle River, NJ: Prentice Hall PTR, 2001.

[Beck 00] Beck, K. *Extreme Programming Explained*. Reading, MA: Addison-Wesley Publishing Co. 2000.

[Beck 01] Beck, K. and M. Fowler. *Planning Extreme Programming*. Reading, MA: Addison-Wesley Publishing Co. 2001.

[Berg] Berg, Clifford. *Advanced Java Development for Enterprise Applications*. Upper Saddle River, NJ: Prentice Hall PTR, 1989.

[Brooks] Brooks, F. *The Mythical Man-Month, Anniversary Edition*. Reading, MA: Addison-Wesley Publishing Co., 1995.

[Coad 96] Coad, Peter, and Mark Mayfield. *Java Design: Building Better Apps and Applets*. Upper Saddle River, NJ: Prentice Hall PTR, 1996.

[Coad 97] Coad, Peter, et al. *Object Models Strategies, Patterns, & Applications*, 2nd ed. Upper Saddle River, NJ: Prentice Hall PTR, 1997.

[Coad 99] Coad, Peter, et al. *Java Modeling in Color with* UML. Upper Saddle River, NJ: Prentice Hall PTR, 1999.

[Crosby] Crosby, Philip B. *Quality Is Free: The Art of Making Quality Certain*. New York: Penguin Books USA, 1980.

[Cusumano] Cusumano, M., and R. Selby. *Microsoft Secrets: How the World's Most Powerful Software Company Creates Technology, Shapes Markets, and Manages People.* New York: Simon & Schuster, 1996.

[De Marco] De Marco, T., and T. Lister. *Peopleware: Productive Projects and Teams*. 2nd ed. New York: Dorset House, 1999.

[Dobbs] http://www.digitalfocus.com/ddj/code/

[E & Y] Ernst & Young, U.S., Organizational Development Research, Inc., (ODR). *Organizational Change Management* (OCM), 1994.

263

[Fagan] Fagan, M.E. "Design and Code Inspections to Reduce Errors in Program Development." IBM *Systems Journal*, 15(3): 182–211 (1976).

[Fairley] Fairley, R. *Software Engineering Concepts*. New York: McGraw Hill, 1985.

[Fowler] Fowler, M., and K. Scott. UML *Distilled: Applying the Standard Object Modeling Language*. Reading, MA: Addison-Wesley Publishing Co., 1997.

[Freedman] Freedman, D.P., and G.M. Weinberg. "Software Inspections: An Effective Verification Process." IEEE *Software*. May 31–36 (1982).

[Gamma] Gamma, E., et al. *Design Patterns: Elements of Reusable Object-Oriented Software*. Reading, MA: Addison-Wesley Publishing Co., 1995.

[Gilb 88] Gilb, T. *Principles of Software Engineering Management*, 205–226 and 403–442. Reading, MA: Addison-Wesley Publishing Co., 1988.

[Gilb 93] Gilb, T., and D. Graham. *Software Inspection*. Reading, MA: Addison-Wesley Publishing Co., 1993.

[Hohmann] Hohmann, Luke. *Journey of the Software Professional: The Sociology of Computer Programming*. Upper Saddle River, NJ: Prentice Hall PTR, 1997.

[Jacobson 92] Jacobson, I., et al. *Object-Oriented Software Engineering: A Use Case Driven Approach*. Reading, MA: Addison-Wesley Publishing Co., 1992.

[Jacobson 99] Jacobson, I., et al. *The Unified Software Development Process*. Reading, MA: Addison-Wesley Publishing Co., 1999.

[Jones] Jones, C.L. "A Process-Integrated Approach to Defect Prevention." IBM *Systems Journal*, 24(2):150–167 (1985).

[Kassem] Kassem, Nicholas, Enterprise Team. *Designing Enterprise Applications with the Java™ 2 Platform, Enterprise Edition*. Reading, MA: Addison-Wesley Publishing Co., 2000.

[McConnell 93] McConnell, S. *Code Complete*. Redmond, Washington: Microsoft Press, 1993.

[McConnell 98] McConnell, S. *Software Project Survival Guide*. Redmond, Washington: Microsoft Press, 1998.

[Miller] Miller, G., and F. Armour. *Advanced Use Case Modeling*. Reading, MA: Addison-Wesley Publishing Co., 2001.

[ODR] ODR®-USA, Inc. Organizational Change Management (OCM) Course Material. 2900 Chamblee-Tucker Road NW Building 16, Atlanta, GA 30341-4129 (1994).

[Palmer] Palmer, Stephen R., ed. *The Coad Letter*. www.togethercommunity.com. 2000–2002.

[Paramount Picture Corporation] Paramount Picture Corporation. *Star Trek III: The Search for Spock*, 1984.

[Rosenberg] Rosenberg, Doug, and Kendall Scott. *Use Case Driven Object Modeling with UML*. Reading, MA: Addison-Wesley Publishing Co., 1999.

[Satir] Satir, V., J. Banmen, J. Gerber, and M. Gomori. *The Satir Model: Family Therapy and Beyond*. Palo Alto, CA: Science and Behavior Books, 1991.

[Tennyson] Tennyson, Lord Alfred. *Charge of the Light Brigade.*

[Tolkien] Tolkien, J.R.R. *The Lord of the Rings Part One.* London, UK: Unwin Hyman Limited, 1955.

[Tufte] Tufte, E. *Envisioning Information.* Cheshire, CT: Graphics Press, 1990.

[Weinberg 92] Weinberg, G. *Quality Software Management vols.* 1–4. New York: Dorset House, 1992–1997.

[Weinberg 98] Weinberg, G. *The Psychology of Computer Programming: Silver Anniversary Edition.* New York: Dorset House, 1998.

Index

A

architectural framework, 20
assign classes to developers task, 152–154
assign feature sets to chief programmers task,
    150–152
attracting good people, 25

B

Beck, Kent, 76
best practices, list of, 36
Brooks, Fred, 22–23
build, layers and, 214–215
Build a Features List, 65–66
    build the features list task, 139–142
    exit criteria, 143–144
    form the features list team task, 138–139
    overview, 135–138
    verification, 143
Build by Feature, 71–72
    conduct a code inspection task, 185–188
    exit criteria, 193–196
    implement classes and methods task, 182–184
    overview, 181–182
    promote to the build task, 191–192
    unit test task, 189–190
    verification, 192
build engineer, 30
build the features list task, 139–142
business data, 244

C

capacity of FDD project team, increasing, 237
change
    people and, 250–253
    process and, 259–261
    in requirements, 234–235
    shelfware, 258–259
    single-user-oriented tools, 259
    technology and, 253–259
chief architect
    described, 28–29
    tips for, 107–112
chief facilitator, tips for, 107–112
chief programmer work packages, 93–95
chief programmers, 29
    hints for, 159–161
    plan dates, tracking progress and, 87–91
    reporting to, 80–84
clarifications of requirements, 233–234
class (code) ownership, 42–46
class owners, 29–30
code inspection milestone, 77
code milestone, 77

FDD Process 5: Build by Feature. *See* Build by Feature
FDD process template, 60–61
feature kills, 91
feature set testing, 227–228
feature teams, 46–49
feature testing, 227
features, 57
finding failures, 226–229
fixes, 218–220
fixing faults, 230–231
form a feature team task, 161–164
form the features list team task, 138–139
form the modeling team task, 112–114
form the planning team task, 145–147
formal documentation, 100
four-stage development cycle, 108
Fowler, Martin, 76

H

heavy process approach, 4–5
Hohmann, Luke, 23

I

implement classes and methods task, 182–184
individual productivity, 24
inspections, 49–51
integration testing, 222
intelligent help systems, 242

J

Journey of the Software Professional: The Sociology of Computer Programming (Hohmann), 23

L

language, 9–12
language guru, 30
layers, 205–207
Lister, Timothy, 23

M

magic help, 242
major feature set testing, 228
major feature sets, 57
milestones, 77–78
Mythical Man-Month, The (Brooks), 22–23

N

norms, 109–110

O

online manuals with user guides, 241
organizational chart, sample abstract, 21

P

PD layer, 207
people
    attracting good people, 25
    build engineer, 30
    change and, 250–253
    chief architect, 28–29
    chief programmers, 29
    class owners, 29–30
    core values of an organization and attracting, 25
    deployers, 31
    development manager, 29
    domain experts, 30
    domain manager, 30
    individual productivity, 24
    keeping good people, 27
    language guru, 30
    process and, 23–27
    project manager, 28
    project roles, 28–30
    recognizing good people, 26
    release manager, 30
    supporting roles, 30–31
    system administrator, 31
    technical writers, 31
    testers, 31
    toolsmith, 31
Peopleware: Productive Projects and Teams (De Marco and Lister), 23
Plan by Feature (FDD Process 3), 67–68
    assign classes to developers task, 152–154
    assign feature sets to chief programmers task, 150–152
    determine the development sequence task, 147–150
    exit criteria, 154–157
    form the planning team task, 145–147
    overview, 145
    verification, 154
planning development of user documentation, 242–244
Planning Extreme Programming (Fowler and Beck), 76

practices
    best practices, list of, 36
    class (code) ownership, 42–46
    configuration management, 52–53
    develop by feature, 38–42
    domain object modeling, 36–38
    feature teams, 46–49
    inspections, 49–51
    overview, 35
    progress reporting, 53
    regular build schedule, 51–52
    reporting/visibility of results, 53
    version control, 52–53
processes, 23–27
    change, 259–261
    ETVX template, 60–62
    FDD Process 1: Develop an Overall Model. *See*
      Develop an Overall Object Model
    FDD Process 2: Build a Features List. *See* Build a
      Features List
    FDD Process 3: Plan by Feature. *See* Plan by Feature
    FDD Process 4: Design by Feature. *See* Design by
      Feature
    FDD Process 5: Build by Feature. *See* Build by
      Feature
    FDD process template, 60–61
    features, 57
    major feature sets, 57
    overview, 57–59
    set of well-bounded, 20
progress
    chief programmers, reporting to, 80–84
    code inspection milestone, 77
    code milestone, 77
    design inspection milestone, 77
    design milestone, 77
    development team, reporting to, 78–80
    domain walkthrough milestone, 77
    estimating, 76–77
    feature kills, 91
    milestones, 77–78
    project manager, reporting to, 80–84
    promote to build milestone, 77
    sponsors, reporting to, 84–87
    tracking by feature, 77–78
    upper management, reporting to, 84–87
progress reporting, 53
project manager
    described, 28
    reporting to, 80–84
project patterns, 31–32
project roles, 28–30

promote to build milestone, 77
promote to the build task, 191–192
Psychology of Computer Programming, The (Weinberg), 23

Q

quality, 13–17
quality spectrum, 14

R

Racey, Fred, 110
Rajashima, M. A., 60
recognizing good people, 26
recommended materials, 110–111
reference data, 244–245
refine object model task, 171–173
refine overall object model task, 126–129
regular build schedule, 51–52
release manager, 30
reporting failures, 229–230
reporting/visibility of results, 53
requirements
    capacity of FDD project team, increasing, 237
    changes in, 234–235
    clarifications of, 233–234
    defects in, 234
    schedule, extending, 236–237
    scope of project, reducing, 236
    10% slippage rule, 235–236
roles, list of, 19

S

schedule, extending, 236–237
scope of project, reducing, 236
set of technologies, 20
set of well-bounded processes, 20
severity of failure, 229–230
shelfware, 258–259
SI layer, 207–209
single-user-oriented tools, 259
skills and experience, people with, 19
software development process
    building in quality, 14–17
    communication, 8–12
    complexity, 12–13
    heavy process approach, 4–5
    language, 9–12
    overview, 3–18
    purpose of, 17
    quality, 13–17

quality spectrum, 14
waterfall approach, 14–15
software development project
architectural framework, 20
components of, 19–20
processes, set of well-bounded, 20
roles, list of, 19
set of technologies, 20
set of well-bounded processes, 20
skills and experience, people with, 19
statement of purpose, 19
Software Engineering Concepts (Fairley), 23
sponsors, reporting to, 84–87
statement of purpose, 19
study documents task, 118–119
study referenced documents task, 166–168
supporting roles, 30–31
system administrator, 31
system testing, 223–225

T

technical architecture, 203–207
build, layers and, 214–215
dependencies between components, reducing, 215–216
DM layer, 213–214
domains, 205
layers, 205–207
overview, 199–203
PD layer, 207
SI layer, 207–209
UI layer, 210–213
technical writers, 31
technology and change, 253–259
10% slippage rule, 235–236
test cases
characteristics, 228–229
domain area testing, 228
feature set testing, 227–228
feature testing, 227
major feature set testing, 228
testers, 31
testing
customer/user acceptance testing, 225
defect board, 231
diagnosing defects, 230
failures, 218–220
faults, 218–220
finding failures, 226–229
fixes, 218–220
fixing faults, 230–231

integration testing, 222
overview, 217–218
reporting failures, 229–230
severity of failure, 229–230
system testing, 223–225
test cases. *See* test cases
types of, 218
unit testing, 220–222
time constraints, 75–76
tool tips, 238–239
toolsmith, 31
track by feature, 77–78
Tufte, Edward, 60

U

UI layer, 210–213
UML, 22
Unified Modeling Language, 22
unit test task, 189–190
unit testing, 220–222
upper management, reporting to, 84–87
user documentation
context sensitive help, 240–241
embedded help, 238
error and warning messages, 240
intelligent help systems, 242
magic help, 242
online manuals with user guides, 241
overview, 237–238
planning development of, 242–244
tool tips, 238–239

V

verification
Build a Features List, 143
Build by Feature, 192
Design by Feature, 175–177
Develop an Overall Object Model, 132–133
Plan by Feature, 154
version control, 52–53

W

waterfall approach, 14–15
Weinberg, Gerald, 12, 23
work packages
chief programmer work packages, 93–95
described, 99–100
examples, 96–98
write class and method prologue task, 173–175
write model notes task, 129–132